Learn
Python
Generative AI

*Journey from autoencoders to
transformers to large language models*

Zonunfeli Ralte

Indrajit Kar

www.bpbonline.com

First Edition 2024

Copyright © BPB Publications, India

ISBN: 978-93-55518-972

To View Complete
BPB Publications Catalogue
Scan the QR Code:

Dedicated to

My beloved Parents:
R. Zohmingthanga *and* **Sangthangseii**

− Zonunfeli Ralte

My beloved Parents:
Avijit Kar *and* **Puspa Kar**

− Indrajit Kar

About the Authors

- **Zonunfeli Ralte,** a seasoned professional with a Master's in Business Administration and Economics, boasts 15 years of experience in Analytics, Finance, and AI. Currently, she is the CEO and Founder of RastrAI, while also serving as a Principal AI Consultant, developing GenAI applications for diverse industries. Zonunfeli has an impressive academic contribution with 6 IEEE research papers including **Large Language Models (LLM)**, Deep learning and computer vision, 3 of which received best paper awards. Her multifaceted expertise and leadership make her a notable figure in the AI community. Additionally, she has filed 1 patent in GenAI.

- **Indrajit Kar,** a master's graduate in Computational Biology from Bengaluru, also holds a Bachelor's in Science from the same institution with more than two decades of experience in AI and ML. He is an experienced intrapreneur, having built AI teams at Siemens, Accenture, IBM, and Infinite Data Systems. Presently, he is the AVP and Global Head of AI and ML leading AI research (ZAIR) and Data Practices. Indrajit has published 22 research papers across IEEE, Springers, Wiley Online Library, and CRC press, covering topics like LLM, Computer Vision, NLP, and more. He has 14 patents, including Generative AI. He is a mentor for startups and a recipient of multiple awards, including the 40 Under 40 Data Scientists award. He is also author of 2 AI books.

About the Reviewers

❖ **Utkarsh Mittal** is a Machine Learning manager at Gap Inc., a global retail company. He has more than ten years of practice experience in machine learning automation and is a leader of big AI-based database projects. He received his Master's in Industrial Engineering with a Supply Chain and Operations Research major from Oklahoma State University, USA. He is closely associated with research groups and editorial boards of high-profile International Journals and research organizations. He is passionate about solving complex business challenges and encouraging innovation through upcoming technologies. He is a Senior member of the IEEE Computer Society.

❖ **Arun Naudiya**l wears many hats, but they all share a common thread - a love for building, learning, and driving meaningful impact. As a Senior Product Engineer at a Big 4 Firm, his eight years of experience translate into a potent blend of expertise. He's the go-to for crafting and deploying Machine Learning pipelines on AWS, wielding frameworks like Kubernetes and Sagemaker with masterful hands. Arun's passion extends beyond code. He's an avid learner, constantly upskilling in MLOps and beyond. This thirst for knowledge led him to explore the fascinating world of Large Language Models. Under his guidance, teams have crafted projects that revolutionized document summarization for EdTech, unearthed customer sentiment like a treasure hunter, and even built an AI code assistant that boosts programmer productivity.

Acknowledgements

O   **Zonunfeli Ralte:** To my family, especially my parents, sisters, and cousins, your unwavering encouragement and belief in my abilities have been the bedrock of my journey. Your support has been a guiding light, empowering me to pursue and accomplish this endeavor.

I also wish to express my heartfelt appreciation to the people of Mizoram, particularly the community of Ramthar Veng. Our rich culture and vibrant spirit have been a constant source of motivation and have deeply influenced my perspectives and writing.

A special acknowledgment goes to BPB Publications and my co-author Indrajit Kar for their patience and trust in my vision. Your flexibility in allowing the book to be published in multiple parts has been crucial in adequately covering the expansive and evolving field of AI.

Lastly, I thank my companies for providing an environment that fosters learning and growth. The opportunities to explore and develop GenAI applications have been fundamental in accumulating the knowledge shared in this book.

To all, your hidden and visible support has shaped this journey in countless ways, and for that, I am forever grateful.

O   **Indrajit Kar:** I extend my deepest appreciation to my family, particularly my parents, wife, in-laws and children, whose steadfast encouragement and unwavering belief in my abilities have formed the cornerstone of my journey. Your support has illuminated my path, empowering me to pursue and fulfill this endeavor with confidence and dedication.

I must also express my profound gratitude to BPB Publications for their patience and trust in my vision. Their flexibility in allowing this book to be published in multiple segments has been pivotal in thoroughly addressing the broad and dynamic landscape of AI.

Furthermore, I am immensely thankful to my companies for creating an environment that nurtures learning and growth. The opportunities they have provided to delve into and develop GenAI applications have been instrumental in gathering the insights shared in this book.

To everyone involved, both in visible and unseen ways, your support has profoundly shaped this journey. For this, I am eternally grateful.

Preface

Learn Python Generative AI is an extensive and comprehensive guide that delves deep into the world of generative artificial intelligence. This book provides a thorough understanding of the various components and applications in this rapidly evolving field. It begins with a detailed analysis, laying a solid foundation for exploring generative models. The combination process of different generative models is discussed in depth, offering a roadmap to understand the complexities involved in integrating various AI models and techniques.

The early chapters emphasize the refinement of TransVAE, an advanced variational autoencoder, showcasing improvements in its encoder-decoder structure. This discussion sets the stage for a broader examination of the evolution of AI models, particularly focusing on the incorporation of the SWIN-Transformer in generative AI.

As the book progresses, it shifts focus to the practical applications of generative AI in diverse sectors. In-depth chapters explore its transformative potential in healthcare, including applications in hospital settings, dental, and radiology, underscoring the impact of AI in medical diagnostics and patient care. The role of GenAI in retail and finance is also thoroughly examined, with a special emphasis on corporate finance and insurance, demonstrating how AI can revolutionize customer engagement, risk assessment, and decision-making.

Each sector-specific chapter is enriched with real-world examples, challenges, and innovative solutions, offering a comprehensive view of how generative AI is reshaping various industries. The concluding chapters synthesize the key learnings from all topics, providing insights into the future trajectory of generative AI.

Chapter 1: Introducing Generative AI - The objective of this chapter is to provide a comprehensive understanding of generative models, including an overview of generative models, a comparison of discriminative vs generative models, an introduction to the types of discriminative and generative models, as well as their strengths and weaknesses. By the end of the content, readers should be able to differentiate between discriminative and generative models, understand the different types of each, and make informed decisions about which type of model is most appropriate for their needs.

Chapter 2: Designing Generative Adversarial Networks - In this chapter, the objective is to delve into the multifaceted landscape of GANs by comprehensively exploring various types of GANs and their intricate architectures. By the end of this chapter, readers will be equipped with a solid understanding of the architecture, equations, and crucial design factors associated with different GAN variants. The chapter will dissect discriminator and generator losses, shed light on pivotal GAN types, including Vanilla GAN, Deep Convolutional GAN, Wasserstein GAN, Conditional GAN, CycleGAN, Progressive GAN, StyleGAN, and Pix2Pix, and address the major challenges encountered in designing effective GAN architectures. Through an in-depth analysis of each architecture, readers will gain the knowledge necessary to make informed decisions when selecting and designing GANs for various generative tasks.

Chapter 3: Training and Developing Generative Adversarial Networks - The objective of this book chapter is to provide readers with a comprehensive understanding of the process of training and tuning GANs, including the latest techniques and best practices for improving the stability and performance of GAN models.

Chapter 4: Architecting Auto Encoder for Generative AI - The primary goal of this chapter is to explore the fascinating world of autoencoders in the context of generative AI. We will delve into the inner workings of autoencoders, discussing their architectural variations, training strategies and their applications in generating diverse and high-quality outputs across various domains. Furthermore, we will examine advanced techniques that leverage autoencoders, such as Variational AutoEncoders (VAE) and Generative Adversarial Networks (GAN), which push the boundaries of generative AI even further.

Throughout this chapter, and the next, we will also discuss the key challenges associated with autoencoders for generative tasks, including issues like mode collapse, blurry outputs, and training instability. We will explore solutions and strategies to mitigate these challenges, providing practical insights and recommendations for building robust and effective generative models using autoencoders.

By the end of this chapter, readers will have gained a comprehensive understanding of autoencoders as a powerful tool in the realm of generative AI. They will have a solid grasp of the fundamental concepts, practical considerations, and cutting-edge advancements that can enable them to apply autoencoders effectively in their own projects and unlock the potential of generative models to create realistic and novel outputs.

Chapter 5: Building and Training Generative Autoencoders - The key objectives of this chapter are to provide the reader with a deep understanding of autoencoders and their applications. By the end of this chapter, readers will gain a comprehensive understanding of the concept of latent space and its significance in autoencoders, explore the concept of dual input autoencoders and their usefulness in handling missing values and multi-modal data, and familiarize themselves with various loss functions commonly used in autoencoders and their role in training and reconstruction.

The readers will also learn about potential issues during training, such as overfitting, vanishing gradients, and noisy data, along with strategies to mitigate them, discover optimization techniques specific to autoencoders for effective model training and performance enhancement, as well as understand the differences between autoencoders and variational autoencoders and their respective benefits.

Lastly, the reader will acquire the knowledge and skills to leverage autoencoders in practical scenarios for data representation, generation, and anomaly detection.

Chapter 6: Designing Generative Variation Auto Encoder - By the end of this chapter, the reader will be able to understand the fundamental differences between VAEs and traditional AEs. We will also explore the network architecture of VAEs, including the encoder and decoder networks, and their role in learning latent representations. The reader will also gain insight into the mathematical principles underlying VAEs, including the reparameterization trick and the ELBO objective function.

The chapter will then move to advanced techniques in VAEs, such as employing different prior distributions, utilizing various forms of the encoder network, and handling missing or incomplete data. We will also discover methods for interpreting the latent space of a VAE and visualizing its representations, explore the generative capabilities of VAEs by generating novel samples using the decoder network, and lastly, acquire the necessary knowledge and skills to apply VAEs in practical applications, including image generation, natural language processing, and anomaly detection.

By achieving these key objectives, readers will develop a comprehensive understanding of VAEs and be able to leverage their power and flexibility in various domains, ultimately enhancing their ability to learn and generate meaningful representations from complex data.

Chapter 7: Building Variational Autoencoders for Generative AI - By the end of this chapter, the reader will have explored various architectural choices, including convolutional or Non convolution networks, to handle complex dependencies in VAEs. We will also investigate the impact of KL divergence and different prior distributions on the generative process of VAEs, and develop strategies to effectively handle missing or incomplete data within the VAE framework. The reader will also understand the role of loss functions and address potential issues during training to ensure stable convergence, as well as optimize VAE performance and generative capabilities for diverse data modalities.

By achieving these key objectives, readers will develop a comprehensive understanding of VAEs and be able to leverage their power and flexibility in various domains, ultimately enhancing their ability to learn and generate meaningful representations from complex data.

Chapter 8: Fundamental of Designing New Age Generative Vision Transformer - By the end of this chapter, readers will have a solid understanding of transformers, their underlying principles, and their various applications in natural language processing and computer vision. They will also have the necessary knowledge to build, train, and fine-tune transformer models for their own use cases. The readers will gain a comprehensive introduction to transformers as a class of neural networks. This includes explaining their significance in revolutionizing natural language processing and their current applications in computer vision. Then, we will explore fundamental transformer concepts, delve into the basic principles and key components of transformers, such as self-attention mechanisms and the transformer architecture. This chapter will cover generative transformers and highlight the main differences between regular transformers and those designed for generative tasks. Apart from this, the reader will also be able to analyze different types of attention, such as self-attention, cross-attention, and multi-headed attention, and elucidate their specific applications in image processing.

Lastly, we will explore transformer math and positional encoding.

Chapter 9: Implementing Generative Vision Transformer - In this chapter, our primary objective is to explore and understand the fundamental distinctions between Generative Transformers and conventional Transformers, highlighting their key differences and applications within the realm of image generation. We will then delve into VAE models and their application to the STL dataset, emphasizing their capability to capture latent features and generate images. Building upon this foundation, our objective further extends to the conversion of a VAE model into a Generative Transformer model, showcasing the integration of these two powerful architectures to enhance image synthesis.

Throughout the chapter, we will compare Generative Transformers and Transformers. We will thoroughly dissect the distinctions between Generative Transformers and traditional Transformers in terms of architecture, training methodologies, and their respective strengths and weaknesses. We'll construct VAEs for the STL dataset, then transition to Generative Transformer models, adapting VAE components to fit Transformer's self-attention and positional encodings. Our comprehensive evaluation will compare image quality, diversity, and speed against traditional models. We'll also explore real-world applications, demonstrating the model's capability to produce diverse, contextually coherent images. Ultimately, this chapter aims to deepen understanding of Generative

Transformers versus traditional models, guide in VAE construction, and reveal the innovative transition to Generative Transformer architecture.

Chapter 10: Architectural Refactoring for Generative Modeling - In this chapter, our primary objective is to explore the combination process, and delve into the process of synergistically combining an encoder-decoder architecture with a transformer model for enhanced generative modeling in computer vision. We will investigate how to enhance the transformer model by introducing modifications and optimizations, contributing to improved performance and suitability for specific tasks, and provide an in-depth exploration of the SWIN transformer implementation, including detailing its architecture, components, and distinctions from other transformer variants.

Moreover, this chapter will introduce readers to advanced concepts encompassing combining hyper parameter tuning and model refactoring and aims to equip readers with a comprehensive understanding of the entire process, encompassing motivations for combining architectures, technical implementation details, and an appreciation of the intricacies of the SWIN transformer model.

Through this holistic approach, readers will gain both theoretical insights and practical skills, setting the stage for innovative generative modeling using combined encoder-decoder-transformer architectures.

Chapter 11: Major Technical Roadblocks in Generative AI and Way Forward - The designated sections of this chapter aim to unravel the challenges and innovative solutions in the fields of data representation, retrieval, and cross-modal understanding. Obstacles and technical hurdles delve into the multifaceted challenges faced in various domains, such as generative AI and computer vision.

Text and image embeddings provide insights into the pivotal role of embeddings in transforming textual and visual data into condensed, meaningful vectors. It examines how embeddings facilitate the understanding of semantic relationships and contextual nuances within language and images. The objective is to showcase how embeddings bridge the gap between raw data and AI models, contributing to better comprehension, representation, and manipulation of diverse data types.

Vector databases delves into the construction and application of databases where items are represented as vectors. The section emphasizes efficient retrieval through indexing, particularly similarity searches. It aims to elucidate the construction of structures that enable quick and accurate querying of semantically related items, illustrating their significance in real-world applications.

Image-to-image search utilizing the liberated pinecone vector databases explores the practical implementation of vector databases for image search tasks. It sheds light on the liberation of these databases for open exploration and outlines how they power efficient image retrieval mechanisms. This section aims to demonstrate how vector databases can revolutionize image search, transforming the way users discover visually similar content across a spectrum of applications.

Chapter 12: Overview and Application of Generative AI Models - In this chapter, we embark on a journey through the dynamic landscape of technology's role in various industries, without delving into complex code or algorithms. Imagine a world where cutting-edge innovations like LLM and Gen AI are not just buzzwords but integral tools reshaping healthcare, retail, finance, and insurance.

The story begins in healthcare, where LLM streamlines compliance, analyzes intricate medical documents, and guides professionals through complex regulatory mazes. Meanwhile, Gen AI steps in to provide personalized medical advice, automate appointment scheduling, and deliver vital information to patients and healthcare providers, ensuring the highest quality of care. Transitioning to the retail sector, LLM ensures contractual accuracy, compliance, and vendor agreement efficiency. Gen AI transforms the customer experience, captivating shoppers with personalized recommendations and dynamic marketing strategies, creating a retail environment tailored to each individual. In the financial realm, LLM takes center stage, enhancing risk assessment, detecting fraud, and analyzing contracts with unparalleled precision. Simultaneously, Gen AI optimizes customer service through AI-powered chatbots and virtual assistants, providing real-time and context-aware responses to financial inquiries.

Finally, in the insurance sector, LLM drives claims efficiency, fraud detection, and regulatory compliance. Gen AI revolutionizes insurance by reshaping underwriting processes, crafting personalized policy offerings, and elevating customer interactions.

Chapter 13: Key Learnings - The objective of this chapter is to synthesize and distill the core teachings and insights from chapters one through twelve. It aims to provide readers with a comprehensive summary, highlighting the key concepts, important takeaways, and significant learnings obtained from each preceding chapter. By consolidating this knowledge, the chapter seeks to offer a holistic understanding of the subject matter, reinforcing key ideas, and preparing readers for further exploration or application of the discussed principles. Ultimately, the objective is to enhance comprehension, retention, and practical application of the cumulative wisdom acquired throughout the previous chapters.

Code Bundle and Coloured Images

Please follow the link to download the
Code Bundle and the *Coloured Images* of the book:

https://rebrand.ly/7cicq52

The code bundle for the book is also hosted on GitHub at
https://github.com/bpbpublications/Learn-Python-Generative-AI.
In case there's an update to the code, it will be updated on the existing GitHub repository.

We have code bundles from our rich catalogue of books and videos available at **https://github.com/bpbpublications**. Check them out!

Errata

We take immense pride in our work at BPB Publications and follow best practices to ensure the accuracy of our content to provide with an indulging reading experience to our subscribers. Our readers are our mirrors, and we use their inputs to reflect and improve upon human errors, if any, that may have occurred during the publishing processes involved. To let us maintain the quality and help us reach out to any readers who might be having difficulties due to any unforeseen errors, please write to us at :

errata@bpbonline.com

Your support, suggestions and feedbacks are highly appreciated by the BPB Publications' Family.

Did you know that BPB offers eBook versions of every book published, with PDF and ePub files available? You can upgrade to the eBook version at www.bpbonline.com and as a print book customer, you are entitled to a discount on the eBook copy. Get in touch with us at :

business@bpbonline.com for more details.

At **www.bpbonline.com**, you can also read a collection of free technical articles, sign up for a range of free newsletters, and receive exclusive discounts and offers on BPB books and eBooks.

Piracy

If you come across any illegal copies of our works in any form on the internet, we would be grateful if you would provide us with the location address or website name. Please contact us at **business@bpbonline.com** with a link to the material.

If you are interested in becoming an author

If there is a topic that you have expertise in, and you are interested in either writing or contributing to a book, please visit **www.bpbonline.com**. We have worked with thousands of developers and tech professionals, just like you, to help them share their insights with the global tech community. You can make a general application, apply for a specific hot topic that we are recruiting an author for, or submit your own idea.

Reviews

Please leave a review. Once you have read and used this book, why not leave a review on the site that you purchased it from? Potential readers can then see and use your unbiased opinion to make purchase decisions. We at BPB can understand what you think about our products, and our authors can see your feedback on their book. Thank you!

For more information about BPB, please visit **www.bpbonline.com**.

Join our book's Discord space

Join the book's Discord Workspace for Latest updates, Offers, Tech happenings around the world, New Release and Sessions with the Authors:

https://discord.bpbonline.com

Table of Contents

CHAPTER 1

Introducing Generative AI

Introduction

In this chapter, you will learn about the evolution of generative AI and how it has progressed over the years. It also highlights the approaches previously used for generative models, and how these have changed with the emergence of deep learning and vast amounts of data. Some of the latest techniques, such as **Generative Adversarial Networks (GANs)** and **Variational Autoencoders (VAEs)**, and their applications in generating high-quality images, audio, and text are also discussed.

In addition, you can learn about the difference between discriminative and generative models and how generative models aim to generate new data that follows the original data distribution. An introduction to generative models and an overview of the various generative models available are also provided.

Finally, the chapter discusses the strengths and weaknesses of generative models and highlights that there is still much room for further innovation and improvement in generative AI. Overall, the chapter provides an excellent introduction to the evolution of generative AI and the different techniques used in the field.

Structure

In this chapter, we will learn about the following topics:

- Overview of generative models
- Discriminative vs generative modes
- Types of discriminative and generative models
- Strengths and weaknesses

Objectives

The objective of this chapter is to provide a comprehensive understanding of generative models, including an overview of generative models, a comparison of discriminative vs generative models, an introduction to the types of discriminative and generative models, as well as their strengths and weaknesses. By the end of the content, readers should be able to differentiate between discriminative and generative models, understand the different types of each, and make informed decisions about which type of model is most appropriate for their needs.

Overview of generative models

Generative AI refers to a type of artificial intelligence that can generate new data or content, such as images, videos, or text, with similar characteristics to the training data it was given. Generative AI has progressed rapidly over the years, and much of this progress has been driven by advances in deep learning.

One of the earliest examples of generative AI was the autoencoder, developed in the 1980s. Autoencoders are neural networks that can learn to compress and reconstruct data, and they can also be used to generate new data by sampling from the known compressed representation. However, autoencoders have limitations regarding the types of data they can develop and the quality of the generated output.

In the 1990s, Boltzmann machines were developed, which are neural networks that can model the joint probability distribution of a set of input variables. Boltzmann Machines can be used for generative modeling by sampling from the learned distribution, but they are challenging to train and scale to large datasets.

More recently, deep learning has enabled significant progress in generative AI, particularly with the development of GANs and VAEs. GANs were first introduced in 2014. They consist of two neural networks: a generator network that generates new data and a discriminator network that distinguishes between generated and real data. The generator is trained to produce indistinguishable data from real data, while the discriminator is trained to correctly classify the data as real or fake. Through this adversarial training process, GANs can generate high-quality data in a variety of domains, including images, videos, and music.

VAEs were also introduced in 2014, they are similar to autoencoders, with the addition of a probabilistic encoder that learns a distribution over the compressed representation. VAEs can generate new data by sampling from the learned distribution, and they have been used for generative modeling in various domains, including images and text.

More recent advancements in generative AI have focused on improving the quality and diversity of generated data, such as using attention mechanisms and self-attention, as well as exploring new domains for generative modeling, such as 3D object generation and interactive storytelling. Generative AI has also made significant progress in **natural language processing (NLP)**, where language models such as OpenAI's **Generative Pre-trained Transformer (GPT)** series have achieved remarkable performance in tasks such as language generation, language understanding, and even question answering. These models use a generative approach to learn the underlying structure and patterns of human language, allowing them to generate coherent and fluent sentences almost indistinguishable from those written by humans.

Moreover, generative AI has also been used in creative domains such as art, music, and fashion, enabling new forms of artistic expression and creativity. For example, DeepDream, a generative model developed by Google, has been used to create surreal and psychedelic images by altering the features of an input image. Similarly, the Magenta project by Google has developed generative models for music creation that can generate original compositions in various styles and genres. In recent years, there have been several new generative models that have emerged, which have shown impressive results in generating realistic and diverse outputs. Two such models are the **Stable Diffusion (SDE)** and DALL-E.

Stable Diffusion (SDE) is a recently proposed generative model that builds upon the idea of continuous-time stochastic processes. The model is based on the diffusion process, a stochastic process that describes the movement of particles in a fluid or gas. The SDE model uses a **Markov Chain Monte Ca]rlo (MCMC)** approach to learn a stochastic differential equation that describes the dynamics of the diffusion process. This allows the model to understand the complex correlations between the inputs and generate high-quality samples that exhibit a high degree of diversity.

DALL-E is another recently proposed generative model that OpenAI developed. DALL-E is a transformer-based model that can generate high-quality images from textual descriptions. The model uses a conditioning mechanism that takes in a textual description as input and generates an image that corresponds to the description. DALL-E is trained on a massive dataset of text-image pairs, which allows it to learn the complex relationships between text and images.

One of the advantages of these new generative models is that they are capable of generating high-quality and diverse outputs that are difficult to distinguish from real data. This has important implications for a range of applications, such as image and video synthesis, text-to-image generation, and natural language processing.

Discriminative vs. generative models

Discriminative modeling involves directly learning the decision boundary between classes, which allows for the direct classification of new examples. For example, in a binary classification problem, a discriminative model learns to predict whether an input belongs to class A or class B. Discriminative models do not attempt to model the underlying distribution of the data, but rather focus on learning the boundary between classes. Common discriminative models include logistic regression, support vector machines, and neural networks.

On the other hand, generative modeling involves modeling the underlying distribution of the data and using that model to generate new examples like the training data. Generative models can also be used for classification by computing the probability of a new example belonging to each class and choosing the class with the highest probability. Common generative models include Naive Bayes, Gaussian mixture models, and Hidden Markov models.

One advantage of generative models is that they can generate new data points, which can be useful in scenarios where the amount of training data is limited. However, generative models may be more computationally expensive than discriminative models, as they require modeling the entire data distribution. In addition, generative models may not perform as well as discriminative models in situations where the decision boundary between classes is complex.

Both discriminative and generative modeling is important in today's deep learning era.

Discriminative models, such as convolutional neural networks and recurrent neural networks, are commonly used in tasks such as image classification, object detection, and natural language processing. These models are highly effective at learning complex decision boundaries between classes and can achieve state-of-the-art performance on many tasks.

Generative models, such as variational autoencoders and generative adversarial networks, have become increasingly popular recently. These models can generate new data points that are similar to the training data, which can be useful in scenarios where the amount of training data is limited. Generative models are also being used in applications such as image and video synthesis, text generation, and data augmentation.

Overall, both discriminative and generative models have essential roles in the deep learning era, and the choice between them depends on the specific task and available resources. As deep learning continues to advance, it is likely that both types of models will continue to play essential roles in different applications. In the following figure, we can clearly see the difference between discriminative and generative models and how they illustrate the decision boundary. Understanding these concepts is crucial for anyone looking to work with machine learning models:

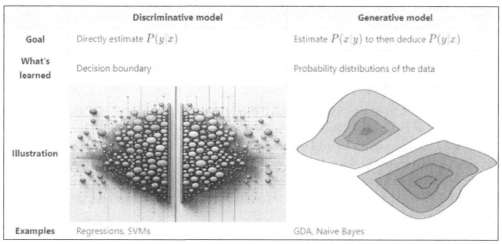

Figure 1.1: *Difference between discriminative and generative models*

Discriminative models learn the boundary between classes directly, while generative models learn the joint probability distribution of the input and output variables. Let's delve deeper into these topics and explore the various types of discriminative and generative models, as well as their strengths and weaknesses. Let us understand the significance of these modeling in today's Deep learning era. Discriminative models, such as convolutional neural networks and recurrent neural networks, are commonly used in tasks such as image classification, object detection, and natural language processing. These models are highly effective at learning complex decision boundaries between classes and can achieve state-of-the-art performance on many tasks.

Generative models, such as variational autoencoders and generative adversarial networks, have become increasingly popular recently. These models can generate new data points similar to the training data, which can be useful in scenarios where the amount of training data is limited. Generative models are also being used in applications such as image and video synthesis, text generation, and data augmentation.

Overall, both discriminative and generative models have essential roles in the deep learning era, and the choice between them depends on the specific task and available resources. As deep learning continues to advance, it is likely that both types of models will continue to play essential roles in many different applications.

Let us clarify a common misconception about **convolutional neural networks (CNNs)** and **recurrent neural networks (RNNs)** The question many ask, are they generative models? CNNs are primarily used for discriminative modeling tasks such as image classification and object detection. They learn to extract features from the input data and use those features to make predictions about the class of the input.

RNNs are commonly used for sequence modeling tasks such as natural language processing and speech recognition. They can model sequences of input data by maintaining a hidden state that captures information from previous inputs.

On the other hand, Generative models explicitly model the underlying probability distribution of the input data and use that distribution to generate new data points. Examples of generative models include Naive Bayes, Gaussian mixture models, and variational autoencoders.

While CNNs and RNNs are not generative models, some variations of these architectures can be used for generative modeling. For example, **generative adversarial networks (GANs)** use a CNN or other neural network as a generator to produce new data points that are similar to the training data. Similarly, some types of RNNs can be used for sequence generation tasks, such as generating new text or music. However, these variations of CNNs and RNNs are not typically used for discriminative modeling tasks like image classification or object detection.

Types of discriminative and generative models

There are various types of discriminative and generative models used in machine learning. Here are some examples:

Discriminative models:

- Logistic regression

- **Support Vector Machines (SVMs)**

- Decision trees

- Random forests

- **Gradient Boosting Machines (GBMs)**

- Neural networks (multilayer perceptron, convolutional neural networks, recurrent neural networks)

Generative models:

- Naive Bayes

- **Gaussian Mixture Models (GMMs)**

- **Hidden Markov Models (HMMs)**

- Autoencoders

- **Variational Autoencoders (VAEs)**

- **Generative Adversarial Networks (GANs)**

- Boltzmann machines

Let us understand each with an equation:

Discriminative models: Following are the types of discriminative models:

- **Logistic regression**: A linear classification algorithm that estimates the probability of an input belonging to a particular class. The model estimates the probability of an input x belonging to a particular class y:

$$P(y = 1 \mid x) = \frac{1}{1 + e^{-(w_0 + w_1 x_1 + w_2 x_2 + z \ldots + w_p x_p)}}$$

  Where $w_0, w_1, w_2, \ldots, w_p$ \$ are the model parameters and $x_1, x_2, \ldots, x_p$ are the input features.

- **Support Vector Machines (SVMs)**: A discriminative model that finds the optimal hyperplane to separate different classes of input data. The model finds the optimal hyperplane to separate different classes of input data. For a linearly separable dataset, the decision boundary is given by:

  $w \cdot x + b = 0$

  where W is the weight vector and b is the bias term.

- **Decision trees**: A classification algorithm that recursively splits the input data into smaller subsets based on the values of input features.

  Decision trees recursively split the input data into smaller subsets based on the values of input features. The decision boundary can be represented as a tree structure, where each internal node represents a decision based on a particular feature, and each leaf node represents a class label. An example decision rule might be:

  if $x_1 < 0.5$ and $x2 < 0.2$ then class $y = 1$

- **Random forests**: An ensemble of decision trees that combines the predictions of multiple trees to improve accuracy.

- **Gradient Boosting Machines (GBMs)**: Another ensemble method that sequentially builds decision trees, with each tree trying to correct the mistakes of the previous tree.

  GBMs sequentially build decision trees, with each tree trying to correct the mistakes of the previous tree. The predicted class label is determined by a weighted sum of the individual decision trees:

$$f(x) = \sum_{i=1}^{T} \alpha_i h_i(x)$$

where T is the number of decision trees, α_i is the weight of the ith tree, and $h_i(x)$ is the prediction of the ith tree.

- **Neural networks**: A class of models that are inspired by the structure and function of the human brain. Examples include Multilayer Perceptron, Convolutional Neural Networks, and Recurrent Neural Networks.

  Neural networks consist of layers of interconnected nodes, or neurons, that process input data. A basic feedforward neural network can be represented as:

  $y = \sigma(W_2 \sigma(W_1 x + b_1) + b_2)$ where x is the input vector, y is the output vector, W_1 and W_2 are the weight matrices, b_1 and b_2 are the bias vectors, and $\sigma(\cdot)$ is an activation function.

Generative models: Different types of generative models are explained as follows:

- **Naive bayes**: A probabilistic model that estimates the likelihood of a particular input belonging to a class based on its feature values. The model estimates the joint probability distribution of the input features and the class label, and uses Bayes' rule to make predictions. For example, for a binary classification problem with input features $x_1, x_2, ..., x_n$ and class label y, the Naive Bayes model can be written as:

$$P(y \mid x_1, x_2, ..., x_n) = \frac{P(x_1, x_2, ..., x_n \mid y)P(y)}{P(x_1, x_2, ..., x_n)}$$

Assuming the input features are conditionally independent given the class label (the "naive" assumption), we can simplify this expression to:

$P(y \mid x_1, x_2, ..., x_n) \propto P(y) \prod_{i=1}^{n} P(x_1 \mid y)$ where $P(y)$ is the prior probability of the class label and $P(x_i \mid y)$ is the conditional probability of the ith feature given the class label.

- **Gaussian Mixture Models (GMMs)**: A probabilistic model that assumes that the input data is generated from a mixture of Gaussian distributions.

  A GMM assumes that the data is generated from a mixture of Gaussian distributions, with each Gaussian component corresponding to a particular class label. The probability density function of a GMM can be written as:

  $p(x) = \sum_{k=1}^{K} \pi_k N(x \mid \mu_k, \Sigma_k)$ where x is the input vector, K is the number of Gaussian components, π_k is the mixing coefficient of the kth component, μ_k is the mean vector of the kth component, and Σ_k is the covariance matrix of the kth component.

- **Hidden Markov Models (HMMs)**: A type of generative model that is used for sequential data, such as speech recognition or natural language processing.

Let $X = (X_1, X_2, ..., X_T)$ denote a sequence of observed variables and $Z = (Z_1, Z_2, ..., Z_T)$ denote a corresponding sequence of hidden (latent) variables. An HMM assumes that the hidden variables Z_t form a Markov chain and that the observed variables X_t are conditionally independent of all other observed variables given the corresponding hidden variable Z_t. The joint probability of the observed and hidden variables can be written as:

$$p(X, Z \mid \theta) = p(Z_1 \mid \pi) \prod_{t-2}^{T} p(Z_t \mid Z_{t-1}, A) \prod_{t-2}^{T} p(X_t \mid Z_t, \phi)$$

Where $\theta = (\pi, A, \phi)$ are the model parameters, π is the initial distribution over hidden states, A is the transition matrix between hidden states, and ϕ is the emission probabilities (that is, the probability of observing a particular output given a hidden state).

- **Autoencoders**: A neural network architecture that is used for unsupervised learning and dimensionality reduction.

  Autoencoders are neural networks that learn to encode input data into a lower-dimensional representation and then decode it back into the original data. The autoencoder loss function can be written as:

  $$\mathcal{L}(x, \hat{x}) = ||\, x - \hat{x}\, ||_2^2$$ where **x** is the input data and $\hat{x}$ is the reconstructed data.

- **Variational Autoencoders (VAEs)**: A type of autoencoder that is used for generative modeling by learning a low-dimensional representation of the input data.

  VAEs are a type of autoencoder that learn a probabilistic model of the input data. The VAE loss function consists of two terms: a reconstruction loss and a regularization term that encourages the learned distribution to match a prior distribution. For example, the VAE loss function for a Gaussian prior can be written as:

  $$\mathcal{L}(x, \hat{x}, \mu, \sigma) = ||\, x - \hat{x}\, ||^{2+} \frac{1}{2} \Sigma i = 2^k (\sigma_i^2 + \mu_i^2 - \log \sigma_i^2 - 11)$$ where **x** is the input data, $\hat{x}$ is the reconstructed data, μ and σ are the mean and standard deviation vectors of the learned distribution, and **k** is

- **Generative Adversarial Networks (GANs)**: A type of generative model that uses two neural networks (a generator and a discriminator) to generate new data points that are similar to the training data.

  GANs consist of a generator network and a discriminator network that play a two-player minimax game. The generator network takes a random noise vector **z** as input and generates fake data samples x_{fake} while the discriminator network takes a data sample **x** as input and outputs a probability that **x** is real. The GAN objective function can be written as:

  $$\min_{G} \max_{D} V(D, G) = \mathbb{E}x \sim p\text{data}(x)[\log D(x)] + \mathbb{E}z \sim pz(z)[\log(1 - D(z)))]$$

Where **G** is the generator network, **D** is the discriminator network, P_{data} is the true data distribution, and P_z is the noise distribution.

- **Boltzmann machines**: A type of generative model that models the joint probability distribution of the input data using energy-based learning.

$$E(v,h) = -\sum_{i=1}^{N_v} a_i v_i - \sum_{i=1}^{N_v} b_j h_j - \sum_{i=1}^{N_v} \sum_{j=1}^{Nh} v_i w_{ij} h_j$$

Where v is the visible unit vector, h is the hidden unit vector, a_i and b_j are the biases for visible unit i and hidden unit j respectively, w_{ij} is the weight between visible unit i and hidden unit j, and N_v and N_h is the number of visible and hidden units, respectively.

Strengths and weaknesses

In this section, we will discuss the strengths and weaknesses:

- **Naive Bayes**: Following are the strengths and weaknesses.

  Strengths:

  o Naive Bayes is a simple and fast algorithm that can be trained on small datasets.

  o It performs well in text classification and spam filtering tasks.

  o It works well with high dimensional data.

  Weaknesses:

  o Naive Bayes assumes that all features are independent of each other, which is often not the case in real-world scenarios.

  o It can result in poor accuracy if the training data is not representative of the test data.

  o It may also suffer from the problem of rare events, where it assigns a zero probability to a feature that has not been observed in the training set.

- **Gaussian Mixture Models (GMMs)**: Following are the strengths and weaknesses:

  Strengths:

  o GMMs are flexible probabilistic models that can capture complex data distributions.

  o They can be used for clustering, density estimation, and dimensionality reduction.

  o GMMs can handle both continuous and discrete data.

Weaknesses:

o GMMs are sensitive to the choice of the number of components or clusters, which is often not known in advance.

o They can be computationally expensive to train, especially when the number of components is large.

o GMMs may converge to local optima and are prone to overfitting.

- **Hidden Markov Models (HMMs)**: Following are the strengths and weaknesses:

Strengths:

o HMMs can model sequential data with a natural probabilistic framework.

o They have been successfully applied to speech recognition, natural language processing, and handwriting recognition.

o HMMs can handle missing data and noisy observations.

Weaknesses:

o HMMs assume that the underlying process is Markovian, which may not always be true in practice.

o The performance of HMMs heavily depends on the quality of the initial state and transition probabilities.

o HMMs can be sensitive to the choice of the number of hidden states.

- **Autoencoders**: Following are the strengths and weaknesses:

Strengths:

o Autoencoders can learn compressed representations of high-dimensional data, which can be useful for data compression, feature extraction, and visualization.

o They can be trained on unlabeled data and then used for supervised tasks.

o Autoencoders can handle missing data and noisy observations.

Weaknesses:

o Autoencoders may suffer from overfitting, especially when the number of hidden units is large.

o They may not capture all relevant information in the data and may result in lossy compression.

o They can be computationally expensive to train, especially when the input dimensionality is high.

- **Variational Autoencoders (VAEs)**: Following are the strengths and weaknesses:

Strengths:

o   VAEs can generate new samples from the learned data distribution.

o   They can handle missing data and noisy observations.

o   They can be used for unsupervised and semi-supervised learning.

Weaknesses:

o   VAEs can suffer from mode collapse, where the model generates only a few distinct samples.

o   The training of VAEs can be computationally expensive and requires careful tuning of hyperparameters.

o   The quality of generated samples heavily depends on the choice of the prior distribution.

- **Generative Adversarial Networks (GANs)**: Following are the strengths and weaknesses:

Strengths:

o   GANs can generate high-quality samples that are visually realistic.

o   They can be used for image and video generation, data augmentation, and style transfer.

o   GANs can learn complex non-linear mappings between input and output domains.

Weaknesses:

o   GANs are notoriously difficult to train and require careful tuning of hyperparameters.

o   They can suffer from mode collapse, where the generator produces a limited set of samples.

o   GANs may produce artifacts and distortions in generated samples.

- **Boltzmann machines**: Following are the strengths and weaknesses:

Strengths:

o   Boltzmann machines can model complex data distributions and can be used for unsupervised learning.

o   They can be trained using a simple and scalable learning algorithm called **Contrastive D**

Weaknesses:

o   **Computational complexity**: Boltzmann machines, particularly when dealing with large networks, can be computationally expensive and inefficient. This is mainly due to the need for repeated sampling to approximate the distribution of the network, which is a process that requires significant computational resources. This challenge becomes more pronounced as the size of the network increases, leading to longer training times and higher computational costs.

o **Difficulty in training**: Training boltzmann machines, especially deep architectures like Deep Boltzmann Machines, can be quite challenging. This is because the learning process involves calculating gradients of a log-likelihood function, which can be difficult due to the intractability of partition functions in these models. As a result, approximations like Contrastive Divergence are used, but these can lead to suboptimal learning and convergence issues. The training process is also sensitive to the choice of hyperparameters, which can make it difficult to optimize and apply these models effectively in different scenarios.

Let us understand generative model in detail:

A generative model is a probabilistic model that describes how a dataset is generated. It can be used to generate new data by sampling from this model. For instance, we can use generative modeling to generate a new image of a horse that has never existed but still looks realistic. To build such a model, we need a dataset consisting of many examples of the entity we are trying to generate. Each observation consists of many features, and our goal is to build a model that can generate new sets of features that look as if they have been created using the same rules as the original data. The model must be probabilistic rather than deterministic and include a stochastic element that influences the individual samples generated by the model. We can imagine some unknown probabilistic distribution explaining why some images are likely to be found in the training dataset and others are not. Our job is to build a model that mimics this distribution as closely as possible and then sample from it to generate new, distinct observations that look as if they could have been included in the original training set. While discriminative modeling has been driving advances in machine learning, in recent years there have been notable breakthroughs in generative modeling using deep learning techniques. Projects such as StyleGAN and GPT-2 have demonstrated the impressive capabilities of generative models in creating hyper-realistic images and completing text passages. The potential applications of generative modeling extend beyond industries such as game design and cinematography, with the possibility of creating fake news and novels using generative models raising ethical concerns.

There are three key reasons why generative modeling is considered essential in unlocking a more sophisticated form of artificial intelligence beyond what discriminative modeling can achieve:

- First, it is important to understand how data is generated, not just categorize it.

- Second, generative modeling can drive developments in other fields of machine learning such as reinforcement learning by allowing agents to learn in their own simulated environments.

- Finally, to achieve true artificial intelligence comparable to humans, generative modeling must be part of the solution. Our perception of reality is believed to be a generative model, and a deep understanding of how machines can acquire this ability is crucial for general artificial intelligence.

The journey into generative modeling starts with understanding more straightforward examples and building towards more complex architectures. Discriminative models, on the other hand, are used when you want to learn the decision boundary between classes in the data. They focus on finding the most discriminative features that separate the different classes. Some common uses for discriminative models include:

- Classification
- Regression
- Ranking
- Information retrieval
- Pattern recognition

Whereas generative models and discriminative models are two different approaches to machine learning that are used for different purposes. Here is a brief explanation of when you might use one or the other.

Generative models are used when you want to model the underlying probability distribution of the data. In other words, they learn to generate new data that is like the data they were trained on. Some common uses for generative models include:

- Image and video generation
- Text generation
- Data augmentation
- Outlier detection
- Density estimation
- Digital twins

Note: Generative models can be used to generate synthetic data that can be used to train digital twins. This is particularly useful in situations where the data is scarce or expensive to collect. For example, in manufacturing, generative models can be used to generate synthetic sensor data to train digital twins that can predict equipment failures.

Generative models can be useful for synthetic data generation when there is a need to augment or balance an existing dataset. For example, in the case of image classification, if there is a class with a limited number of samples, a generative model can be trained to generate more examples of that class. This can help improve the performance of a classifier by providing more data for the underrepresented class.

Class imbalance scenario

Let us understand class imbalance scenario: How to use the generative model in multi class classification where there are imbalance classes.

Suppose we have a multi-class classification problem where we have three classes: A, B, and C. However, the data is highly imbalanced, with class A having only 10% of the samples, class B having 20%, and class C having 70%.

To address this imbalance, we can use a generative model to generate synthetic data for the minority classes. Specifically, we can use a GAN to generate new samples for classes A and B. The GAN consists of a generator and a discriminator. The generator generates new samples that mimic the training data, while the discriminator tries to distinguish between the real and fake samples.

Here are the steps for using a GAN for synthetic data generation:

1. Separate the data by classes A, B, and C.

2. Train the discriminator on the original data, using class labels as targets. The discriminator will learn to distinguish between the classes.

3. Train the generator to produce synthetic samples for class A and class B. The generator takes random noise as input and produces synthetic samples as output. The generator is trained to fool the discriminator into thinking that the synthetic samples are real.

4. Once the generator is trained, use it to generate new synthetic samples for classes A and B. You can generate as many samples as you need to balance the data.

5. Combine the original data with the synthetic data, creating a new dataset with balanced classes.

6. Train a classifier on the new dataset, using class labels as targets. You can use any classifier that works well for multi-class classification, such as a decision tree, a support vector machine, or a neural network.

7. Evaluate the classifier on a holdout dataset to measure its accuracy and performance.

Additionally, generative models can be used for data augmentation, where new samples are generated by adding small variations to existing data. This can help to increase the size and diversity of a dataset, which can be beneficial for improving the accuracy of a model.

However, it's important to note that generative models may not always be the best approach for addressing data imbalance. In some cases, discriminative models may be more appropriate, such as when the class distribution is highly imbalanced or when the class boundaries are difficult to separate. Discriminative models can also be more efficient to train and require less data.

Ultimately, the choice between using a generative or discriminative model depends on the specific problem at hand and the available data. It's important to carefully consider the strengths and limitations of both approaches and choose the one that is most suitable for the task.

Generative modeling framework

There are some benefits of using a framework for generative AI:

- **Increased flexibility**: Generative models provide a flexible approach to modeling data, allowing for a wide range of data types and structures to be modeled.

- **Improved performance**: Generative models can improve the performance of a model by increasing the amount of data available for training and reducing overfitting.

- **Better understanding**: Generative models can provide a better understanding of the underlying structure of the data and the relationships between the variables.

- **Improved efficiency**: Generative models can improve efficiency by reducing the need for manual feature engineering and data preprocessing.

- **Enhanced creativity**: Generative models can be used for creative applications such as art generation, music generation, and story generation, which can be used in various fields including entertainment, marketing, and advertising.

Now that we understand the benefits let us understand the framework:

- **Data preprocessing**: The first step is to prepare your data for use with the model. This may involve cleaning, normalizing, or transforming the data to make it more suitable for the task at hand.

- **Model selection**: There are many types of generative models, so it is important to choose the one that is best suited for your particular problem. Common types include VAEs, GANs, and autoregressive models.

- **Model design**: Once you have selected a model, you need to design its architecture. This involves determining the number of layers, the types of activation functions to use, and the number of neurons in each layer.

- **Model training**: After you have designed your model, you need to train it on your data. This involves feeding the data into the model and adjusting the weights of the model's neurons based on the error between the predicted output and the actual output.

- **Model evaluation**: Once your model has been trained, you must evaluate its performance. This involves using metrics such as accuracy, precision, recall, and F1 score to assess how well the model is able to generate new data.

- **Model optimization**: If your model is not performing well, you may need to optimize it by adjusting its hyperparameters or changing its architecture.

- **Model deployment**: Once your model has been optimized, you can deploy it for use in your application. This may involve integrating it into a larger system or making it available as a standalone tool.

- **Model maintenance**: Finally, it is important to maintain your model over time. This may involve retraining it on new data, updating its architecture, or optimizing its hyperparameters to ensure that it continues to generate accurate and useful results.

Let us understand how to implement the framework in MLops.

Note: MLOps, short for Machine Learning Operations, is a practice that combines the principles of DevOps with the specific needs of Machine Learning (ML) workflows. It focuses on the management and automation of ML pipelines, from data preparation and model training to deployment and maintenance.

Note: MLOps aims to streamline the ML process and make it more efficient, reliable, and scalable. It brings together teams of data scientists, developers, and IT professionals to collaborate on building and deploying ML models in a consistent, reproducible, and scalable manner. By implementing MLOps practices, organizations can improve their ability to deliver ML-powered applications to production faster, with higher quality, and at lower cost.

There are several tools that can be used to implement a generative model framework in **Machine Learning Operations (MLOps)**, which involves integrating machine learning models into production pipelines. Some of these tools include:

- **TensorFlow Extended (TFX)**: TFX is an end-to-end platform for deploying machine learning models in production. It includes a set of libraries and tools for building, training, and deploying models, as well as monitoring and managing them in production environments.

- **Kubeflow**: Kubeflow is a popular open-source platform for deploying machine learning workflows on Kubernetes clusters. It provides a set of tools and APIs for building, training, and deploying models, as well as monitoring and managing them in production environments.

- **MLflow**: MLflow is an open-source platform for managing the complete machine learning lifecycle, including building, training, and deploying models. It includes a set of libraries and tools for building and deploying models, as well as tracking and managing experiments and workflows.

- **Hugging Face**: Hugging Face is a popular library for building and deploying natural language processing models, including generative models. It includes a set of pre-trained models that can be fine-tuned for specific use cases, as well as a set of tools for building and deploying custom models.

- **Amazon SageMaker**: Amazon SageMaker is a cloud-based platform for building, training, and deploying machine learning models at scale. It includes a set of tools and APIs for building and deploying models, as well as monitoring and managing them in production environments.

- **Google Cloud AI Platform**: Google Cloud AI Platform is a cloud-based platform for building, training, and deploying machine learning models at scale. It includes a set of tools and APIs for building and deploying models, as well as monitoring and managing them in production environments.

There are several MLOps tools that can be used for each section of the generative model framework:

- **Data preprocessing**: For data preprocessing, popular tools include Pandas for data manipulation, NumPy for numerical computing, and Scikit-Learn for data preprocessing tasks such as scaling, encoding, and feature selection.

- **Model selection**: Popular libraries for model selection include TensorFlow and PyTorch, which provide pre-built functions for implementing popular generative models such as VAEs and GANs.

- **Model design**: For model design, TensorFlow and PyTorch provide tools for building custom architectures and pre-built models that can be modified for specific use cases.

- **Model training**: TensorFlow and PyTorch provide tools for model training, including built-in functions for backpropagation and optimization.

- **Model evaluation**: Scikit-Learn and TensorFlow provide metrics for evaluating generative models, including accuracy, precision, recall, and F1 score.

- **Model optimization**: TensorFlow and PyTorch provide tools for hyperparameter tuning and architecture optimization, including automatic differentiation and hyperparameter search.

- **Model deployment**: Once the model is trained and optimized, it can be deployed using tools such as TensorFlow Serving, Kubernetes, or AWS Lambda.

- **Model maintenance**: For maintaining the model over time, it is important to keep it up to date with the latest data, regularly retrain it, and monitor its performance to ensure that it continues to generate accurate and useful results. Tools such as MLflow and Kubeflow can help with model versioning and tracking.

The following section will describe the key concepts to understand before starting with the next chapter.

Sample Space

In the context of generative models, the sample space refers to the set of all possible outcomes that the model can generate. It is the space of all possible samples that the model can produce given some input or random noise.

A generic equation for the sample space of a generative model can be represented as:

$$X = G(Z; \theta)$$

Where X represents the sample space of the generative model, Z represents the input or noise space, θ represents the model parameters, and G represents the function that maps the input or noise space to the sample space.

The sample space X can be continuous, as in the case of Gaussian mixture models or variational autoencoders, or discrete, as in the case of generative adversarial networks or autoregressive models. The size and complexity of the sample space depends on the complexity of the underlying model and the dimensionality of the input or noise space.

In the context of generative models such as GANs and VAEs, the sample space refers to the set of all possible outputs that can be generated by the model.

In GANs, the sample space corresponds to the space of generated samples that are produced by the generator network. These samples are generated by feeding random noise into the generator network and then mapping it to a high-dimensional space of images or other data types. The goal of the generator network is to learn to generate samples that are indistinguishable from real samples.

In VAEs, the sample space corresponds to the space of possible data points that can be generated by sampling from the learned latent space. The encoder network maps the input data into a lower-dimensional latent space, while the decoder network maps point in the latent space back to the original data space. The VAE model learns to generate new samples by sampling points in the latent space and decoding them using the decoder network.

The generic equation for the sample space in a generative model is:

$$S = \{x \mid x = G(z), z \sim p(z)\}$$

Where S is the sample space, G is the generator network, z is a random noise vector sampled from a prior distribution $p(z)$, and x is the generated sample.

Probability density function

Probability density function (PDF) is a mathematical function that describes the probability distribution of a continuous random variable. It gives the probability of the variable falling within a particular range of values, rather than taking on any one specific value.

More formally, a PDF is a function $f(x)$ that maps each value x in the domain to a non-negative value representing the relative likelihood of x occurring. The total area under the PDF curve over the entire domain is equal to 1, since the probability that the variable falls within the whole range of possible values is 1.

In practice, PDFs are used in a variety of applications, such as statistical inference, machine learning, and signal processing. They provide a way to quantify the uncertainty associated with continuous random variables and to model the underlying probability distributions of the data:

$$f(x) = \frac{d}{dx} F(x)$$

Where $F(x)$ is the **cumulative distribution function (CDF)** of the random variable X. The PDF and CDF are related as follows:

$$F(x) = P(X \le x) = \int_{-\infty}^{x} f(x) dx$$

Where $F(x)$ is the CDF of the random variable X, $f(x)$ is the PDF of X, and the integral represents the area under the PDF curve up to x.

In other words, the CDF gives the probability that the random variable X takes a value less than or equal to x, while the PDF gives the rate at which the probability density changes with x. The PDF is the derivative of the CDF:

$$f(x) = \frac{dF(x)}{dx}$$

Conversely, the CDF is the integral of the PDF:

$$F(x) = \int_{-\infty}^{x} f(x) dx$$

Therefore, the PDF and CDF are two complementary ways of describing the same underlying distribution. Here is an example of a Python function to calculate the PDF of a normal distribution:

```python
import numpy as np
import matplotlib.pyplot as plt

def normal_pdf(x, mu, sigma):
    """
    Computes the PDF of a normal distribution with mean mu and standard
deviation sigma
    at point x.
    """
    return (1 / (np.sqrt(2 * np.pi) * sigma)) * np.exp(-((x - mu) ** 2) / (2
* sigma ** 2))

# Example usage:
x_values = np.linspace(-5, 5, 100)
```

```
mu = 0
sigma = 1
pdf_values = normal_pdf(x_values, mu, sigma)

plt.plot(x_values, pdf_values)
plt.title("Normal PDF with mean = 0 and std dev = 1")
plt.xlabel("x")
plt.ylabel("PDF(x)")
plt.show()
```

In the following figure, we can see the PDF of a normal distribution. The normal distribution, also known as the **gaussian distribution**, is a fundamental concept in probability theory and statistics:

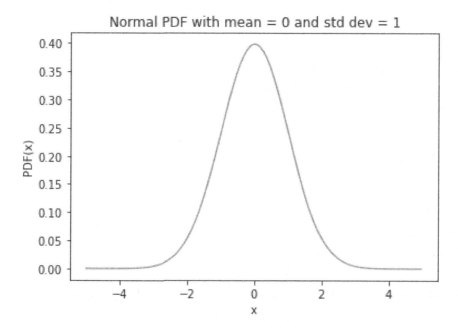

Figure 1.2: probability density function

It is a bell-shaped curve that is symmetric around the mean and describes the distribution of a continuous random variable. Understanding the properties of the normal distribution is important for a wide range of applications, including data analysis, hypothesis testing, and machine learning.

Although there is only one actual density function p that is believed to have produced the observed dataset, there are countless other density functions p that can be utilized to estimate p. To streamline our search for a suitable $p(X)$, we can employ a method known as parametric modeling.

Parametric modeling. parametric modeling is a technique used in statistical inference where the PDF is assumed to belong to a known family of distributions with a finite set of parameters. These parameters can be estimated using **maximum likelihood estimation (MLE)** or Bayesian methods.

The PDF is expressed as a function of the observed variable X and the unknown parameters θ:

$p(X \mid \theta)$

For example, if we assume that the data is normally distributed, the PDF can be written as:

$$p(X \mid \mu, \sigma) = \frac{1}{\sigma\sqrt{2\pi}} \cdot \exp\left(-\frac{(X-\mu)^2}{2\sigma^2}\right)$$

Here, the PDF belongs to the normal family of distributions with parameters μ (mean) and σ (standard deviation). Once the parameters are estimated, we can use the PDF to make predictions about the data or generate new data from the same distribution:

```python
import numpy as np
import matplotlib.pyplot as plt
from scipy.stats import norm


# Generate some data from a normal distribution
mu = 5
sigma = 2
data = np.random.normal(mu, sigma, 1000)


# Estimate the mean and standard deviation of the distribution from the data
mu_hat, sigma_hat = norm.fit(data)


# Plot a histogram of the data with the estimated distribution overlaid
plt.hist(data, bins=50, density=True, alpha=0.5)
x = np.linspace(mu - 4*sigma, mu + 4*sigma, 100)
plt.plot(x, norm.pdf(x, mu_hat, sigma_hat), 'r-', lw=2)
plt.show()
```

In the following figure, we can see a histogram of a dataset with the estimated distribution overlaid:

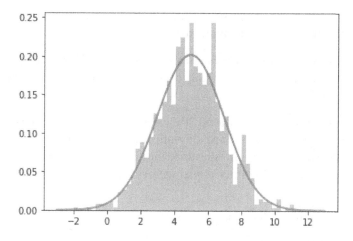

***Figure 1.3**: Histogram of a dataset with the estimated distribution overlaid*

Histograms are a graphical representation of the distribution of a dataset, where the data is divided into a set of intervals and the number of data points falling within each interval is plotted. Overlaid on the histogram is the estimated distribution, which is a probability distribution function that represents the underlying probability distribution of the data. This approach is commonly used in data analysis to gain insight into the characteristics of a dataset, and it can be particularly useful when exploring the properties of large datasets.

Likelihood is a function that measures how well a statistical model fits a set of observations. It is defined as the probability of the observed data given a set of model parameters. In other words, it measures the plausibility of the data given a specific model.

Log-likelihood is simply the logarithm of the likelihood function. It is used instead of likelihood in practice because it is often easier to work with, and it avoids numerical underflow when dealing with very small probabilities.

Mathematically, if we have a set of observations X and a statistical model with parameters θ, then the likelihood function $L(\theta \mid X)$ is:

$$L(\theta \mid X) = p(X \mid \theta)$$

Where $p(X \mid \theta)$ is the PDF or **probability mass function (PMF)** of the observations given the parameters θ.

The log-likelihood function is:

$$log\, L(\theta \mid X) = log\, p(X \mid \theta)$$

Using the logarithm makes it easier to handle large datasets, as well as to calculate derivatives of the likelihood function for optimization purposes.

One advantage is that it can help avoid numerical underflow or overflow, which can occur when dealing with very small or very large likelihood values. Additionally, the log-likelihood function is a more convenient function to work with mathematically, as it can simplify certain calculations and derivations.

Therefore, we may use likelihood when the values are not too extreme and use log-likelihood when working with very small or very large values, or when mathematical convenience is desired.

Here is Python code for Log likelihood, this code generates a dataset from a normal distribution with mean 5 and standard deviation 2 and calculates the log-likelihood of different combinations of mean and standard deviation values using the log-likelihood function. It then plots the log-likelihood surface over a range of mu and sigma values:

```python
import numpy as np
import matplotlib.pyplot as plt
from scipy.stats import norm


# Generate a dataset
data = np.random.normal(5, 2, 1000)


# Define the log-likelihood function
def log_likelihood(theta, x):
    mu, sigma = theta
    return np.sum(norm.logpdf(x, loc=mu, scale=sigma))


# Define the range of mu and sigma values to evaluate the likelihood over
mus = np.linspace(0, 10, 100)
sigmas = np.linspace(0.1, 5, 100)


# Create a grid of mu and sigma values
mu_grid, sigma_grid = np.meshgrid(mus, sigmas)


# Calculate the log-likelihood over the grid of mu and sigma values
ll_grid = np.zeros_like(mu_grid)
for i in range(mu_grid.shape[0]):
    for j in range(mu_grid.shape[1]):
        ll_grid[i,j] = log_likelihood([mu_grid[i,j], sigma_grid[i,j]], data)


# Plot the log-likelihood surface
fig = plt.figure(figsize=(8,6))
```

```
ax = fig.add_subplot(111, projection='3d')
ax.plot_surface(mu_grid, sigma_grid, ll_grid, cmap='viridis')
ax.set_xlabel('mu')
ax.set_ylabel('sigma')
ax.set_zlabel('log likelihood')
plt.show()
```

In the following figure, we can see the log-likelihood surface plotted for a given dataset:

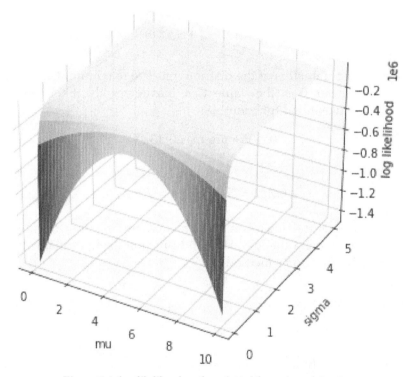

Figure 1.4: log-likelihood surface plotted for a given dataset

The log-likelihood surface is a visualization of the log-likelihood function, which is a measure of how well a statistical model fits the data. By plotting the log-likelihood surface, we can gain insight into the properties of the model and the likelihood of various parameter values. This approach is commonly used in statistical modeling and machine learning to estimate the parameters of a model and to assess the goodness-of-fit of the model to the data.

If we have a dataset X the equation would be $L(\theta \mid X) = \prod_{i=1}^{n} f(X_i \mid \theta)$ where θ is the parameter vector of the distribution, $f(x_i \mid \theta)$ is the probability density function of the distribution evaluated at X_i.

Maximum likelihood

Maximum likelihood is a statistical method used to estimate the parameters of a probability distribution, given a set of observations. The goal of maximum likelihood is to find the values of the parameters that maximize the likelihood of the observed data.

The likelihood function is defined as the probability of the observed data given the parameters of the distribution. For a set of independent and identically distributed random variables $X = \{x_1, x_2, ..., x_n\}$ with probability density function $p(x \mid \theta)$, the likelihood function can be defined as:

$$L(\theta \mid X) = \prod_{i=1}^{n} p(x_i \mid \theta)$$

Where θ is the set of parameters of the distribution. The **maximum likelihood estimator (MLE)** of the parameter θ is the value that maximizes the likelihood function, or equivalently, the log-likelihood function:

$$\hat{\theta}MLE = \arg\max \theta L(\theta \mid X)$$

Or

$$\hat{\theta}MLE = \arg\max \theta \log L(\theta \mid X)$$

Where $\log$ is the natural logarithm. In practice, finding the maximum likelihood estimate involves optimizing the log-likelihood function using numerical methods such as gradient descent or Newton's method.

KL divergence

KL stands for Kullback-Leibler divergence, which is a measure of the difference between two probability distributions. It is often used in machine learning and information theory to compare the *true* probability distribution with a model's estimated distribution.

The KL divergence between two probability distributions $p(x)$ and $q(x)$ is defined as:

$$KL(p \mid \mid q) = \int_{-\infty}^{\infty} p(x) \log \frac{p(x)}{q(x)} dx$$

Where the integral is taken over the entire domain of x.

This equation essentially measures how much information is lost when we approximate the true distribution $p(x)$ with the estimated distribution $q(x)$. The KL divergence is always non-negative, and is zero only when the two distributions are exactly the same.

```python
import numpy as np
def kl_divergence(p, q):
    """
```

```
Computes KL divergence between two probability distributions p and q.
"""

p = np.asarray(p, dtype=np.float)
q = np.asarray(q, dtype=np.float)
return np.sum(np.where(p != 0, p * np.log(p / q), 0))
```

```
# Example usage:
p = [0.2, 0.3, 0.5]
q = [0.25, 0.25, 0.5]
kl_div = kl_divergence(p, q)
print("KL divergence:", kl_div)
KL divergence: 0.010067756775344432
```

The KL divergence for discrete random variables with probability mass functions P and Q is defined as:

$$D_{KL}(P \mid Q) = \sum_i P(i) \log\left(\frac{P(i)}{Q(i)}\right)$$

Where i ranges over all possible values of the discrete random variable. For two continuous probability distributions with probability density functions $p(x)$ and $q(x)$, the **Kullback-Leibler (KL)** divergence is defined as:

$$D_{KL}(p \mid\mid q) = \int_{-\infty}^{\infty} p(x) \log\frac{p(x)}{q(x)} dx$$

Where $D_{KL}(p \mid\mid q)$ represents the relative entropy of p with respect to q.

In the following figure, we can see a plot of the KL divergence between two probability distributions:

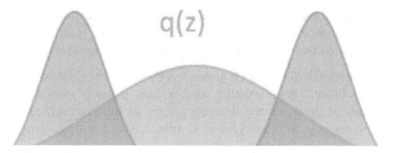

Figure 1.5: KL divergence between two probability distributions

The KL divergence is a measure of the difference between two probability distributions, and it is commonly used in information theory, statistics, and machine learning. By calculating the KL divergence between two distributions, we can assess the similarity or dissimilarity of the distributions and gain insight into the properties of the data.

Maximum likelihood, PDF, KL divergence, and parametric modeling are all important concepts in generative modeling, particularly in VAEs and GANs.

In VAEs, the maximum likelihood principle is used to estimate the parameters of the generative model, which is typically a parametric model such as a Gaussian mixture model. The goal is to find the parameters that maximize the likelihood of the observed data given the latent variables. This is achieved by minimizing the KL divergence between the true posterior distribution and the approximate posterior distribution, which is used to encode the input data into the latent space.

In GANs, the generator network learns to approximate the true data distribution by minimizing the KL divergence between the generated data distribution and the true data distribution. The discriminator network provides feedback to the generator by estimating the probability that the generated samples are real, and the generator updates its parameters to increase the likelihood of generating realistic data.

PDF and parametric modeling are used in both VAEs and GANs to model the data distribution and the latent space. In VAEs, the generative model is typically a parametric model with a known PDF, such as a Gaussian distribution. In GANs, the generator network typically learns a parametric model of the data distribution, which is used to generate new samples.

Let us build a Gaussian Mixture Model from MNIST dataset.

As described above, a **Gaussian Mixture Model (GMM)** is a probabilistic model used for unsupervised learning. It is a model for representing complex probability distributions as a mixture of simpler Gaussian distributions. GMMs are widely used for tasks such as clustering, density estimation, and feature extraction.

In a GMM, each data point is assumed to be generated by one of several Gaussian distributions. The mixture model assumes that there are K Gaussian distributions, where K is a hyperparameter chosen by the user. Each Gaussian distribution is characterized by a mean and a covariance matrix. The mean and covariance matrix of each Gaussian distribution are estimated from the data using maximum likelihood estimation.

The GMM assumes that each data point is generated by one of the K Gaussian distributions with a certain probability. The probability that a data point is generated by the k-th Gaussian distribution is given by the mixture weight or mixing coefficient denoted by π_k. The sum of the mixing coefficients for all Gaussian distributions is equal to 1.

Given a set of data points, the goal of the GMM is to estimate the parameters of the mixture model, including the mixing coefficients, means, and covariances of the Gaussian distributions. Once these parameters are estimated, the GMM can be used to generate new data points that are similar to the observed data.

To estimate the parameters of the GMM, the **expectation-maximization (EM)** algorithm is used. The EM algorithm is an iterative algorithm that alternates between computing the expected probabilities that each data point belongs to each Gaussian distribution (E-step) and updating the parameters of the Gaussian distributions based on these probabilities (M-step). The algorithm continues to iterate until convergence.

In the following figure, we can see a cluster of data points or Gaussian distributions. Clustering is a technique used in unsupervised learning to group similar data points together.

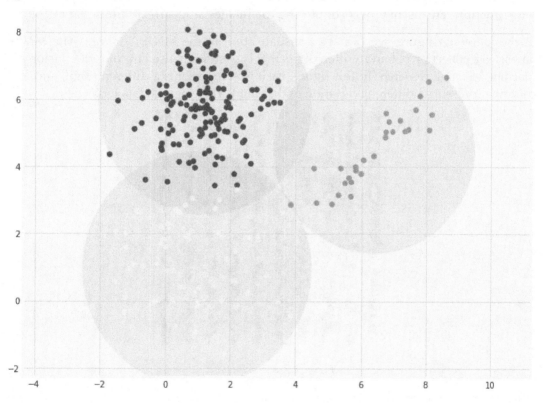

Figure 1.6: Cluster of data points or Gaussian distributions

In this figure, the data points are represented as Gaussian distributions, which are probability distributions that describe the likelihood of a continuous random variable. By grouping the data points into clusters, we can gain insight into the underlying structure of the data and identify patterns or anomalies that may be present. Clustering is a powerful tool that has a wide range of applications, including data analysis, image segmentation, and anomaly detection.

```
import numpy as np
import matplotlib.pyplot as plt
from sklearn.datasets import load_digits
```

```
from sklearn.mixture import GaussianMixture

# Load MNIST dataset
digits = load_digits()
X, y = digits.data, digits.target
```

Note: load_digits is a function from the sklearn.datasets module that loads a popular digit dataset called the MNIST dataset. It contains a set of images of hand-written digits (0-9) that are commonly used for image classification tasks in machine learning. The function returns an object containing the images and corresponding labels.

In the following figure, we can see a visualization of the MNIST dataset. The MNIST dataset is a collection of handwritten digits that is commonly used in computer vision and machine learning research. In this figure, each row represents a different digit, and each column represents a different variation of that digit. The original data looks like:

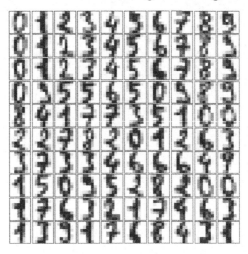

Figure 1.7: *MNIST dataset*

```
# Fit GMM to the data
n_components = 20
gmm = GaussianMixture(n_components=n_components, covariance_type='full',
random_state=42)
gmm.fit(X)
# Generate new samples from the GMM
n_samples = 100
samples, _ = gmm.sample(n_samples)
# Reshape the samples into images
samples = np.reshape(samples, [n_samples, 8, 8])
# Visualize the generated samples
```

```
fig, axes = plt.subplots(10, 10, figsize=(10, 10))
for i in range(10):
    for j in range(10):
        axes[i][j].imshow(samples[i * 10 + j], cmap='gray')
        axes[i][j].axis('off')
plt.show()
```

In the following figure, we can see a visualization of a generated MNIST dataset from our model. Generating new data that is similar to existing data is a key task in machine learning, and generative models are designed to do just that. In this figure, the generated dataset resembles the original MNIST dataset, but with some variations:

Figure 1.8: Generated MNIST dataset from our model

GMM code using TensorFlow probability

TensorFlow Probability (TFP) is a library for probabilistic modeling and statistical inference in TensorFlow. It is an extension of the TensorFlow ecosystem that allows users to specify and train probabilistic models using standard TensorFlow APIs, while also providing additional functionality for building and training probabilistic models.

TFP provides a wide range of probabilistic distributions, including continuous and discrete distributions, mixture distributions, and hierarchical distributions. These distributions can be used to model a wide range of data types and generate random samples from these distributions.

In addition to distributions, TFP provides tools for performing statistical inference on probabilistic models. This includes methods for calculating the likelihood of data given a model, estimating the parameters of a model using maximum likelihood or Bayesian methods, and performing posterior inference using techniques such as MCMC and variational inference.

One of the key features of TFP is the ability to use probabilistic models within the context of deep learning. This allows users to combine the flexibility and expressiveness of deep learning models with the uncertainty and probabilistic reasoning of probabilistic models. TFP provides tools for building and training probabilistic deep learning models, such as variational autoencoders and Bayesian neural networks.

In summary, TensorFlow Probability is a library for probabilistic modeling and statistical inference in TensorFlow. It provides a wide range of probabilistic distributions, tools for performing statistical inference, and functionality for building and training probabilistic deep learning models. TFP is useful for a wide range of applications, including uncertainty quantification, generative modeling, and decision-making under uncertainty. TensorFlow to build a GMM using the TFP library. TFP provides a wide range of distributions, including Gaussian mixture distributions, and tools for performing statistical inference on probabilistic models, including the EM algorithm that is commonly used to estimate the parameters of a GMM:

```python
import numpy as np
import tensorflow as tf
import tensorflow_probability as tfp


# Load MNIST dataset
(x_train, y_train), _ = tf.keras.datasets.mnist.load_data()
x_train = x_train.astype('float32') / 255.
x_train = x_train.reshape(x_train.shape[0], -1)


# Define model
num_components = 100
num_features = x_train.shape[1]
batch_size = 1000
gmm = tfp.distributions.MixtureSameFamily(
    mixture_distribution=tfp.distributions.Categorical(
        probs=tf.ones([num_components], dtype=tf.float32) / num_components),
    components_distribution=tfp.distributions.MultivariateNormalDiag(
        loc=tf.Variable(tf.zeros([num_components, num_features], dtype=tf.float32)),
        scale_diag=tfp.util.TransformedVariable(tf.ones([num_components, num_features], dtype=tf.float32),
                        bijector=tfb.Softplus())
```

```
    )
)


# Define loss function
@tf.function
def nll_loss(x):
    return -tf.reduce_mean(gmm.log_prob(x))


# Define optimizer
optimizer = tf.optimizers.Adam(learning_rate=0.001)


# Train model
num_epochs = 100
num_batches = x_train.shape[0] // batch_size


for epoch in range(num_epochs):
    epoch_loss = 0.
    for batch in range(num_batches):
        x_batch = x_train[batch*batch_size:(batch+1)*batch_size]
        with tf.GradientTape() as tape:
            loss = nll_loss(x_batch)
        gradients = tape.gradient(loss, gmm.trainable_variables)
        optimizer.apply_gradients(zip(gradients, gmm.trainable_variables))
        epoch_loss += loss
    print('Epoch: {}, Loss: {}'.format(epoch, epoch_loss / num_batches))


# Generate samples from the trained model
num_samples = 10
samples = gmm.sample(num_samples)
samples = tf.reshape(samples, [num_samples, 28, 28])
samples = tf.clip_by_value(samples, 0, 1)
```

Conclusion

In this chapter, we covered a range of topics related to machine learning and deep learning, including probability density functions, maximum likelihood estimation, KL divergence, parametric modeling, and generative models like VAE and GAN. We started by discussing the basics of probability density functions, including the PDF equation and the relationship between the PDF and the cumulative distribution function. We then moved on to maximum likelihood estimation and the log-likelihood function, which is commonly used in machine learning to estimate model parameters. We also discussed KL divergence and how it is used to measure the difference between two probability distributions.

Next, we looked at the importance of parametric modeling, which involves fitting a model with a fixed number of parameters to a given dataset. We discussed how this approach can be used to estimate the parameters of a PDF and generate new data samples. We then looked at generative models like VAE and GAN and how they can be used to generate new data samples by learning the underlying probability distribution of a given dataset.

Finally, we built a GMM from MNIST dataset. A GMM is a probabilistic model that represents complex probability distributions as a mixture of simpler Gaussian distributions. The parameters of the GMM are estimated using the EM algorithm, and once these parameters are estimated, the GMM can be used for various unsupervised learning tasks such as clustering and density estimation. Overall, this session covered a range of topics related to machine learning and deep learning, providing an overview of key concepts and equations that are commonly used in these fields.

In the next chapter, we will focus on Generative Adverserial Network and their typesClus.

Join our book's Discord space

Join the book's Discord Workspace for Latest updates, Offers, Tech happenings around the world, New Release and Sessions with the Authors:

https://discord.bpbonline.com

## CHAPTER 2

Designing Generative Adversarial Networks

Introduction

The idea of whether machines are capable of thinking predates the existence of computers. In 1950, *Alan Turing*, a well-known mathematician, logician, and computer scientist who played a key role in breaking the Nazi's Enigma code during World War II, wrote a paper titled *Computing Machinery and Intelligence*, which became famous for proposing the **Turing test**. The test involves an observer conversing with two entities behind a closed door, one being a human and the other being a computer. Turing suggested that if the observer cannot distinguish between the two, the computer can be considered intelligent. While computers have not yet passed this test convincingly, they have surpassed human abilities in certain tasks such as facial recognition and playing the game of Go.

Machine learning algorithms excel at identifying patterns in existing data and using that knowledge for tasks like classification and regression. However, generating new data has been a significant challenge for computers. While computers can beat human experts in tasks like chess, stock prediction, and fraud detection; conversing naturally or creating original works remains difficult for even the most advanced supercomputers.

In 2014, *Ian Goodfellow*, a PhD student at the University of Montreal, developed **Generative Adversarial Networks (GANs)** that use two separate neural networks to generate realistic data. GANs have produced unprecedented results in data generation, such as generating realistic images from scribbles, converting video footage of a horse into a running zebra, and creating synthetic faces that rival high-resolution photographs. This breakthrough has revolutionized machine data generation and is the focus of this chapter.

Structure

In this chapter, we will cover the following chapter:

- Introduction to GAN architectures
- Fundamentals of GAN architecture
- Foundational GAN types
- Specialized GAN architectures
- Advanced GAN architectures
- Comparative analysis and case studies
- Future directions and emerging trends

By the end of this chapter, readers will have a comprehensive understanding of various GAN architectures, their underlying principles, design considerations, and practical applications in the field of generative AI.

Objectives

In this chapter, the objective is to delve into the multifaceted landscape of GANs by comprehensively exploring various types of GANs and their intricate architectures. By the end of this chapter, readers will be equipped with a solid understanding of the architecture, equations, and crucial design factors associated with different GAN variants. The chapter will dissect Discriminator and generator losses, shed light on pivotal GAN types, including Vanilla GAN, Deep Convolutional GAN, Wasserstein GAN, Conditional GAN, CycleGAN, Progressive GAN, StyleGAN, and Pix2Pix, and address the major challenges encountered in designing effective GAN architectures. Through an in-depth analysis of each architecture, readers will gain the knowledge necessary to make informed decisions when selecting and designing GANs for various generative tasks.

Generative Adversarial Networks

Generative Adversarial Networks (GANs) are a type of machine learning method that comprises two models trained simultaneously: a Generator, which produces fake data, and the Discriminator, which distinguishes between the fake and real data. The aim of GANs is to generate new data, with the specific type of data generated depending on the training set used. For instance, if we want to generate images resembling da Vinci's paintings, we will train the GAN on a dataset of da Vinci's artwork.

The term **adversarial** refers to the competitive relationship between the Generator and the Discriminator, in which the Generator seeks to produce data that is indistinguishable from the real examples in the training set while the Discriminator attempts to distinguish between the fake and real data. The two networks continuously strive to outsmart each other, with the Generator creating more convincing fake data and the Discriminator improving its ability to identify real versus fake examples.

The Generator and the Discriminator are usually implemented using neural networks, which can vary in complexity depending on the specific GAN implementation. For example, GANs may employ simple feed-forward neural networks, more complex convolutional neural networks, or even more advanced models such as the U-Net. The main goal of GANs is to enable machines to generate new data, which was previously a challenge for computer algorithms.

Types of GANs available

There are two types of taxonomy in GANs based on architecture:

- **Pure GAN:** In the context of machine learning models, a pure GAN would refer to a GAN that is not combined or mixed with any other type of model, whereas a hybrid GAN would refer to a GAN that is combined with another type of model, such as a **Variational Autoencoders (VAE)** or **Autoencoders (AE)**. There are several types of GANs that have been developed since the introduction of the original GAN model in 2014. Some of the most commonly used types of GANs include:

  o **Deep Convolutional GANs (DCGANs):** These GANs use **Convolutional Neural Networks (CNNs)** in both the Generator and Discriminator networks to generate high-resolution images.

  o **Wasserstein GANs (WGANs):** These GANs use a different loss function than traditional GANs, which helps to prevent problems such as mode collapse and instability.

  o **Conditional GANs (cGANs):** These GANs take additional input, such as class labels or image descriptions, to generate images that meet specific criteria.

  o **CycleGANs:** These GANs are used for image-to-image translation tasks, such as converting images from one style to another.

  o **Progressive GANs (PGANs):** These GANs generate images with increasing resolution in a step-by-step manner; allowing the generation of high-quality images at high resolutions.

  o **StyleGANs:** These GANs allow for the generation of high-resolution images with diverse styles, such as human faces with different facial expressions or animal images with different features.

o **Pix2Pix:** This is another type of GAN used for image-to-image translation, where the Generator takes an input image and generates an output image that matches a specific target.

There are many other types of GANs being developed and studied, each with their own unique strengths and limitations.

- **Hybrid GAN:** There are hybrid GANs that combine the generative power of GANs with the encoding capability of AE or VAE. These models are known as **Variational Autoencoder-Generative Adversarial Network (VAE-GAN)** and **Adversarial Autoencoder-Generative Adversarial Network (AAE-GAN),** respectively.

In VAE-GANs, the encoder part of the VAE is replaced by the Generator of the GAN. The Generator produces a sample from the prior distribution, which is then fed to the Discriminator. The Discriminator, in turn, learns to distinguish between the generated samples and the real samples. The loss function for this model is a combination of the VAE loss and the GAN loss.

In AAE-GANs, the encoder part of the autoencoder is replaced by the Discriminator of the GAN. The encoder maps the input data to a latent space, which is then fed to the Generator to produce a sample. The Discriminator then learns to distinguish between the encoded samples and the samples generated by the Generator. The loss function for this model is a combination of the reconstruction loss and the GAN loss.

Hybrid GANs have been shown to produce better quality samples and to be more stable during training than traditional GANs. They also allow for more control over the generated samples, as the encoder or the Generator can be used to manipulate the latent space to produce specific outputs.

Architecture of a GAN

The GAN architecture resembles that of a **Variational Autoencoder (VAE)**, which comprises an encoder and a decoder. The Generator is equivalent to the VAE's decoder, while the Discriminator corresponds to the VAE's encoder. The Generator converts low-dimensional and simple distributions into high-dimensional images, like a decoder does, and the input to the Generator typically comes from a normal distribution. We feed the Discriminator both real and fake images in different minibatches, with real images sourced from the dataset and fake images produced by the Generator. The Discriminator is a binary classifier that determines the probability of the input being real or fake and can be implemented using CNN. Despite having different purposes, the Discriminator and the encoder reduce the dimensionality of their input.

Equation

The value function captures the fundamentals of how a GAN works. The equation is as follows:

$$min_G max_D V(D,G) = E_{X \sim Pdata}(x)[\log D(x)] + E_{Z \sim Pz(z)}[\log(1 - D(G(z)))]$$

Here:

- **D** stands for Discriminator.

- **G** is the Generator.

- **x** is input data and **z** is a latent variable.

The notation used in the mathematical formula for the loss function will be the same notation used in the code implementation. The goal of the Generator is to minimize this function, while the Discriminator aims to maximize it.

Once you understand the loss function, implementing it in code will become easier and more understandable. Additionally, much of the discussion about the challenges and advancements of GANs revolves around the loss function, so it is worth studying in detail. Some literature also refers to the GAN loss function as the adversarial loss. Although the formula may appear complicated at first, we will simplify it through steps to transform it into manageable loss functions that we can implement.

Discriminator loss

The value function has two terms on the right-hand side, with the first one representing the value of correctly classifying a real image. On the left-hand side, we know that the Discriminator aims to maximize this term. The term **expectation** refers to a mathematical concept that represents the sum of weighted averages of all possible outcomes of a random variable. In this equation, the weight is the probability of data, and the variable is the logarithm of the Discriminator's output, which can be expressed as:

$$E_X(\log D(x)) = \sum_{i=1}^N p(x) \log D(x) = \frac{1}{N} \sum_{i=1}^N y \log p(y_i)$$

The probability of data, p(x), in a minibatch of size N is equal to $1/N$, since x represents a single image. Rather than maximizing this probability, we can minimize it by changing the sign to minus. To achieve this, we use the log loss equation as follows:

$$min_D V(D)) = \frac{1}{N} \sum_{=1} \log D(x) = -\frac{1}{N} \sum_{i=1}^N y \log p(y_i)$$

Here:

- **yi** is the label, which is 1 for real images.

- **p(yi)** is the probability of the sample being real.

The next term in the value function deals with fake images generated by the Generator. Here, **z** represents random noise and **G(z)** represents the generated fake images. **D(G(z))** represents the Discriminator's confidence score for determining the likelihood of the image being real. By assigning a label of 0 for fake images, we can apply the same approach as before and express it as follows:

$$-E_{z\square pz(z)}[\log(1 - D(G(z)))] = -\frac{1}{N}\Sigma_{=1}^{N}(1 - y_i)\log(1 - p(y_i))$$

Now, putting everything together, we have our Discriminator loss function, which is binary cross-entropy loss:

$$\min_D V(D)) = -\frac{1}{N}\Sigma_{i=1}^{N} y_i \log p(y_i) + (1 - y_i)1 - p(y_i))$$

During the training process, we first pass the real and fake images through the model separately, with both groups having the same size of minibatches. As a result, we can calculate the binary cross-entropy loss for each group separately. Finally, we take the average of both losses to obtain the overall loss.

Generator loss

The Generator comes into play only during the evaluation of fake images. Hence, we need to focus on the second right-hand term of the value function and simplify it to the following:

$$min_G V(G) = E_{z \sim Pz(z)}[log(1 - D(G(z))]$$

During the initial stage of training, the Generator's performance in generating images is poor. Hence, the Discriminator confidently classifies the generated images as 0, causing the Discriminator's output to always be 0. As a result, log (1 – 0) is also always 0. If the model's output error is constantly 0, then no gradient is available for backpropagation. Therefore, the Generator's weights remain unchanged, and the Generator does not learn. This problem is known as the **saturating gradient problem**, which occurs because the Discriminator's sigmoid output has almost no gradient. To overcome this issue, the equation is modified from minimizing **1-D(G(z))** to maximizing **D(G(z))**, as shown below:

$$max_G V(G) = E_{z \sim Pz(z)}[log(D(G(z))]$$

GANs that utilize this loss function are referred to as **Non-Saturating GANs (NS-GANs)**. It is worth noting that most implementations of the original GAN use this loss function instead of the original one.

Vanilla GAN

After GANs were invented, many researchers became interested and gave them different names. There were so many GANs that it became difficult to keep track of all of them. The term **Vanilla GAN** is used to refer to the basic GAN without any fancy modifications. Vanilla GAN is usually implemented with two or three hidden dense layers.

To calculate the generator loss, we can employ the same mathematical procedures used for the Discriminator. This results in a similar loss function for the Discriminator, with the only difference being the use of a label of one for real images. It might be confusing for beginners to understand why real labels are used for fake images, but we can clarify this by deriving the equation or understanding that we aim to deceive the Discriminator into believing that the generated images are real, so we use the real labels.

Outline crucial factors in GAN architecture design

Here are some key considerations while designing a GAN architecture:

- **Discriminator and generator architecture:** The Discriminator and Generator architectures should be carefully designed to balance the trade-off between model capacity and computational efficiency. Experimenting with different architectures and hyperparameters is important to find the optimal balance.

- **Loss function:** The choice of loss function can greatly impact the performance of the GAN. Different loss functions can be used, such as binary cross-entropy, Wasserstein loss, and hinge loss. The loss function should be carefully chosen based on the specific task and data being used.

- **Normalization techniques:** Normalization techniques, such as batch normalization, can help stabilize training and improve performance.

- **Regularization techniques:** Regularization techniques, such as weight decay and dropout, can help prevent overfitting and improve generalization performance.

- **Training strategy:** The training strategy, such as the learning rate, batch size, and number of training iterations, can greatly impact the performance of the GAN. It's important to experiment with different training strategies to find the optimal combination.

- **Data augmentation:** Data augmentation techniques, such as random cropping and flipping, can help increase the diversity of the training data and improve the performance of the GAN.

- **Evaluation metrics:** Evaluation metrics, such as the Inception Score and Fréchet Inception Distance, can be used to evaluate the quality of the generated samples and the overall performance of the GAN.

Major challenges in designing GANs architecture

There are several challenges in designing GAN architectures, including:

- **Mode collapse:** GANs can sometimes generate only a limited set of output, ignoring other valid modes in the dataset.

- **Vanishing gradients:** GANs are trained using backpropagation, which can suffer from vanishing gradients, making it difficult to optimize deep architectures.

- **Discriminator saturation:** In the early stages of training, the Discriminator can become too confident in its predictions, leading to a lack of gradient signals that can prevent the Generator from learning.

- **Training instability:** GANs can suffer from instability during training, where the Generator and Discriminator can become too dominant or too weak, leading to poor-quality generated samples.

- **Evaluation:** There is no clear metric for evaluating GANs, making it difficult to compare and improve different models.

- **Overfitting:** GANs can be prone to overfitting, particularly when working with small datasets, leading to poor generalization of new data.

- **Computational complexity:** GANs are computationally expensive to train, particularly when working with high-resolution images or complex datasets.

Architecture of Deep Convolutional GANs

DCGANs are a type of GAN architecture specifically designed for image generation tasks. They were first introduced in a paper by Radford et al. in 2015 and have since become one of the most popular architectures for GANs.

The architecture of DCGANs consists of a generator network and a Discriminator network, similar to other GANs. However, there are several key differences in the design of these networks that make them particularly effective for generating high-quality images:

- **Generator network:** The generator network takes a random noise vector as input and produces an image as output. The architecture of the Generator typically consists of several deconvolutional layers (also known as transpose convolution or fractionally-strided convolution), followed by batch normalization and ReLU activation functions. The final layer usually has a tanh activation function to ensure that the output values are within the range of [-1, 1], which is the typical range for image pixel values.

- **Discriminator network:** The Discriminator network takes an image as input and outputs a probability score indicating whether the image is real or fake. The architecture of the Discriminator typically consists of several convolutional layers, followed by batch normalization and LeakyReLU activation functions. The final layer usually has a sigmoid activation function to produce a probability score between 0 and 1.

Some of the key design choices that make DCGANs effective include:

- **Removing fully connected layers:** Unlike other GAN architectures, DCGANs do not include fully connected layers. This reduces the number of parameters in the model and allows for larger input images to be processed.

- **Using stride instead of pooling:** DCGANs use strided convolutions instead of pooling layers to downsample the feature maps. This helps to preserve spatial information and avoid loss of details.

- **Using batch normalization:** Batch normalization is applied after each convolutional or deconvolutional layer to help stabilize the training process and prevent internal covariate shift.

Overall, the design of DCGANs is focused on creating a stable and scalable architecture that can generate high-quality images. The use of convolutional and deconvolutional layers, along with batch normalization and ReLU activation functions, allows for the model to learn complex patterns and generate realistic images.

Architecture of Wasserstein GANs

WGANs are a type of Generative Adversarial Networks that differ from traditional GANs in the way they measure the distance between the real and fake distributions. Rather than using the binary cross-entropy loss function as in traditional GANs, WGANs use the Wasserstein distance, also known as **Earth Mover's distance (EMD)**, which is a more meaningful and stable measure of distance between probability distributions.

The WGAN architecture has several key components that make it different from traditional GANs:

- **Critic network:** Instead of the discriminator network used in traditional GANs, WGANs use a critical network that maps the input data to a scalar output. The critic network does not produce a probability output like the Discriminator, but rather a score that measures the distance between the real and fake data distributions.

- **Wasserstein distance:** The critical network output is used to compute the Wasserstein distance between the real and fake distributions. The Wasserstein distance is defined as the minimum cost of transforming one distribution into the other, where the cost is defined by the critical network output.

- **Weight clipping:** To enforce the Lipschitz continuity constraint required for the critic network, WGANs clip the weights of the critic network to a fixed range. This ensures that the gradient of the critical network remains bounded and helps stabilize the training process.

- **Generator network:** The generator network in WGANs is similar to that of traditional GANs, but instead of minimizing the binary cross-entropy loss, it minimizes the negative Wasserstein distance between the real and fake data distributions. This is achieved by maximizing the critical network output on the generated data.

- **Training:** WGANs are trained using the gradient descent algorithm, where the critic and generator networks are updated alternatively in a min-max game. The critic network is updated to minimize the Wasserstein distance between the real and fake distributions, while the generator network is updated to minimize the negative Wasserstein distance between the fake and real data distributions.

Overall, the WGAN architecture is designed to address some of the stability and convergence issues that are commonly encountered in traditional GANs. By using the Wasserstein distance and a critic network, WGANs provide a more meaningful and stable measure of distance between probability distributions, which leads to more stable training and better-quality generated images.

Architecture of Conditional GANs

Conditional GANs are a type of GANs that allow the user to control the output of the Generator by conditioning it on additional information. This additional information can be any type of data, such as text, images, or audio.

The architecture of a cGAN is similar to that of a DCGAN, with the addition of a conditional vector that is concatenated with the input noise vector. The Generator takes in both the noise vector and the conditional vector as input, and outputs an image. The Discriminator takes in both the generated image and the conditional vector as input, and outputs a probability that the image is real.

Here is a detailed explanation of the architecture of cGANs:

- **Generator:** The Generator in a cGAN is similar to that in a DCGAN, with the addition of a conditional vector. The input to the Generator is a noise vector of size (Nz, 1, 1), where Nz is the size of the noise vector. The conditional vector, which contains the additional information that the Generator is conditioned on, is also of size (Nc, 1, 1), where Nc is the size of the conditional vector.

  The Generator typically consists of several transpose convolution layers, also known as **deconvolution layers**, followed by batch normalization and a non-linear activation function such as ReLU. The output layer of the Generator uses a Tanh activation function to ensure that the pixel values of the generated image are within the range of [-1, 1].

- **Discriminator:** The Discriminator in a cGAN takes in both the generated image and the conditional vector as input, and outputs a probability that the image is real. The input to the Discriminator is an image of size (3, 64, 64), which is the same size as the output of the Generator.

The Discriminator consists of several convolution layers, followed by batch normalization and a non-linear activation function such as LeakyReLU. The output layer of the Discriminator uses a linear activation function to output a scalar value between [-infinity, infinity].

- **Loss function**: The loss function for a cGAN is similar to that of a vanilla GAN, with the addition of the conditional vector. The Generator and Discriminator are trained using a binary cross-entropy loss function, where the Generator tries to minimize the probability that the Discriminator correctly classifies the generated image as fake, and the Discriminator tries to maximize the probability that it correctly classifies the generated image as fake and the real image as real.

  The conditional vector is also included in the loss function to ensure that the Generator is conditioned on the additional information. The conditional vector is concatenated with the noise vector and fed into the Generator, and then fed into the Discriminator along with the conditional vector.

cGANs have been successfully applied to various tasks, such as image-to-image translation, text-to-image synthesis, and image super-resolution. The conditional vector allows for greater control over the output of the Generator and enables the generation of more specific and diverse images.

Architecture of CycleGANs

CycleGAN is a type of GAN architecture that is used for image-to-image translation tasks, where the aim is to learn a mapping between two image domains without the need for paired training data. CycleGANs are designed to learn mapping between two image domains, say, domain X and domain Y, such that an image from domain X can be translated to domain Y and vice versa.

The architecture of CycleGAN is based on the basic GAN architecture but with some modifications. The architecture consists of two generators (G and F) and two Discriminators (DX and DY). Generator G learns to translate images from domain X to domain Y, while generator F learns to translate images from domain Y to domain X. The Discriminators DX and DY learn to differentiate between real images from their respective domains and fake images generated by the generators.

The architecture can be summarized as follows:

- The input image from domain X is passed through the Generator G to generate a corresponding image in domain Y. Similarly, the input image from domain Y is passed through the Generator F to generate a corresponding image in domain X.

- The generated images from step 1 are then passed through their respective Discriminators DX and DY. The Discriminators classify the images as real or fake and provide feedback to the Generators.

- The Generators receive feedback from the Discriminators and adjust their parameters to improve the quality of the generated images.

- To enforce the cycle consistency, an additional loss function is added to the training process. The loss function ensures that if an image from domain X is translated to domain Y and then back to domain X, it should be similar to the original image. Similarly, if an image from domain Y is translated to domain X and then back to domain Y, it should be similar to the original image.

The cycle consistency loss is defined as follows:

$$Lcycle(G,F) = ||F(G(x)) - x||1 + ||G(F(y)) - y||1$$

Where **x** is an image from domain X, **y** is an image from domain Y, **G** is the Generator that maps from X to Y, **F** is the Generator that maps from Y to X, and $||.||1$ denotes the L1 distance.

By minimizing the cycle consistency loss, the Generator is forced to learn a bijective mapping between the two domains, which ensures that the translation is consistent and reversible.

CycleGANs have been used for a variety of image-to-image translation tasks, such as converting horses to zebras, turning day-time images into night-time images, and more.

Architecture of progressive GANs

Progressive GANs are an extension of the basic GAN architecture that utilizes a progressive growing method to generate high-resolution images progressively. The architecture is designed to generate high-quality images by training the GAN network on low-resolution images and gradually increasing the resolution over time. This approach allows for the network to learn increasingly complex features and generate higher quality images as it progresses through the training process.

The architecture of PGANs is composed of two main components: the generator and the discriminator, which are as follows:

- **Generator:** The Generator consists of a series of convolutional layers that upsample the input noise vector to generate images. The Generator starts with a low-resolution image and then gradually increases the resolution by adding more convolutional layers. Each layer generates a higher resolution image than the previous one until the final image is produced. The Generator also includes skip connections that allow the network to learn features at different scales.

- **Discriminator:** The Discriminator is also a series of convolutional layers that downsample the input image to produce a probability score indicating whether the image is real or fake. The Discriminator starts with a low-resolution image and then gradually increases the resolution by adding more convolutional layers. Each layer processes a higher-resolution image than the previous one until the final output is produced.

The PGAN architecture is trained in multiple stages, each stage consisting of a Generator and Discriminator pair. In the initial stage, the Generator generates a low-resolution image, and the Discriminator evaluates the realism of the generated image. Once the Generator produces realistic images at the current resolution level, the resolution is increased, and a new set of Generator and Discriminator networks are added to the architecture to continue the training process. This process is repeated until the desired resolution is achieved.

The progressive growing method allows for the network to learn increasingly complex features as it progresses through the training process, resulting in high-quality images. Additionally, the use of skip connections allows the network to learn features at different scales and reduces the risk of losing information during the training process. Overall, PGANs are an effective approach to generating high-quality images with a progressive growing method.

Architecture of StyleGANs

StyleGAN is a GAN architecture introduced by NVIDIA researchers in 2018, which extends the idea of GANs to learn a generative model of high-quality natural images with fine-grained control over the style of the generated images.

The architecture of StyleGANs can be broken down into three main components: the Generator, the Discriminator, and the mapping network.

The generator network takes a random input vector (z) and passes it through several intermediate layers that gradually increase the spatial resolution of the output, eventually generating a high-resolution image. Unlike traditional GANs, where the input vector is mapped to a single image, StyleGAN maps the input vector to a set of intermediate latent vectors at different resolutions, which are then fed into a set of style modulation blocks. The style modulation blocks inject style information into each layer of the generator network by scaling and biasing the feature maps using learnable parameters, which are obtained by mapping the intermediate latent vectors through a style mapping network.

The Discriminator network is a typical convolutional neural network that takes an image as input and outputs a scalar value indicating whether the image is real or fake. However, instead of using the typical cross-entropy loss to train the Discriminator, StyleGAN uses a hinge loss, which has been shown to produce more stable and higher-quality results.

The mapping network is used to map the input random vector (z) to the intermediate latent vectors that are fed into the style modulation blocks. It is a fully connected neural network that takes the random input vector and maps it to a sequence of intermediate latent vectors that have the same dimensionality as the output of the generator network.

In addition to these three main components, StyleGAN also introduces a number of other architectural features that help improve the quality and diversity of the generated images. For example, it uses a progressive growing technique where the Generator and Discriminator are trained on images of increasing resolution. It also uses a feature vector normalization technique that helps improve the diversity of the generated images and a truncation trick that limits the influence of the input vector on the output, producing more consistent and high-quality images.

Overall, the StyleGAN architecture is a powerful tool for generating high-quality and diverse images with fine-grained control over the style of the generated images. Its ability to learn continuous mapping from input vectors to output images makes it particularly useful for tasks such as image editing, style transfer, and data augmentation.

Architecture of Pix2Pix

Pix2Pix is a type of conditional GAN that was introduced in 2016 by Isola et al. The goal of Pix2Pix is to generate an output image given an input image, where the output image is directly related to the input image. For example, the input image could be a black and white image, and the output image could be a colorized version of that image.

The architecture of Pix2Pix is based on an encoder-decoder architecture with skip connections. The encoder takes in the input image and produces a feature map, which is then passed to the decoder. The decoder takes the feature map and generates the output image. The skip connections allow the network to copy information from the input image to the output image, resulting in more visually pleasing results.

The Generator in Pix2Pix consists of a series of downsampling and upsampling layers. The downsampling layers reduce the spatial resolution of the input image while increasing the number of channels, and the upsampling layers increase the spatial resolution while decreasing the number of channels. The skip connections between the encoder and decoder are implemented using a concatenation operation.

The Discriminator in Pix2Pix is a patch-based Discriminator, which means that it looks at patches of the input and output images rather than the entire image. This allows the Discriminator to focus on local details rather than global features. The Discriminator is trained to distinguish between real and fake images by computing a binary classification loss.

The loss function used in Pix2Pix is a combination of an adversarial loss and a pixel-wise loss. The adversarial loss encourages the Generator to produce images that are similar to the real images, while the pixel-wise loss encourages the Generator to produce images that are visually similar to the input images. The total loss is a weighted sum of the two losses, where the weights are determined by a hyperparameter.

Overall, Pix2Pix is a powerful tool for many image-to-image translation tasks, including image colorization, image denoising, and style transfer.

Conclusion

In conclusion, the readers will gain a comprehensive understanding of the diverse landscape of GAN architectures and their profound implications for the field of generative AI. Throughout this chapter, readers embark on a journey that covers fundamental GAN concepts, equations, and essential components, providing a solid foundation for grasping the intricacies of GANs. The exploration extends to the intricate roles of discriminator and generator losses, unveiling their pivotal contributions to the adversarial training process.

This chapter delves into a spectrum of GAN architectures, ranging from the foundational Vanilla GAN to specialized versions like Conditional GAN, CycleGAN, and Pix2Pix. Through these architectural adaptations, readers will discover the versatility of GANs in excelling across various generative tasks. The discussion also extends to advanced architectures such as StyleGAN, which introduces the integration of artistic style into the generative process, harmonizing creativity with technological innovation.

Importantly, readers will confront the challenges faced by GAN architects, including stability during training and the complex issue of mode collapse. By exploring these challenges, readers are equipped to appreciate the forefront of GAN research and the complexities inherent in designing effective GAN architectures.

This chapter not only encapsulates the current state of GAN architecture but also hints at future trends and developments, urging readers to remain attentive to the evolving landscape of GANs. Ultimately, the reader will grasp that GAN architectures symbolize the interplay of competition and collaboration, mirroring the dance between generator and discriminator. As the chapter concludes, it is evident that GANs continually redefine the boundaries of generative capabilities, fostering innovation and imagination in equal proportions.

In the next chapter, readers can expect to gain a detailed understanding of training and fine-tuning **Generative Adversarial Networks (GANs)**. It will cover advanced methods and best practices essential for enhancing the stability and performance of GAN models, ensuring they are well-optimized and effective in various applications.

Multiple choice questions

1. **What is the primary purpose of Discriminator and generator losses in a GAN architecture?**

    a. Discriminator loss enhances image resolution.

    b. Generator loss improves training stability.

    c. Discriminator loss generates new data samples.

    d. Generator loss evaluates the authenticity of generated data.

2. **Which type of GAN architecture addresses mode collapse and provides better training stability?**

    a. Vanilla GAN

    b. Deep Convolutional GAN (DCGAN)

    c. Wasserstein GAN

    d. Conditional GAN

3. **Which GAN architecture is specifically designed for unpaired image-to-image translation tasks?**

    a. Vanilla GAN

    b. Deep Convolutional GAN (DCGAN)

    c. CycleGAN

    d. Progressive GAN

4. **What does StyleGAN primarily introduce into GAN architecture?**

    a. Conditional information

    b. Cycle consistency

    c. Artistic style integration

    d. Progressive growth

5. **What is one of the major challenges in designing GAN architectures?**

    a. Selecting the right loss function for the generator

    b. Generating high-resolution images efficiently

    c. Minimizing the role of Discriminator in training

    d. Reducing the impact of adversarial training

6. **Which aspect does NOT fall under consideration for successful GAN architecture design?**

    a. Training stability

    b. Mode collapse prevention

    c. Optimization of Discriminator loss only

    d. Effective interplay between Discriminator and generator

7. **Which type of GAN architecture involves incremental growth for generating high-resolution images?**

    a. Conditional GAN

    b. Progressive GAN

    c. StyleGAN

    d. Wasserstein GAN

8. **What does CycleGAN leverage to perform image-to-image translation when paired data is not available?**

    a. Adversarial training

    b. Cycle consistency

    c. Conditional information

    d. Progressive growth

9. **In the context of GANs, what is the role of the generator?**

    a. To assess the authenticity of data samples

    b. To generate new data samples

    c. To discriminate between real and fake data

    d. To optimize the loss function of the Discriminator

Answers

1. b

2. c

3. c

4. c

5. a

6. c

7. b

8. b

9. b

Join our book's Discord space

Join the book's Discord Workspace for Latest updates, Offers, Tech happenings around the world, New Release and Sessions with the Authors:

https://discord.bpbonline.com

CHAPTER 3

Training and Developing Generative Adversarial Networks

Introduction

Generative Adversarial Networks (GAN) have revolutionized the field of artificial intelligence by allowing machines to generate realistic and diverse data. However, training GANs is a challenging and iterative process that requires careful consideration of several factors, including selecting appropriate loss functions and hyperparameters and dealing with common issues like mode collapse and vanishing gradients.

In this chapter, we will delve into the process of training and tuning GANs, exploring various techniques for stabilizing GAN training. We will cover topics such as spectral normalization, gradient penalty, and progressive growing, which have been shown to improve the stability and robustness of GAN models. We will also discuss strategies for selecting appropriate loss functions and hyperparameters, which can greatly affect the performance and convergence of GANs.

Additionally, the chapter will examine the common issues that arise during GAN training, such as mode collapse and vanishing gradients, and provide practical solutions for overcoming these challenges. We will provide code examples and practical advice for effectively training GANs, allowing readers to gain a deeper understanding of the challenges and complexities involved in creating these powerful models. Let us start from where we left from.

Structure

In this chapter, we will cover the following topics:

- Generative Adversarial Training
- Generating MNIST data: Basic GAN implementation
- Issues during training a GANs
- Case study: Common practical implementation of GANs for augmentation and balancing classes

Objectives

The objective of this chapter is to provide readers with a comprehensive understanding of the process of training and tuning GANs, including the latest techniques and best practices for improving the stability and performance of GAN models.

Generative Adversarial Training

Generative Adversarial Training, also known as **GAN training**, is a type of deep learning training method used to generate realistic and diverse data. It involves training two neural networks, a generator and a discriminator, simultaneously in a zero-sum game framework.

The generator is trained to create synthetic data that is similar to the training data, while the discriminator is trained to distinguish between the real and fake data. During the training process, the generator tries to produce data that can fool the discriminator into thinking it is real, while the discriminator tries to correctly identify the fake data generated by the generator.

The training process is iterative and continues until the generator produces data that is indistinguishable from the real data. Once the generator has been trained, it can be used to generate new data that is similar to the training data.

The advantage of GAN training is that it does not require the explicit formulation of a probability distribution for the generated data, which can be challenging in many real-world scenarios. Instead, GANs can learn the distribution implicitly by optimizing the generator and discriminator networks together.

It is crucial to note that the examples the Generator will be able to produce, are determined by the training dataset. Suppose the objective is to generate lifelike images of cats. In that case, it is necessary to provide the GAN with a dataset containing cat images. The Generator's goal is to produce examples that are similar to the data distribution of the training dataset.

From a technical perspective, images are represented as matrices of pixel values, with grayscale images being two-dimensional and color images being three-dimensional (RGB). These pixel values create the visual elements of an image, such as lines, edges, and contours, which follow a complex distribution across each image in the dataset. If there is no distribution followed, the image would be nothing more than random noise. Object recognition models identify the patterns in images to recognize the image's content. Conversely, the Generator's task is to learn to produce these patterns, essentially synthesizing them instead of recognizing them.

Generating MNIST data: Basic GAN implementation

Creating a GAN using TensorFlow to work with the MNIST dataset is a complex task. However, there are a few points to clarify:

- GANs typically do not have a direct measure of *accuracy* as in classification tasks. Instead, we monitor the generator and discriminator losses.

- Training a GAN for 1000 epochs on the MNIST dataset might be time-consuming and computationally expensive. We will create the code but running it may require substantial resources depending on your hardware.

- Generating images every 250 epochs is feasible. We can set up the code to save or display images at these intervals.

Let us proceed with the steps:

1. **Setting up the environment**: Install TensorFlow and other required libraries.

2. **Loading the MNIST dataset**: Use TensorFlow to load the dataset.

3. **Building the GAN**: Create the generator and discriminator models.

4. **Training the GAN**: Train the models, with checkpoints every 250 epochs.

5. **Plotting Losses**: Plot the generator and discriminator losses over epochs.

6. **Generating Images**: Generate and display images at specified epochs.

In the following *Figure 3.1*, we can see a GANS architecture where the model is trying to generate 8 so it has first learned how to generate a 3:

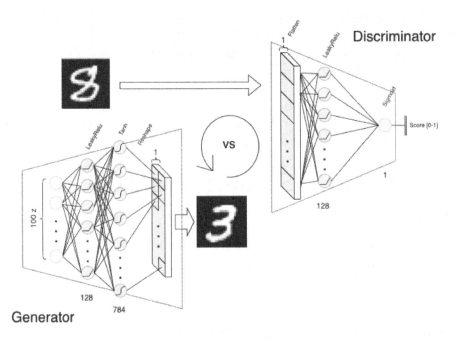

Figure 3.1: *GANS architecture where the model is trying to generate 8*
so it has first learned how to generate a three.

Utilizing TensorFlow, we embark on crafting a state-of-the-art **Generative Adversarial Network (GAN)** to revolutionize the realm of machine learning:

```python
import tensorflow as tf

from tensorflow.keras.layers import Dense, Flatten, Reshape

from tensorflow.keras.models import Sequential

import numpy as np

import matplotlib.pyplot as plt

from tensorflow.keras.layers import Dense, Flatten, Reshape, BatchNormalization, LeakyReLU, Conv2DTranspose, Conv2D


# Load MNIST dataset
(train_images, _), (_, _) = tf.keras.datasets.mnist.load_data()
train_images = train_images.reshape(train_images.shape[0], 28, 28, 1).astype('float32')
train_images = (train_images - 127.5) / 127.5  # Normalize the images to [-1, 1]


# Buffer size and batch size
BUFFER_SIZE = 60000
BATCH_SIZE = 256
```

```
# Batch and shuffle the data
train_dataset    =    tf.data.Dataset.from_tensor_slices(train_images).
shuffle(BUFFER_SIZE).batch(BATCH_SIZE)


# Generator model
def make_generator_model():
    model = Sequential()
    model.add(Dense(7*7*256, use_bias=False, input_shape=(100,)))
    model.add(BatchNormalization())
    model.add(LeakyReLU())
    model.add(Reshape((7, 7, 256)))

     model.add(Conv2DTranspose(128, (5, 5), strides=(1, 1), padding='same',
use_bias=False))
    model.add(BatchNormalization())
    model.add(LeakyReLU())

     model.add(Conv2DTranspose(64, (5, 5), strides=(2, 2), padding='same',
use_bias=False))
    model.add(BatchNormalization())
    model.add(LeakyReLU())

    # Output layer with tanh activation
     model.add(Conv2DTranspose(1, (5, 5), strides=(2, 2), padding='same',
use_bias=False, activation='tanh'))
    return model


# Discriminator model
def make_discriminator_model():
    model = Sequential()
     model.add(Conv2D(64, (5, 5), strides=(2, 2), padding='same', input_
shape=[28, 28, 1]))
    model.add(LeakyReLU())
    model.add(Flatten())
    model.add(Dense(1))
    return model
```

```python
generator = make_generator_model()
discriminator = make_discriminator_model()

# Define the loss and optimizers
cross_entropy = tf.keras.losses.BinaryCrossentropy(from_logits=True)

def generator_loss(fake_output):
    return cross_entropy(tf.ones_like(fake_output), fake_output)

def discriminator_loss(real_output, fake_output):
    real_loss = cross_entropy(tf.ones_like(real_output), real_output)
    fake_loss = cross_entropy(tf.zeros_like(fake_output), fake_output)
    total_loss = real_loss + fake_loss
    return total_loss

generator_optimizer = tf.keras.optimizers.Adam(1e-4)
discriminator_optimizer = tf.keras.optimizers.Adam(1e-4)

# Training loop
EPOCHS = 1000
noise_dim = 100
num_examples_to_generate = 16

# Seed for visualization
seed = tf.random.normal([num_examples_to_generate, noise_dim])

def train_step(images):
    noise = tf.random.normal([BATCH_SIZE, noise_dim])

    with tf.GradientTape() as gen_tape, tf.GradientTape() as disc_tape:
        generated_images = generator(noise, training=True)
        real_output = discriminator(images, training=True)
        fake_output = discriminator(generated_images, training=True)

        gen_loss = generator_loss(fake_output)
        disc_loss = discriminator_loss(real_output, fake_output)
```

```
        gradients_of_generator = gen_tape.gradient(gen_loss, generator.
trainable_variables)
    gradients_of_discriminator = disc_tape.gradient(disc_loss, discriminator.
trainable_variables)

        generator_optimizer.apply_gradients(zip(gradients_of_generator,
generator.trainable_variables))
    discriminator_optimizer.apply_gradients(zip(gradients_of_discriminator,
discriminator.trainable_variables))

    return gen_loss, disc_loss


def train(dataset, epochs):
    for epoch in range(epochs):
        gen_loss_list = []
        disc_loss_list = []

        for image_batch in dataset:
            t = train_step(image_batch)
            gen_loss_list.append(t[0])
            disc_loss_list.append(t[1])

        # Produce images for the GIF as we go
        if (epoch + 1) % 250 == 0:
            generate_and_save_images(generator, epoch + 1, seed)

        # Save the model every 50 epochs
        if (epoch + 1) % 50 == 0:
            checkpoint.save(file_prefix = checkpoint_prefix)

    return gen_loss_list, disc_loss_list

# Generate and save images
def generate_and_save_images(model, epoch, test_input):
    predictions = model(test_input, training=False)
    fig = plt.figure(figsize=(4,4))
```

```python
for i in range(predictions.shape[0]):
    plt.subplot(4, 4, i+1)
    plt.imshow(predictions[i, :, :, 0] * 127.5 + 127.5, cmap='gray')
    plt.axis('off')

    plt.savefig('image_at_epoch_{:04d}.png'.format(epoch))
    plt.show()

gen_loss_list, disc_loss_list = train(train_dataset, EPOCHS)

# Plotting the training losses
plt.figure(figsize=(10,5))
plt.title("Generator and Discriminator Loss During Training")
plt.plot(gen_loss_list,label="G")
plt.plot(disc_loss_list,label="D")
plt.xlabel("iterations")
plt.ylabel("Loss")
plt.legend()
plt.show()
```

Refer to the following *Figure 3.2:*

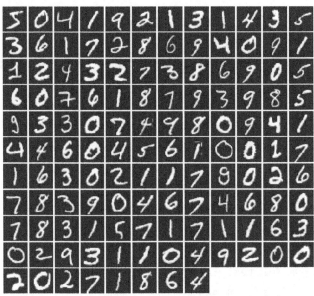

Figure 3.2: *Visualization of MNIST dataset*

Refer to the following figure to see the improved performance of GAN network:

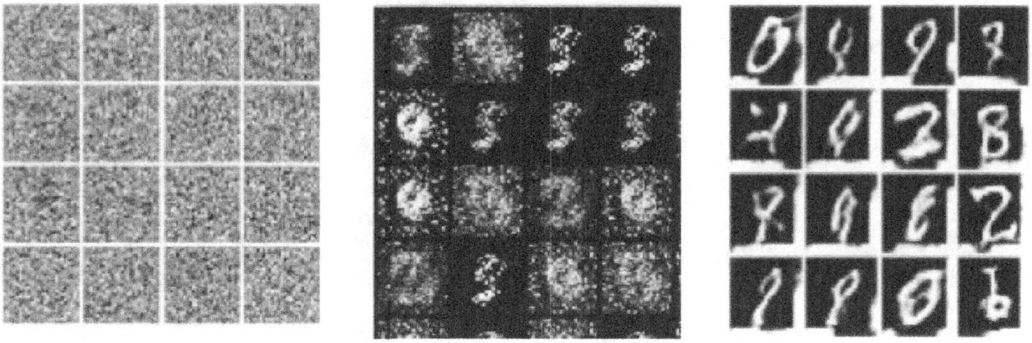

Figure 3.3: *As the number of iterations increases, the diversity of generated images also increases, indicating improved performance of the GAN network (left) Iteration 0: D Loss 1.423, G loss 0.4224 (Middle) Iteration 250: D loss1.248, G loss 0.6211 (Right)Iteration 500: D Loss 1.151, G Loss 1.037*

As the number of iterations increases, the diversity of generated images also increases, indicating improved performance of the GAN network. Initially, during the lower iterations, the network may produce less diverse images with fewer digits. However, with increased iterations, the network becomes capable of generating all available digits, transforming random noise into realistic-looking images.

The discriminator's role is to classify the images as real or fake. When its loss converges to around 0, it means that the discriminator performs classification very accurately, and the generator fails to fool the discriminator. Thus, the generator tries to minimize the probability of the discriminator incorrectly classifying the images. Consequently, the loss would be negative log of the above value, which would be very high.

However, when the discriminator is not getting fooled and performing its work accurately, the probability of incorrectly classifying the images is almost zero. As a result, the negative log of this value is very high at the end of training, indicating that the generator is not a good generator and cannot generate images that look real. Therefore, this situation is not preferred for generating accurate and realistic-looking images.

In the following *Figure 3.4*, we can see a side-by-side comparison of GANs trained on the MNIST dataset. The MNIST dataset is a commonly used benchmark for evaluating generative models, and in this figure, we can see how the GANs improve as the training progresses. Each row in the figure represents a different GAN iteration, and as we move from left to right, we can see the GAN generating more realistic images of handwritten digits.

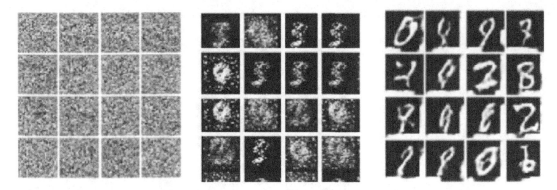

Figure 3.4: Side-by-side comparison of GANs

In *Figure 3.5*, we can see a side-by-side comparison of GANs and **Gaussian Mixture Models (GMM)** trained on the MNIST dataset. GANs are a type of generative model that uses a neural network to generate new data that is similar to the training data, while GMMs are a probabilistic model that represents the data as a mixture of Gaussian distributions. In this figure, we can see that the GANs generate more realistic images of handwritten digits than the output of the GMM. This is because GANs can capture more complex dependencies in the data and generate more diverse and realistic samples, refer to the following figure:

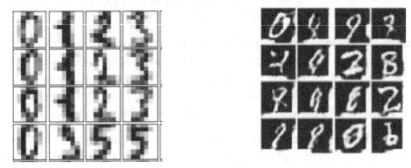

Figure 3.5: Side-by-side comparison of GANs and GMMs

Issues during training a GANs

Although GANs are a significant advancement in generative modeling, they are challenging to train. In this section, we will discuss some of the most common issues faced while training GANs, and then we will explore modifications to the GAN framework that can alleviate many of these problems.

Mode collapse

Imagine you are drawing pictures, and you have a friend who guesses what you are drawing. You are trying to make your drawings so good that your friend thinks they are real. However, if you find out your friend always thinks a picture of a cat is real, you might start drawing only cats. That is like what happens in a special computer program called a GAN, where one part makes pictures and another part guesses if they're real or made-up. If the picture-making part keeps making the same kind of picture because the guessing part always thinks it's real, that's called **mode collapse**. It is like only drawing cats!

When the generator produces very similar outputs, the discriminator can easily distinguish them as fake. As a result, the generator fails to capture the full diversity of the training data.

Mode collapse is a problem that can occur when training GANs. In mode collapse, the generator learns to produce only a limited set of outputs, even though the training data contains a much wider variety of outputs. This can be seen in the learning curve of the generator, which will show that the loss function plateaus after a certain point.

The learning curve of a GAN typically shows the progression of the generator and discriminator losses over the course of training. In the case of mode collapse, the learning curve may exhibit certain distinct patterns that indicate the presence of this issue.

Initially, during the early stages of training, the generator and discriminator losses may decrease steadily, indicating that both networks are improving and learning to generate more realistic samples and distinguish between real and fake data. However, as training progresses, mode collapse may occur, leading to a specific pattern in the learning curve.

One characteristic pattern associated with mode collapse is a sudden drop in the discriminator loss. This drop occurs when the discriminator becomes highly effective at discriminating between real and fake samples. The discriminator loss converges to a very low value, suggesting that the discriminator can easily distinguish between the generated samples and the real data.

Simultaneously, the generator loss may exhibit a different behavior. Instead of steadily decreasing or stabilizing, it may start fluctuating or even increasing. This indicates that the generator is struggling to produce diverse and realistic samples that can fool the discriminator. The generator loss may reach a plateau or oscillate around a certain value, suggesting a lack of progress in improving the generator's performance.

The learning curve in mode collapse can be visually represented as a downward trend in the discriminator loss, while the generator loss either plateaus or shows erratic behavior. This imbalance between the discriminator and generator can result in the generator producing similar outputs, lacking diversity, and failing to capture the full range of the target data distribution.

There are a number of factors that can contribute to mode collapse, including:

- **The choice of hyperparameters:** Some hyperparameters, such as the learning rate, can make it more likely for mode collapse to occur.

- **The quality of the training data:** If the training data is not diverse enough, the generator will not have enough information to learn to produce a wide range of outputs.

- **The architecture of the generator and discriminator:** The architecture of the models can make it more or less difficult for the generator to learn to produce a wide range of outputs.

Refer to the following *Figure 3.6*:

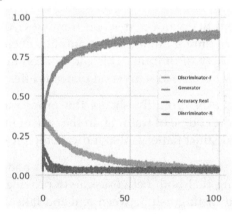

Figure 3.6: Identify mode collapse from training plot

Vanishing gradients

When the gradients propagated through the GAN become very small, and the generator fails to improve. This can happen due to the use of activation functions or a poor choice of hyperparameters.

Vanishing gradients is a problem that occurs during the training of GANs. It happens when the gradients propagated through the network become extremely small or vanish altogether. This can make it difficult for the GAN to learn and converge.

The presence of vanishing gradients can be observed in the learning curve of a GAN. The learning curve typically shows the progression of the generator and discriminator losses over the course of training. In the case of vanishing gradients, the learning curve may exhibit certain patterns that indicate the presence of this issue.

One common pattern associated with vanishing gradients is a plateau or slow convergence of the generator and discriminator losses. The losses may reach a certain value and then show limited progress or become stagnant. This indicates that the gradients flowing through the network are becoming very small, making it difficult for the networks to update their parameters effectively and learn further.

As the gradients diminish, the learning rate of the network decreases, causing slower convergence and longer training times. This phenomenon can significantly impact the GAN's ability to learn complex patterns and generate high-quality samples.

There are several techniques that can be employed to mitigate the issue of vanishing gradients in GANs. One common approach is to use different activation functions, such as LeakyReLU or ReLU, which can alleviate the vanishing gradients problem compared to more traditional activation functions like sigmoid or tanh. Additionally, weight normalization, gradient clipping, and batch normalization can be applied to stabilize the gradients during training and mitigate the vanishing gradients issue.

By addressing vanishing gradients, the GAN can better propagate meaningful gradients through the network, leading to more effective learning and improved convergence, ultimately resulting in better quality generated samples.

Refer to the following *Figure 3.7*:

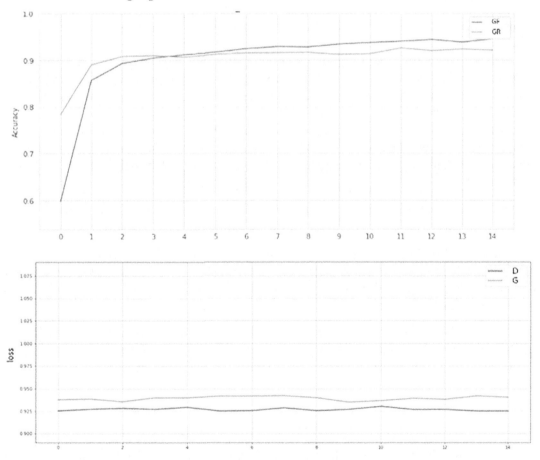

Figure 3.7: *Identify vanishing gradients from training plot*

Here are some additional details about vanishing gradients:

- Vanishing gradients are caused by the use of non-linear activation functions in neural networks. These functions can cause the gradients to become smaller as they propagate through the network, eventually becoming so small that they are effectively zero.

- Vanishing gradients can make it difficult for neural networks to learn, as they can no longer effectively update their parameters. This can lead to slow convergence and poor performance.

- There are a number of techniques that can be used to mitigate the problem of vanishing gradients, including using different activation functions, weight normalization, gradient clipping, and batch normalization.

Oscillation

Imagine you are on a swing, going back and forth, up and down. Now, think of a game where you are trying to stop the swing in the middle, but it's tricky, so sometimes you go too high, and sometimes too low. In a computer program that learns by itself, there is a thing called a loss curve, which is like the path of your swing. It shows if the program is getting better at its game. But sometimes, like your swing, it goes up and down, not staying steady, because the program is having a hard time learning perfectly. That is like the swing not stopping in the middle but going back and forth. That up and down movement of the loss curve is what we call oscillation. When the generator and discriminator are oscillating between two states, without making any real progress, it is called oscillation.

Oscillation is a problem that occurs during the training of GANs. It happens when the generator and discriminator are not effectively learning from each other. This can cause the learning curves of both networks to show instability and lack of convergence.

The presence of oscillation can be observed in the learning curve of a GAN. The learning curve typically shows the progression of the generator and discriminator losses over the course of training. In the case of oscillation, the learning curves may exhibit certain patterns that indicate the presence of this issue.

One characteristic pattern associated with oscillation is a fluctuation or irregular behavior in both the generator and discriminator losses. Instead of steadily decreasing or stabilizing, the losses may show erratic jumps or fluctuations around certain values. This suggests that the networks are not converging or making meaningful progress but rather bouncing back and forth between two states.

There are several factors that can cause oscillation, including:

- **An imbalance in network capacities:** If the generator and discriminator are not evenly matched, it can lead to the generator being unable to produce samples that can fool the discriminator consistently.

- **Inappropriate choice of hyperparameters:** The choice of hyperparameters, such as the learning rate, can have a significant impact on the stability of GAN training.

- **Mismatched learning rates between the generator and discriminator:** If the generator and discriminator are updated with different learning rates, it can lead to oscillation.

Resolving oscillation often requires careful tuning of the network architecture, adjusting hyperparameters, or using alternative training strategies. Some techniques that can be used to mitigate oscillation include:

- **Updating the networks with different frequencies:** This can help to stabilize the learning process by preventing the generator and discriminator from becoming too far apart.

- **Employing techniques like spectral normalization or gradient penalty:** These techniques can help to improve the stability of GAN training by regularizing the gradients and preventing them from becoming too large.

By addressing the oscillation issue, the GAN can achieve more stable and consistent learning, leading to improved convergence and the generation of high-quality samples.

Refer to the following *Figure 3.8*:

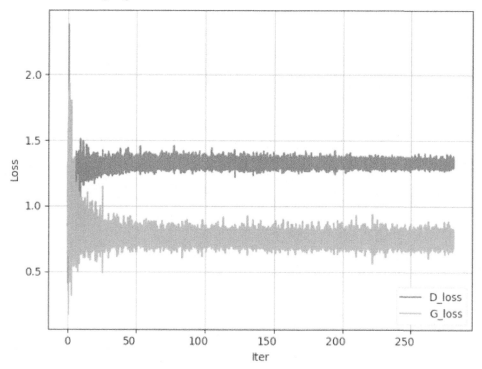

Figure 3.8: Identify oscillation from training plot

Unstability

When the training of the GAN becomes unstable, and the loss function does not converge, there occurs unstability. This can be due to a variety of factors, including the use of inappropriate loss functions, poor choice of hyperparameters, or the presence of noise in the data, as shown:

- **Inadequate hyperparameter selection:** The choice of hyperparameters, such as learning rate, batch size, and network architecture, greatly impacts the stability of GAN training. Poorly selected hyperparameters can hinder convergence and lead to unstable training behavior. Finding the right balance and tuning these hyperparameters is crucial for achieving stable GAN training.

- **Sensitive loss function:** GANs employ an adversarial loss function that involves competing objectives. The generator aims to generate samples that fool the discriminator, while the discriminator aims to correctly classify real and fake samples. Balancing these objectives can be challenging, and slight changes in the loss function formulation can affect the stability of the training process.

Refer to the following figure:

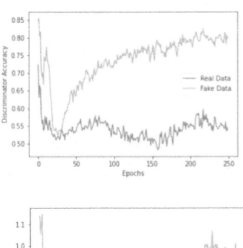

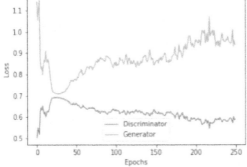

Figure 3.9: Identify unstable training from training plot

To address GAN instability, researchers and practitioners have proposed several techniques:

- **Architecture modifications:** Modifying the GAN architecture can help alleviate instability issues. Techniques such as adding skip connections, using normalization layers (such as, batch normalization), or incorporating residual blocks can improve gradient flow and stabilize training.

- **Regularization techniques:** Applying regularization techniques, such as weight clipping in Wasserstein GANs or adding gradient penalties, can help prevent the discriminator from becoming too dominant and stabilize training.

- **Learning rate scheduling:** Adjusting the learning rate during training, such as using a decaying learning rate schedule, can aid in stabilizing the GAN training process by preventing abrupt updates and allowing the networks to converge more smoothly.

- **Training strategies:** Exploring different training strategies like progressive growing, where the GAN is initially trained on lower-resolution images before gradually transitioning to higher resolutions, can enhance stability and improve the overall quality of generated samples.

Evaluation

It can be difficult to evaluate the quality of GAN-generated samples. The evaluation process is often subjective and relies heavily on human perception. The reliability of loss values obtained during training of GANs is often questionable. In GAN research papers, both qualitative and quantitative evaluation methods are commonly employed to assess the performance of the models. Qualitative evaluation involves subjective judgments made by human observers who determine whether a generated sample looks real or fake. In such cases, the visual quality of the generated sample is considered crucial for the success of GAN training, regardless of the fluctuating loss values. However, qualitative evaluations can be biased and may not provide a comprehensive assessment, particularly in scenarios like mode collapse where the generated images may look good but lack diversity.

Therefore, directly relying on loss values for GAN evaluation is not recommended. Instead, various metrics such as Inception Score, **Frechet Inception Distance (FID** score), and **Learned Perceptual Image Patch Similarity (LPIPS)** measures are used to interpret the results. These quantitative metrics offer a more objective evaluation of GAN performance. For example, early stopping can be implemented by monitoring the FID score or perceptual similarity to halt training when there is degradation in performance.

Furthermore, alternative GAN models like WGAN and WGAN-LP provide better mathematical insights into GAN training by employing the Wasserstein distance calculation and enforcing Lipschitz continuity. These models address some of the challenges faced by traditional GANs and offer improved training stability and performance.

Wasserstein GAN (WGAN) was proposed to address some of the major issues faced by traditional GANs. Here are some reasons why WGAN was introduced to address these issues:

- **Mode collapse:** One of the major problems with GANs is mode collapse, where the generator learns to produce only a limited set of outputs, rather than producing diverse outputs. WGANs use the Wasserstein distance to measure the distance between the real and fake data distributions, which encourages the generator to produce a more diverse set of outputs.

- **Vanishing gradients:** GANs often suffer from the problem of vanishing gradients, where the gradients of the loss function become very small, making it difficult for the network to learn. WGANs address this issue by using a weight clipping technique, which ensures that the gradient magnitudes are kept in a reasonable range.

- **Unstable training:** GANs can be difficult to train, and the training process can be unstable, with the generator and discriminator oscillating between modes. WGANs address this issue by using a more stable training process, where the discriminator is trained to convergence before updating the generator.

Case study: Common practical implementation of GANs for augmentation and balancing classes

Let us go over a case study now:

Improving dental cavity detection with GANs: Balancing imbalanced classes in the CranexD dataset

Dataset can be downloaded from here **https://universe.roboflow.com/pravar-kulbhushan/teeth-fsxmv**

Introduction: Dental cavity detection plays a vital role in preventive dentistry and oral healthcare. However, accurately identifying and classifying cavities from dental X-rays can be a challenging task, especially when dealing with imbalanced classes. In this article, we explore the use of GAN to address class imbalances in the CranexD dataset, enhancing the accuracy of dental cavity detection.

Understanding imbalanced classes in the CranexD dataset: The CranexD dataset, comprising panoramic dental X-rays, contains valuable information for dental imaging applications. However, the dataset suffers from class imbalances, with certain cavity classes being significantly underrepresented compared to others. This imbalance hinders the performance of traditional machine learning algorithms, as they tend to favor the majority classes, leading to suboptimal accuracy in detecting and classifying cavities.

Using GANs to balance classes: To overcome the challenges posed by imbalanced classes, we turn to GANs. GANs have shown remarkable success in generating realistic and diverse samples, which can be leveraged to augment the minority classes and balance the dataset. By training the GAN to generate synthetic samples representing the underrepresented cavity classes, we can effectively address the class imbalance issue.

The GAN training process: The GAN training process involves two components: the generator and the discriminator. The generator learns to generate synthetic cavity images based on random noise input, while the discriminator distinguishes between real and synthetic cavity images. Through an adversarial training process, the generator continually improves its ability to generate realistic cavity samples, while the discriminator becomes more adept at differentiating between real and synthetic images.

Improving accuracy with balanced classes: By incorporating synthetic cavity samples generated by the GAN into the CranexD dataset, we create a balanced training set that better represents all cavity classes. This balanced dataset enables the training of machine learning models that exhibit improved accuracy in detecting and classifying cavities. The presence of augmented samples from the minority classes provides the models with a more comprehensive understanding of cavity variations and enhances their ability to generalize to real-world scenarios. Refer to the following code:

Code:`import tensorflow as tf`

```
# Load the CranexD dataset
dataset = tf.keras.datasets.cranexd
(x_train, y_train), (x_test, y_test) = dataset.load_data()


# Define the generator and discriminator networks
generator = tf.keras.Sequential([
  tf.keras.layers.Input(shape=(224, 224, 3)),
  tf.keras.layers.Conv2D(64, (3, 3), padding='same'),
  tf.keras.layers.LeakyReLU(),
  tf.keras.layers.MaxPooling2D((2, 2)),
  tf.keras.layers.Conv2D(128, (3, 3), padding='same'),
  tf.keras.layers.LeakyReLU(),
  tf.keras.layers.MaxPooling2D((2, 2)),
  tf.keras.layers.Flatten(),
  tf.keras.layers.Dense(1024),
  tf.keras.layers.LeakyReLU(),
  tf.keras.layers.Dense(224 * 224 * 3),
  tf.keras.layers.Reshape((224, 224, 3))
```

```python
])

discriminator = tf.keras.Sequential([
  tf.keras.layers.Input(shape=(224, 224, 3)),
  tf.keras.layers.Conv2D(64, (3, 3), padding='same'),
  tf.keras.layers.LeakyReLU(),
  tf.keras.layers.MaxPooling2D((2, 2)),
  tf.keras.layers.Conv2D(128, (3, 3), padding='same'),
  tf.keras.layers.LeakyReLU(),
  tf.keras.layers.MaxPooling2D((2, 2)),
  tf.keras.layers.Flatten(),
  tf.keras.layers.Dense(1024),
  tf.keras.layers.LeakyReLU(),
  tf.keras.layers.Dense(1, activation='sigmoid')
])

# Compile the generator and discriminator networks
generator.compile(optimizer='adam',          loss='binary_crossentropy',
metrics=['accuracy'])
discriminator.compile(optimizer='adam',          loss='binary_crossentropy',
metrics=['accuracy'])

# Define the GAN loss
gan_loss = tf.keras.losses.BinaryCrossentropy()

# Define the GAN training steps
@tf.function
def train_step(x_batch):
  # Generate fake images
  fake_images = generator(x_batch)

  # Train the discriminator
  real_labels = tf.ones((x_batch.shape[0], 1))
  fake_labels = tf.zeros((x_batch.shape[0], 1))
  discriminator_loss = discriminator.train_on_batch([x_batch, fake_images],
[real_labels, fake_labels])
```

```
# Train the generator
  generator_loss = gan_loss(tf.ones((x_batch.shape[0], 1)), generator(x_
batch))


  return discriminator_loss, generator_loss


# Train the GAN
epochs = 10
for epoch in range(epochs):
  discriminator_loss, generator_loss = train_step(x_train)
  print(f'Epoch {epoch + 1}/{epochs}, Discriminator Loss: {discriminator_
loss}, Generator Loss: {generator_loss}')


# Generate fake images
fake_images = generator.predict(x_test)


# Save the generated images
tf.keras.utils.save_img(fake_images, 'generated_images.jpg')
```

Quantifying the improvement: To evaluate the impact of balancing the classes using GANs, we employ quantitative metrics such as precision, recall, and F1-score. These metrics measure the performance of the cavity detection models on both the majority and minority classes. Through comparative analysis, we observe significant improvements in the accuracy of cavity detection and classification when using the GAN-balanced dataset compared to the original imbalanced dataset.

Conclusion: Addressing class imbalances in the CranexD dataset using GANs has proven to be a valuable approach in improving the accuracy of dental cavity detection. By generating synthetic samples for underrepresented cavity classes, GANs enable the creation of a balanced dataset, enhancing the performance of machine learning models. This advancement in cavity detection technology can contribute to more effective preventive dentistry and early intervention, ultimately improving oral healthcare outcomes for patients.

Refer to the following *Figure 3.10:*

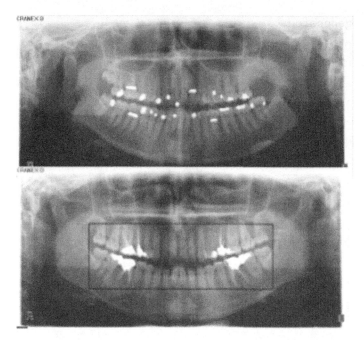

Figure 3.10: Original Cranex D data with Annotation Figure 1.8 Generated Carnex D data

The following figure shows the generated Cranex D data:

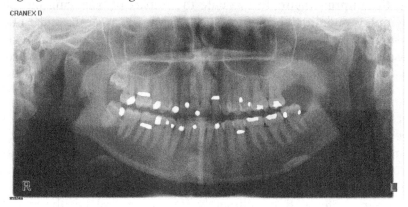

Figure 3.11: Generated Carnex D data

Conclusion

In conclusion, Generative Adversarial Networks are notorious for being among the most difficult models to train in the field of deep learning. GAN training is challenging due to various issues such as instability, mode collapse, vanishing gradients, and inadequate hyperparameter selection. These factors often lead to non-convergence of the loss function and inconsistent generation of samples. However, researchers have made significant progress in addressing these challenges and improving the stability of GAN training. Several solutions have been proposed to mitigate the difficulties associated with GAN training. These include architectural modifications, regularization techniques, learning rate scheduling, training strategies, and effective evaluation and monitoring.

Architectural modifications, such as incorporating skip connections, normalization layers, and residual blocks, can improve the flow of gradients and stabilize the training process. Regularization techniques, such as weight clipping and gradient penalties, help prevent the discriminator from dominating the training dynamics and stabilize the learning process.

Applying learning rate scheduling techniques, such as using a decaying learning rate or adaptive learning rate algorithms, can facilitate more stable and efficient training. Training strategies like progressive growing, where the GAN is initially trained on lower-resolution images before gradually increasing the complexity, can aid in achieving stability and generating high-quality samples.

Additionally, continuous evaluation and monitoring of the training process are essential. Visualizing generated samples, tracking the loss function, and using quantitative metrics like **Fréchet Inception Distance (FID)** or Inception Score provide valuable insights into the performance and progress of the GAN training.

While GAN training remains a challenging task, these proposed solutions offer potential pathways to improve stability and enhance the overall performance of GANs. Continued research and development in this field hold the promise of further advancements, making GANs more accessible and effective for a wide range of applications in generative modeling and artificial intelligence. Also, relying solely on loss values is not advisable in GANs, and a combination of qualitative and quantitative evaluation methods, along with specific metrics and alternative GAN models, should be employed for a more comprehensive assessment of GAN performance.

A comprehensive range of metrics for GAN evaluation is detailed in a referenced paper.

In the next chapter, readers will have gained a comprehensive understanding of autoencoders as a powerful tool in the realm of generative AI. They will have a solid grasp of the fundamental concepts, practical considerations, and cutting-edge advancements that can enable them to apply autoencoders effectively in their own projects, and unlock the potential of generative models to create realistic and novel outputs.

Join our book's Discord space

Join the book's Discord Workspace for Latest updates, Offers, Tech happenings around the world, New Release and Sessions with the Authors:

https://discord.bpbonline.com

CHAPTER 4

Architecting Auto Encoder for Generative AI

Introduction

In recent years, the field of **artificial intelligence (AI)** has witnessed remarkable advancements, particularly in the area of generative models. These models, designed to learn the underlying patterns and structure of data, have opened up new possibilities for applications such as image generation, natural language processing, and even music composition. Among the diverse range of generative models, one approach that has gained significant attention and proven to be highly effective is autoencoders.

Autoencoders represent a class of neural network architectures that have the remarkable ability to learn compact and meaningful representations of input data. They are comprised of an encoder network that maps the input data into a lower-dimensional latent space, and a decoder network that reconstructs the input data from the latent space representation. What makes autoencoders particularly interesting is their inherent capability to capture the essential features and characteristics of the input data, enabling them to generate new, synthetic samples that closely resemble the original distribution.

Join us on this exciting journey as we unravel the intricate workings of autoencoders and discover their immense potential in driving innovation and creativity in the field of generative AI.

Structure

In this chapter, we will cover the following topics:

- Auto Encoders

- Key distinctions with autoencoders

- Importance of regularization in auto encoders

- About Cifar10

- Anomaly detection using Auto Encoder

- Autoencoders with convolutional layers

Objectives

The primary goal of this chapter is to explore the fascinating world of autoencoders in the context of generative AI. We will delve into the inner workings of autoencoders, discussing their architectural variations, training strategies and their applications in generating diverse and high-quality outputs across various domains. Furthermore, we will examine advanced techniques that leverage autoencoders, such as **Variational AutoEncoders (VAE)** and **Generative Adversarial Networks (GAN)**, which push the boundaries of generative AI even further.

Throughout this chapter, and the next, we will also discuss the key challenges associated with autoencoders for generative tasks, including issues like mode collapse, blurry outputs, and training instability. We will explore solutions and strategies to mitigate these challenges, providing practical insights and recommendations for building robust and effective generative models using autoencoders.

By the end of this chapter, readers will have gained a comprehensive understanding of autoencoders as a powerful tool in the realm of generative AI. They will have a solid grasp of the fundamental concepts, practical considerations, and cutting-edge advancements that can enable them to apply autoencoders effectively in their own projects and unlock the potential of generative models to create realistic and novel outputs.

Auto Encoders

An autoencoder is a type of algorithm with the primary purpose of learning an *informative* representation of the data that can be used for different applications by learning to reconstruct a set of input observations well enough.[1]

---

[1] Bank, D., Koenigstein, N., and Giryes, R., Autoencoders, https://arxiv.or g/abs/2003.05991

Neural networks are commonly utilized in supervised settings, where each training observation, denoted as xi, is associated with a corresponding label or expected value, yi. During training, the neural network model learns the relationship between the input data and the expected labels. However, what if we only have unlabeled observations? This means that our training dataset, denoted as ST, solely consists of M observations xi, where i ranges from 1 to M:

$$ST = \{xi \mid i = 1, \ldots, M\} \quad (1)$$

Here, *xi* generally belongs to the real-valued n-dimensional space, denoted as Rn, with *n* being a natural number. In 1986, *Rumelhart, Hinton*, and *Williams* introduced autoencoders with the objective of learning to reconstruct the input observations, *xi*, with the lowest possible error.

Now, you might wonder why one would want to learn to reconstruct the input observations. To illustrate this concept, consider a dataset consisting of images. An autoencoder serves as an algorithm that aims to produce an output image that closely resembles the input image. While this may initially seem perplexing, it is crucial to delve deeper into understanding the usefulness of autoencoders by providing a more informative definition, albeit not yet entirely unambiguous.

To better understand autoencoders, we need to look at their typical architecture. It consists of three main components: an encoder, a latent feature representation, and a decoder. The encoder and decoder are simply functions, while the latent feature representation is a tensor of real numbers.

Generally speaking, we want the autoencoder to reconstruct the input well enough. However, we also want it to create a latent feature representation that is useful and meaningful. For example, latent features for hand-written digits could be the number of lines required to write each number, the angle of each line, and how they connect.

Learning how to write numbers does not require learning the gray values of each pixel in the input image. Humans do not learn to write by filling pixels with gray values. Instead, we extract the essential information that will allow us to solve the problem (writing digits, for example). This latent representation can then be used for various tasks, such as feature extraction, classification, or clustering.

Here are some additional details about the three main components of an autoencoder:

- **Encoder:** The encoder is responsible for taking the input data and compressing it into a lower-dimensional representation. This is done by using a series of layers, such as convolutional layers, pooling layers, and dense layers. The number of layers and the type of layers used will vary depending on the specific application.

- **Latent feature representation:** The latent feature representation is a lower-dimensional representation of the input data. It is typically a tensor of real numbers, but it can also be a categorical variable. The latent feature representation is what allows the autoencoder to reconstruct the input data.

- **Decoder:** The decoder is responsible for taking the latent feature representation and reconstructing the original input data. This is done by using a series of layers that are the opposite of the layers used in the encoder.

Autoencoders are a powerful tool for a variety of tasks, such as:

- **Data compression:** Autoencoders can be used to compress data by reducing the number of dimensions in the input data. This can be useful for storing or transmitting data more efficiently.

- **Feature extraction:** Autoencoders can be used to extract features from data. This can be useful for tasks such as classification, clustering, and dimensionality reduction.

- **Generative modeling:** Autoencoders can be used to generate new data that is similar to the training data. This can be useful for tasks such as creating synthetic data, generating images, and generating text.

Autoencoders are a promising technology with the potential to revolutionize the way we interact with data. Refer to the following figure:

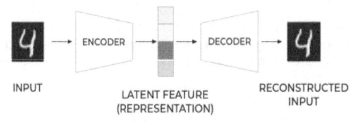

Figure 4.1: General structure of an autoencoder

In typical autoencoder architectures, the encoder and decoder components are implemented using neural networks. This is because neural networks are easy to train using popular software libraries such as TensorFlow or PyTorch.

The encoder can be represented as a function, denoted as g, which depends on certain parameters. When we eValuate the encoder on the input xi, it produces the output hi, representing the latent feature representation. Mathematically, this can be expressed as:

$$h\_i = g(x\_i)$$

Here, hi belongs to the real-valued space Rq, where q denotes the dimensionality of the latent features. It is important to note that g is a function mapping from Rn to Rq.

The decoder, which generates the output of the autoencoder denoted as x^i, can be represented by another generic function, denoted as f, operating on the latent features:

$$\tilde{x}i = f(hi) = f(g(xi)) \ (3)$$

Here, x^i belongs to the real-valued space Rn.

Training an autoencoder essentially involves finding the optimal parameter values for both the encoder function $g(x)$ and the decoder function $f(h)$ that minimize the discrepancy between the input and the output of the autoencoder. This discrepancy, represented by the measure Δ, serves as our loss function and penalizes the difference between the input and the output. Mathematically, the training objective can be expressed as:

$$arg\ min\ f,g < [\Delta(xi, f(g(xi)))] >$$

In this equation, Δ quantifies the difference between the input xi and the output $f(g(xi))$, while $\langle \cdot \rangle$ denotes the average over all observations.

Autoencoders can learn to reconstruct the output perfectly, which is not very useful. Two main strategies can be used to avoid this:

- **Creating a bottleneck:** This is achieved by making the latent feature's dimensionality lower (often much lower) than the input's.

- **Regularization:** This is a technique that adds constraints to the model's parameters to prevent overfitting.

We will first discuss regularization, and then we will discuss creating a bottleneck.

Regularization

Regularization is a technique that adds constraints to the model's parameters to prevent overfitting. Overfitting occurs when the model learns the training data too well and is unable to generalize to new data.

There are many different regularization techniques, but two of the most common are:

- **L1 regularization:** This adds a penalty to the loss function that is proportional to the absolute value of the parameters. This encourages the parameters to be small, which can help to prevent overfitting.

- **L2 regularization:** This adds a penalty to the loss function that is proportional to the square of the parameters. This encourages the parameters to be zero, which can also help to prevent overfitting.

Creating a bottleneck

Creating a bottleneck is a way to force the autoencoder to learn a more compressed representation of the input data. This can be done by adding a hidden layer with a smaller number of neurons than the input layer. This forces the autoencoder to learn to represent the input data in a lower-dimensional space.

The bottleneck approach is often used in conjunction with regularization. This can help to prevent overfitting and improve the generalization performance of the autoencoder.

Key distinctions with autoencoders

Let us understand the key distinctions with autoencoders:

Autoencoders

Autoencoders are trained end-to-end with a single loss function. The loss function measures the error between the input data and the output data. The autoencoder is trained to minimize the loss function.

The loss function for an autoencoder is typically mean squared error, but it can also be other loss functions, such as cross-entropy.

GANs

GANs are trained with two loss functions, one for the generator and one for the discriminator. The generator is trained to generate data that is indistinguishable from real data. The discriminator is trained to distinguish between real data and generated data.

The loss functions for the generator and the discriminator are typically adversarial loss functions. Adversarial loss functions are designed to create a competition between the generator and the discriminator. The generator tries to fool the discriminator, and the discriminator tries to correctly identify real data from generated data.

GANs are a more recent generative model than autoencoders, and they are still under development. GANs have the potential to generate more realistic data than autoencoders, but they are also more difficult to train.

Refer to the following *Table 4.1:*

Feature	Autoencoder	GAN
Training approach	End-to-end	Two separate networks
Loss function	Mean squared error	Adversarial loss
Strengths	Easy to train, less prone to overfitting	More expressive, can generate more realistic data
Weaknesses	Less expressive, can generate less realistic data	More difficult to train, prone to mode collapse

Table 4.1: Different features in autoencoders and GANs

Importance of regularization in auto encoders

Regularization plays a crucial role in autoencoders to prevent overfitting and enhance the generalization capabilities of the model. Overfitting occurs when an autoencoder becomes too specialized in learning the training data and fails to generalize well to unseen data. Regularization techniques help to address this issue by adding constraints or penalties to the training process, encouraging the model to learn more robust and generalized representations.

There are a few reasons why regularization is particularly important in autoencoders:

- **Dimensionality reduction:** Autoencoders are commonly used for dimensionality reduction tasks, where the goal is to learn a lower-dimensional representation of the input data. Regularization techniques such as L1 or L2 regularization (also known as weight decay) can help enforce sparsity or limit the magnitude of the learned weights, reducing the risk of the autoencoder learning redundant or irrelevant features. This helps in achieving more compact and informative latent representations.

- **Noise tolerance:** Autoencoders with regularization techniques are often more resilient to noisy or corrupted input data. By introducing regularization, such as dropout or adding noise to the input, the model learns to be less sensitive to small perturbations or outliers in the data. This improves the ability of the autoencoder to reconstruct clean representations even in the presence of noisy inputs.

- **Generalization:** Regularization methods encourage the autoencoder to learn more generalizable patterns from the data. By avoiding excessive reliance on specific training examples, regularization helps the model capture the underlying data distribution rather than memorizing individual instances. This improves the autoencoder's ability to generate meaningful and coherent outputs when applied to unseen or novel data.

- **Preventing overfitting:** Autoencoders, like other neural network models, are prone to overfitting, especially when the model has a large number of parameters relative to the size of the training data. Regularization techniques help in mitigating overfitting by adding regularization terms to the loss function, which penalize complex or over-parameterized models. This encourages the autoencoder to find a simpler and more generalized solution, reducing the risk of overfitting.

Sparsity in the latent feature output means that only a few of the latent features are active at any given time. This can be useful for a variety of tasks, such as dimensionality reduction and feature selection.

There are a number of ways to enforce sparsity in the latent feature output. One way is to add a regularization term to the loss function. Regularization is a technique that adds constraints to the model's parameters to prevent overfitting.

The most common regularization techniques for autoencoders are L1 and L2 regularization. L1 regularization adds a penalty to the loss function that is proportional to the absolute value of the parameters. This encourages the parameters to be small, which can help to prevent overfitting and sparsity in the latent feature output.

L2 regularization adds a penalty to the loss function that is proportional to the square of the parameters. This encourages the parameters to be zero, which can also help to prevent overfitting and sparsity in the latent feature output.

The following is an example of how to add an L2 regularization term to the loss function for an autoencoder:

$$argmin(E[\Delta(xi,g(f(xi)))]+\lambda i\sum\theta i2)$$
$$f, g$$

Or

$$loss = mean\_squared\_error(x\_hat, x) + lambda * l2\_norm(w)$$

The *argminf,g* represents the argument that minimizes the subsequent expression with respect to *f* and *g*. E denotes the expectation, and $\Delta\Delta$ represents the discrepancy or difference between *xi* and *g(f(xi))*. The term λ is a scalar coefficient, and θi represents the *i*-th element of the vector θ. The $\sum\sum i$ notation indicates the summation over all values of *i*.

In the formula, theta (θ) is the parameter value of the function *f(x)* and *g(x)*. In the case of neural networks, the parameters are the weights. The derivative of the cost function with respect to the parameters is easy to calculate.

Another trick to enforce sparsity is to tie the weights of the encoder to the weights of the decoder. This means that the weights of the encoder and decoder are equal. This technique, and a few others, has the same effect of adding sparsity to the latent feature representation.

The type of autoencoders that build *f(x)* and *g(x)* with feed-forward networks that use a bottleneck are very easy to implement and are very effective.

Here are some additional details about autoencoders with a bottleneck:

- **Feed-forward network**: A feed-forward network is a type of neural network that has no loops. This means that the information flows in one direction, from the input layer to the output layer.

- **Bottleneck**: A bottleneck is a layer in a neural network that has fewer neurons than the layers before and after it. This forces the network to learn a more compressed representation of the input data.

Autoencoders with a bottleneck are a popular choice for a variety of tasks, such as:

- **Dimensionality reduction**: Autoencoders can be used to reduce the dimensionality of data by learning a compressed representation of the data. This can be useful for tasks such as visualization and classification.

- **Feature extraction:** Autoencoders can be used to extract features from data by learning a compressed representation of the data. This can be useful for tasks such as classification and clustering.

- **Generative modeling:** Autoencoders can be used to generate new data that is similar to the training data. This can be useful for tasks such as creating synthetic data, generating images, and generating text.

Autoencoders with a bottleneck are a powerful tool for a variety of tasks. They are easy to implement and can be very effective.

The typical architecture of a feed-forward autoencoder follows a specific pattern where the number of neurons in the layers initially decreases as we move through the network until reaching the middle layer. Then, the number of neurons starts to increase again until the final layer, which has the same number of neurons as the input dimensions.[2]

Figure 4.2 features a feed-forward autoencoder:

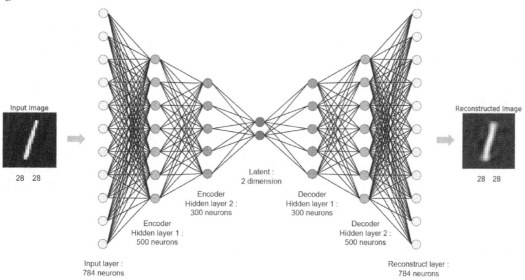

Figure 4.2: *Feed-forward autoencoder*

This architecture can be summarized as follows:

- **Input layer:** The input layer consists of neurons equal to the dimensions of the input data.

- **Encoding layers:** As we move deeper into the network, the number of neurons gradually decreases, forming a bottleneck at the middle layer. The middle layer, also known as the latent or encoding layer, has the lowest number of neurons in the network.

2. *Autoencoder in biology — review and perspectives* | *by Encode Box* | *Medium*

- **Decoding layers:** After the middle layer, the number of neurons starts to increase again, mirroring the structure of the encoding layers. The decoding layers aim to reconstruct the input data based on the information captured in the encoding layers.

- **Output layer:** The final layer of the autoencoder has the same number of neurons as the input layer, allowing the autoencoder to produce output data that closely resembles the input.

This architecture is often referred to as *bottleneck* architecture, as the bottleneck layer in the middle acts as a compressed representation of the input data. By progressively reducing the number of neurons and then expanding them, the autoencoder learns to extract the most essential features from the input data while minimizing information loss.

The architecture enables the autoencoder to learn an efficient representation of the input data by encoding it into a lower-dimensional space and then reconstructing it back to its original dimensions.

Here is an example code snippet that demonstrates how to download the CIFAR-10 dataset, create a TensorFlow autoencoder with two encoder and two decoder layers, and visualize the input and output data.

Cifar10

The CIFAR-10 dataset is a popular benchmark dataset for machine learning and computer vision tasks such as image classification, object detection, and image segmentation. The dataset is relatively small and easy to work with, making it a good choice for beginners. However, the dataset is also challenging, as the images are of high quality and the classes are well-balanced, it includes:

- Airplane

- Automobile

- Bird

- Cat

- Deer

- Dog

- Frog

- Horse

- Ship

- Truck

The CIFAR-10 dataset was created by *Alex Krizhevsky, Ilya Sutskever,* and *Geoffrey Hinton.* It was first made available in 2009. The dataset is available for download from the CIFAR website.

Here are some of the benefits of using the CIFAR-10 dataset:

- It is a large and diverse dataset. The CIFAR-10 dataset contains 60,000 images, which is a large number of data points for training a machine learning model. The dataset also contains a variety of images, which helps to ensure that the model is able to generalize to new data.

- It is a challenging dataset. The CIFAR-10 dataset is challenging because the images are of high quality and the classes are well-balanced. This means that the model must be able to learn to distinguish between the classes accurately.

- It is a well-known dataset. The CIFAR-10 dataset is a well-known dataset in the machine learning community. This means that there are many resources available to help with training and evaluating models on the dataset.

Here are some of the challenges of using the CIFAR-10 dataset:

- It is a small dataset. The CIFAR-10 dataset is relatively small, with only 60,000 images. This can be a challenge for training deep learning models, which require a large number of data points to learn effectively.

- It is a biased dataset. The CIFAR-10 dataset is biased towards certain classes, such as cars and airplanes. This can be a challenge for training models that are fair and unbiased.

- It is an outdated dataset. The CIFAR-10 dataset was created in 2009, and the images are now considered to be outdated. This can be a challenge for training models that are able to generalize to new data.

CIFAR-10 dataset is a valuable resource for machine learning and computer vision research. The dataset is large, diverse, and challenging, and it is well-known in the machine learning community.

Refer to the following code:

```
import tensorflow as tf
import numpy as np
import matplotlib.pyplot as plt


# Download CIFAR-10 dataset
(train_images, _), (test_images, _) = tf.keras.datasets.cifar10.load_data()
train_images = train_images.astype('float32') / 255.0
test_images = test_images.astype('float32') / 255.0
```

```python
# Define the autoencoder model
input_dim = train_images.shape[1:]
encoding_dim = 128

# Encoder layers
encoder = tf.keras.Sequential([
  tf.keras.layers.Flatten(input_shape=input_dim),
  tf.keras.layers.Dense(encoding_dim, activation='relu'),
  tf.keras.layers.Dense(encoding_dim // 2, activation='relu')
])

# Decoder layers
decoder = tf.keras.Sequential([
  tf.keras.layers.Dense(encoding_dim // 2, activation='relu'),
  tf.keras.layers.Dense(encoding_dim, activation='relu'),
  tf.keras.layers.Dense(np.prod(input_dim), activation='sigmoid'),
  tf.keras.layers.Reshape(input_dim)
])

# Autoencoder model
autoencoder = tf.keras.Sequential([encoder, decoder])

# Compile the model
autoencoder.compile(optimizer='adam', loss='binary_crossentropy')

# Train the autoencoder
autoencoder.fit(train_images, train_images,
                epochs=10,
batch_size=128,
                shuffle=True,
validation_data=(test_images, test_images))

# Visualize input and output data
n = 10  # Number of images to visualize
plt.figure(figsize=(20, 4))
```

```
for i in range(n):
    # Original images
    ax = plt.subplot(2, n, i + 1)
plt.imshow(train_images[i])
plt.title("Original")
plt.gray()
ax.get_xaxis().set_visible(False)
ax.get_yaxis().set_visible(False)

    # Reconstructed images
    ax = plt.subplot(2, n, i + n + 1)
        reconstructed = autoencoder.predict(np.expand_dims(train_images[i],
axis=0))
plt.imshow(reconstructed[0])
plt.title("Reconstructed")
plt.gray()
ax.get_xaxis().set_visible(False)
ax.get_yaxis().set_visible(False)

plt.show()
```
```

Make sure to have TensorFlow and matplotlib installed before running the code. The code will download the CIFAR-10 dataset, create a simple autoencoder with two encoder and two decoder layers, and train it using the dataset. Finally, it will visualize the input images alongside their reconstructed counterparts. Following are the steps:

1. The code starts by importing the necessary libraries, including TensorFlow, numpy, and **matplotlib**.

2. It then downloads the CIFAR-10 dataset and pre-processes the images by scaling them to the **range [0, 1]**.

3. The autoencoder model is defined with two encoder layers and two decoder layers using the Sequential API in TensorFlow.

4. The model is compiled with the Adam optimizer and binary cross-entropy loss.

5. The autoencoder is trained using the **fit** function, specifying the training data, number of epochs, batch size, and validation data.

6. After training, the code proceeds to visualize the input and reconstructed images.
```

7. It sets the number of images to display (**n**) and creates a figure to plot the images.

8. For each image, it plots the original image on the top row and the reconstructed image on the bottom row using `matplotlib`.

9. The code hides the x and y axes for better visualization.

10. Finally, it displays the plot with the input and reconstructed images using `plt.show()`.

Refer to the following figure:

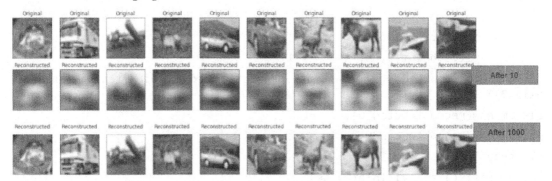

Figure 4.3: Original and reconstructed images after 10 and 1000 epochs

Reconstruction error, also known as **reconstruction loss** or **reconstruction discrepancy**, is a measure of how well an autoencoder can reconstruct its input data. It quantifies the discrepancy between the original input and the output generated by the autoencoder. By minimizing this error, the autoencoder aims to learn an effective representation of the input data.

Mathematically, the reconstruction error is typically computed using a loss function, which measures the dissimilarity between the input and the reconstructed output. One commonly used loss function for reconstruction in autoencoders is the **Mean Squared Error (MSE)**. Let us delve into the details.

Suppose we have an autoencoder with an encoder function, denoted as g, and a decoder function, denoted as f. Given an input sample xi, the autoencoder encodes it into a latent representation $hi = g(xi)$ and then decodes it back into a reconstructed output $\tilde{x}i = f(hi)$.

The reconstruction error for a single input sample xi using the mean squared error loss can be defined as:

$$\Delta(xi, x\raise0pt{\sim}i) = n1\sum j = 1n(xij - x\raise0pt{\sim}ij)2$$

Here, xi_j represents the j-th element of the original input xi, and $\tilde{x}i\_j$ represents the j-th element of the reconstructed output $\tilde{x}i$. The sum calculates the squared differences between the corresponding elements of the input and reconstructed output, and then the average is taken over all elements (n) of the input.

To compute the overall reconstruction error for a dataset with M input samples, we typically take the average of the individual reconstruction errors:

$$E[\Delta(x_i, x\tilde{}_i)] = \frac{1}{M} \sum_{i=1}^{M} \Delta(x_i, x\tilde{}_i)$$

This equation computes the average reconstruction error over all M input samples.

During training, the autoencoder aims to minimize this reconstruction error by adjusting the parameters of the encoder and decoder functions (g and f) using optimization techniques like gradient descent. The optimization process involves iteratively updating the parameters to find the values that minimize the reconstruction error.

By minimizing the reconstruction error, the autoencoder learns to capture the essential features of the input data in the latent representation and generate accurate reconstructions. It effectively learns a compressed representation of the data that can be used for various tasks such as denoising, dimensionality reduction, and generative modeling.

In the above example, reconstruction error was much higher at epoch 10 vs epoch 1000, the reconstruction error quantifies the dissimilarity between the input and the reconstructed output of an autoencoder. By minimizing this error using optimization algorithms, the autoencoder learns to produce accurate reconstructions and extract meaningful representations of the input data.

Anomaly detection using auto encoder

Autoencoders can be used for anomaly detection by training them on a dataset of normal data. Once the autoencoder is trained, it can be used to reconstruct any new data. If the reconstruction error for new data is too high, then the data is likely to be an anomaly.

In the example you provided, an autoencoder was trained on the MNIST dataset, which contains handwritten digits. A single image of a Trouser was then added to the MNIST test dataset. The autoencoder was then used to reconstruct all of the images in the test dataset. The image of the Trouser had the highest reconstruction error, which suggests that it is an anomaly.

This is just one example of how autoencoders can be used for anomaly detection. Autoencoders can be used to detect anomalies in a variety of datasets, including images, text, and time series data.

Here are some of the benefits of using autoencoders for anomaly detection:

- They are unsupervised models, which mean that they do not require labeled data. This makes them a good choice for datasets where labeled data is not available.

- They are able to learn a compressed representation of the data, which can be used to identify anomalies. This is because anomalies are often represented by different features than normal data.

- They are able to detect both point anomalies and contextual anomalies. Point anomalies are individual data points that are different from the rest of the data. Contextual anomalies are groups of data points that are different from the rest of the data.

Here are some of the challenges of using autoencoders for anomaly detection:

- They can be sensitive to the choice of hyperparameters. This means that it can be difficult to find a set of hyperparameters that work well for a particular dataset.

- They can be computationally expensive to train. This is because they require multiple passes over the data.

- They can be prone to overfitting. This means that they can learn the training data too well and not generalize well to new data.

Refer to the following code:

```python
import tensorflow as tf
import numpy as np
import matplotlib.pyplot as plt


# Download MNIST dataset
(train_images, _), (test_images, _) = tf.keras.datasets.mnist.load_data()
train_images = train_images.astype('float32') / 255.0
test_images = test_images.astype('float32') / 255.0


# Download Fashion MNIST dataset
(fashion_train_images, _), (fashion_test_images, _) = tf.keras.datasets.
fashion_mnist.load_data()
fashion_test_images = fashion_test_images.astype('float32') / 255.0


# Isolate Trouser image and save to path
Trouser_image = fashion_test_images[5]  # Assuming the Trouser image is at
index 8
plt.imshow(Trouser_image, cmap='gray')
plt.axis('off')
plt.savefig('Trouser_image.png')


# Define and train the autoencoder on MNIST dataset
input_dim = train_images.shape[1:]
encoding_dim = 32
```

```python
# Encoder layers
encoder = tf.keras.Sequential([
    tf.keras.layers.Flatten(input_shape=input_dim),
    tf.keras.layers.Dense(encoding_dim, activation='relu')
])

# Decoder layers
decoder = tf.keras.Sequential([
    tf.keras.layers.Dense(np.prod(input_dim), activation='sigmoid'),
    tf.keras.layers.Reshape(input_dim)
])

# Autoencoder model
autoencoder = tf.keras.Sequential([encoder, decoder])

# Compile the model
autoencoder.compile(optimizer='adam', loss='binary_crossentropy')

# Train the autoencoder on MNIST dataset
autoencoder.fit(train_images, train_images,
                epochs=10,
                batch_size=128,
                shuffle=True,
                validation_data=(test_images, test_images))

# Reshape Trouser image for testing
Trouser_image_reshaped = Trouser_image.reshape(1, *input_dim)

# Use the trained autoencoder to reconstruct the Trouser image
reconstructed_Trouser = autoencoder.predict(Trouser_image_reshaped)

# Visualize the input Trouser image and reconstructed Trouser image
plt.figure(figsize=(8, 4))
plt.subplot(1, 2, 1)
plt.imshow(Trouser_image, cmap='gray')
plt.title('Input Trouser Image')
```

```
plt.axis('off')
plt.subplot(1, 2, 2)
plt.imshow(reconstructed_Trouser[0], cmap='gray')
plt.title('Reconstructed Trouser Image')
plt.axis('off')
plt.show()
# Set the threshold for anomaly detection
threshold = 0.08
# Print anomaly detection result

if reconstruction_errors[anomaly_index] > threshold:   # Define a threshold
based on the application
    print("Anomaly detected: The Trouser image is likely an anomaly.")
else:
    print("No anomaly detected.")
```

In the following figure, input trouser and reconstructed trouser image are shown:

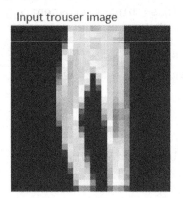 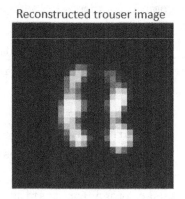

Figure 4.4: Input trouser and reconstructed trouser image

```
Anomaly detected
import tensorflow as tf
import numpy as np
import matplotlib.pyplot as plt

# Download MNIST dataset
(train_images, _), (test_images, _) = tf.keras.datasets.mnist.load_data()
train_images = train_images.astype('float32') / 255.0
test_images = test_images.astype('float32') / 255.0
```

```
# Download Fashion MNIST dataset
(_, _), (fashion_test_images, _) = tf.keras.datasets.fashion_mnist.load_
data()
fashion_test_images = fashion_test_images.astype('float32') / 255.0


# Isolate sandal image and save to path
sandal_image = fashion_test_images[8]   # Assuming the sandal image is at
index 5
plt.imshow(sandal_image, cmap='gray')
plt.axis('off')
plt.savefig('sandal_image.png')


# Define and train the autoencoder on MNIST dataset
input_shape = train_images.shape[1:]
encoding_dim = 32


# Encoder layers
encoder = tf.keras.Sequential([
    tf.keras.layers.Reshape(input_shape + (1,), input_shape=input_shape),
    tf.keras.layers.Conv2D(16, (3, 3), activation='relu', padding='same'),
    tf.keras.layers.MaxPooling2D((2, 2), padding='same'),
    tf.keras.layers.Conv2D(8, (3, 3), activation='relu', padding='same'),
    tf.keras.layers.MaxPooling2D((2, 2), padding='same'),
    tf.keras.layers.Flatten(),
    tf.keras.layers.Dense(encoding_dim, activation='relu')
])


# Decoder layers
decoder = tf.keras.Sequential([
    tf.keras.layers.Dense(np.prod((7, 7, 8)), activation='relu'),
    tf.keras.layers.Reshape((7, 7, 8)),
        tf.keras.layers.Conv2DTranspose(16,   (3,   3),   strides=(2,   2),
activation='relu', padding='same'),
         tf.keras.layers.Conv2DTranspose(1,   (3,   3),   strides=(2,   2),
activation='sigmoid', padding='same')
])
```

```python
# Autoencoder model
autoencoder = tf.keras.Sequential([encoder, decoder])

# Compile the model
autoencoder.compile(optimizer='adam', loss='binary_crossentropy')

# Reshape and normalize train and test images for CNN
train_images_cnn = train_images.reshape(-1, *input_shape, 1)
test_images_cnn = test_images.reshape(-1, *input_shape, 1)

# Train the autoencoder on MNIST dataset
autoencoder.fit(train_images_cnn, train_images_cnn,
                epochs=10,
                batch_size=128,
                shuffle=True,
                validation_data=(test_images_cnn, test_images_cnn))

# Reshape sandal image for testing
sandal_image_reshaped = sandal_image.reshape(1, *input_shape, 1)

# Use the trained autoencoder to reconstruct the sandal image
reconstructed_sandal = autoencoder.predict(sandal_image_reshaped)

# Visualize the input sandal image and reconstructed sandal image
plt.figure(figsize=(8, 4))
plt.subplot(1, 2, 1)
plt.imshow(sandal_image, cmap='gray')
plt.title('Input Sandal Image')
plt.axis('off')
plt.subplot(1, 2, 2)
plt.imshow(reconstructed_sandal[0, ..., 0], cmap='gray')
plt.title('Reconstructed Sandal Image')
plt.axis('off')
plt.show()
```

In the following figure, we can see the input sandal and reconstructed sandal image:

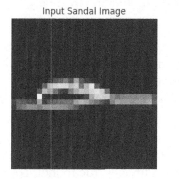 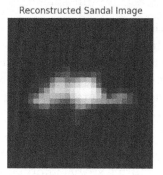

Figure 4.5: Input sandal and reconstructed sandal image

Anomaly detected.

Autoencoders with convolutional layers

The major difference between a dense layer autoencoder and a **Convolutional Neural Network (CNN)** autoencoder lies in their architecture and their ability to capture spatial information.

Let us go over them now:

Architecture

Following the architecture of Autoencoder is explained:

- **Dense Layer Autoencoder:** A dense layer autoencoder consists of fully connected (dense) layers. The input data is flattened into a 1D vector and fed into the encoder. The encoder and decoder are typically composed of multiple dense layers. This type of autoencoder is well-suited for handling structured or tabular data.

- **CNN Autoencoder:** A CNN autoencoder incorporates convolutional layers in the encoder and decoder. Convolutional layers are specifically designed to capture spatial relationships in images. The input data retains its original structure and is processed through convolutional and pooling layers. This makes CNN autoencoders more suitable for image-related tasks.

Capturing spatial information

In this section, capturing the spatial information is discussed:

- **Dense Layer Autoencoder:** Dense layers do not consider the spatial structure of the input data. They treat each input feature independently and do not exploit the locality or correlations present in the data. As a result, dense layer autoencoders may struggle to capture spatial patterns in images effectively.

- **CNN Autoencoder:** CNNs are designed to capture spatial information. Convolutional layers apply filters across small regions of the input image, enabling them to learn local patterns and spatial hierarchies. Pooling layers reduce the spatial dimensions while retaining important features. By leveraging these operations, CNN autoencoders can better preserve and reconstruct the spatial structure of images.

So dense layer autoencoders are suitable for structured or tabular data where spatial relationships are less relevant. On the other hand, CNN autoencoders excel at capturing spatial information in images due to their convolutional layers, making them a preferred choice for image-related tasks.

CNN versus ANN Autoencoders

Convolutional Neural Network (CNN) autoencoders and **Artificial Neural Network (ANN)** autoencoders serve different purposes based on their architecture and are suitable for various real-world applications. Here are five examples where each might be used:

CNN Autoencoders

CNN autoencoders are excellent for tasks involving spatial data, like images or videos, due to their convolutional layers that can capture hierarchical spatial features:

- **Image denoising:** CNN autoencoders can remove noise from images, making them ideal for improving image quality in medical imaging, satellite imagery, or photography.

- **Anomaly detection in surveillance videos:** They can detect anomalies in video feeds by learning normal patterns and identifying deviations, useful in security and surveillance systems.

- **Face recognition:** CNN autoencoders can be used to encode facial features for recognition systems, benefiting security systems or personalized user experiences in tech devices.

- **Automatic colorization of black and white images:** They can learn to add color to grayscale images, which is helpful in media restoration or artistic endeavors.

- **Self-driving car vision systems:** CNN autoencoders can process and interpret visual data from a vehicle's surroundings, crucial for autonomous driving technologies.

ANN Autoencoders

ANN autoencoders are more generalized and are well-suited for less spatially structured data:

- **Feature reduction in text data:** They can reduce the dimensionality of text data for natural language processing tasks, aiding in language translation or sentiment analysis.

- **Fraud detection in finance:** By learning normal transaction patterns, ANN autoencoders can identify unusual patterns indicative of fraud.

- **Data compression:** ANN autoencoders can compress data without significant loss of information, useful in reducing data storage and transmission costs.

- **Bioinformatics:** They can be used for gene expression data analysis, helping in identifying patterns related to genetic diseases or drug responses.

- **Recommender systems:** ANN autoencoders can process user preferences and historical data to make personalized recommendations in e-commerce or content streaming services.

The choice between CNN and ANN autoencoders depends largely on the nature of the data and the specific requirements of the application.

Conclusion

In this chapter, we learnt about autoencoders in the context of generative AI, inner workings of autoencoders, discussing their architectural variations, training strategies and their applications in generating diverse and high-quality outputs across various domains. We also examined advanced techniques that leverage autoencoders, such as **Variational AutoEncoders (VAE)** and **Generative Adversarial Networks (GAN)**, which push the boundaries of generative AI even further.

In the upcoming chapter, we will delve into several important topics related to autoencoders. Firstly, we will explore the concept of latent space, which refers to the compact and meaningful representation of input data learned by the encoder. Understanding the latent space is crucial for leveraging the power of autoencoders in various applications.

We will also explore the concept of dual input autoencoders, which involve using two separate inputs to the autoencoder. This approach can be useful in scenarios where the input data consists of both observed and missing values or when dealing with multi-modal data.

Furthermore, we will discuss different loss functions commonly used in autoencoders. These loss functions play a vital role in training the model and determining how well the reconstructed output matches the original input.

Additionally, we will address potential issues that may arise during the training process of autoencoders. We will explore common challenges such as overfitting, vanishing gradients, and noisy data, and discuss strategies to mitigate these problems.

Optimization techniques specific to autoencoders will also be covered, focusing on how to effectively train the model and optimize its performance. We will explore approaches such as **Stochastic Gradient Descent (SGD)**, adaptive optimization algorithms, and regularization techniques.

Lastly, we will compare **autoencoders (AE)** with **variational autoencoders (VAE)**. While both are generative models, VAEs introduce a probabilistic framework that enables more controlled generation of new data samples. We will discuss the differences and benefits of using AE and VAE architectures in various scenarios.

Join our book's Discord space

Join the book's Discord Workspace for Latest updates, Offers, Tech happenings around the world, New Release and Sessions with the Authors:

https://discord.bpbonline.com

## CHAPTER 5

Building and Training Generative Autoencoders

Introduction

In this chapter, we embark on a thorough exploration of autoencoders, highlighting their facets and applications. We begin with the concept of latent space, which is the encoder's ability to learn a concise representation of input data, crucial for maximizing autoencoder utility. We then explore dual input autoencoders, which use two distinct inputs, beneficial for handling observed and missing data or multi-modal data, thus offering a deeper understanding of complex data structures.

A significant portion is dedicated to the discussion on loss functions in autoencoders, which guide training and measure the alignment between reconstructed output and original input. We address challenges in autoencoder training, including overfitting, vanishing gradients, and noisy data. Furthermore, the chapter touches upon the issues faced by autoencoders in generative tasks, such as mode collapse and training instability, while also suggesting mitigative strategies.

Optimization techniques tailored for autoencoders are discussed, with an emphasis on methods like **Stochastic Gradient Descent (SGD)** and adaptive optimization algorithms. The chapter concludes with a comparison between **Autoencoders (AE)** and **Variational Autoencoders (VAE)**, distinguishing the probabilistic framework of VAEs that facilitates controlled data generation.

Overall, this chapter aims to provide a holistic understanding of autoencoders, empowering readers to apply them effectively in data representation, generation, and anomaly detection.

Structure

In this chapter, we will cover the following topics:

- Latent space
- Difference between GANs latent space and AE latent space
- Key distinctions between autoencoders latent space
- Adding color to a grayscale image using autoencoders
- Coding Advances auto encoders
- Loss in Auto Encoders
- Challenges in training auto encoders and mitigation
- AE vs VAE

Objectives

The key objectives of this chapter are to provide the reader with a deep understanding of autoencoders and their applications. By the end of this chapter, readers will gain a comprehensive understanding of the concept of latent space and its significance in autoencoders, explore the concept of dual input autoencoders and their usefulness in handling missing values and multi-modal data, and familiarize themselves with various loss functions commonly used in autoencoders and their role in training and reconstruction.

The readers will also learn about potential issues during training, such as overfitting, vanishing gradients, and noisy data, along with strategies to mitigate them, discover optimization techniques specific to autoencoders for effective model training and performance enhancement, as well as understand the differences between autoencoders and variational autoencoders and their respective benefits.

Lastly, the reader will acquire the knowledge and skills to leverage autoencoders in practical scenarios for data representation, generation, and anomaly detection.

Latent space

Imagine you have a big box of magic crayons. Each crayon can draw things that are not just a single color, but many different things like animals, cars, or even dreams! But these magic crayons are special because when you pick up one crayon, you do not just get one thing, you get a mix of many things.

For example, let us say you pick a crayon that you think is for drawing a cat. When you start drawing, you might see parts of a cat, but also parts of a dog, a lion, or even a fluffy cloud! That is because this crayon has a bit of all these things mixed in it. This is like the latent space – it is like a big, magical box where everything is mixed together in a way we cannot see.

When someone uses a computer to make new pictures, they are like reaching into this magic box and picking a crayon. They don not know exactly what they will get, but they have an idea. And when they draw with it, they can get something new and surprising, like a cat with a lion's mane or a dog with the paws of a bear!

So, latent space is like a magical box of crayons where all sorts of ideas and images are mixed up, and you can create new, fun, and sometimes surprising things with it.

The concept of the latent space in the context of autoencoders and neural networks can be attributed to the field of artificial neural networks and machine learning as a whole. The idea of using a latent space as an intermediate representation in neural network models has been explored by various researchers over the years.

Refer to the following figure:

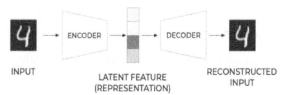

Figure 5.1: *General structure of an autoencoder*

One of the early influential works in this area was the invention of autoencoders by *Geoffrey Hinton, Terrence Sejnowski,* and *David E. Rumelhart* in 1986. They introduced autoencoders as neural network models with the goal of learning to reconstruct the input data with minimal error. In the process of training autoencoders, the models learn to encode the input data into a lower-dimensional latent space representation.

Since then, researchers and practitioners in the field have continued to advance and refine the concept of the latent space in autoencoders and other neural network architectures. The latent space has proven to be a powerful tool for various applications, including data compression, dimensionality reduction, generative modeling, and anomaly detection.

It is important to note that while the concept of the latent space was popularized through the work on autoencoders, the idea of using a lower-dimensional representation or code to capture important features of data can be traced back to earlier works in fields such as information theory and signal processing.

The latent space of an **Autoencoder (AE)** refers to the compressed and meaningful representation of input data that is learned by the encoder component of the AE. It can be understood as a lower-dimensional space that captures the most important features or characteristics of the original data.

In simpler terms, let us consider an AE with an encoder that takes an input data point x and maps it to a latent representation z using a function $Encoder(x) = z$. The latent space is represented by the variable z, which typically has a lower dimensionality than the input x.

The goal of the encoder is to learn a mapping that captures the essential information of x in z. By doing so, the encoder condenses the information into a more compact representation. This latent representation z can be thought of as a summary or compressed version of the input x, containing the most relevant features for reconstruction.

Mathematically, the latent space can be represented as:

$z = Encoder(x)$

The decoder component of the AE takes the latent representation z and aims to reconstruct the original input x using a decoding function $Decoder(z) = x$. The reconstruction should be as close as possible to the original input x, while using the information contained in the latent space z.

The overall objective of the AE is to minimize the reconstruction error between the original input x and the reconstructed output x. This can be measured using various distance metrics, such as **Mean Squared Error (MSE)** or binary cross-entropy.

By learning the latent space representation, the AE can effectively capture the underlying structure and patterns in the data, allowing for tasks such as data compression, denoising, and anomaly detection.

Let us understand using code. This code loads the CIFAR-10 dataset, preprocesses the data, and defines an autoencoder model with a specified latent dimensionality. It then trains the model on the dataset and obtains the latent space representation of the test data using the trained encoder. Finally, it visualizes the latent space using a scatter plot.

Note that this code assumes you have TensorFlow and Matplotlib installed. Moreover, keep in mind that a 2-dimensional latent space might not capture the full complexity of the CIFAR-10 dataset, but it can still provide a meaningful visualization. Adjusting the latent dimensionality and model architecture can be explored to improve the representation.

Refer to the following code:

```
import tensorflow as tf
import matplotlib.pyplot as plt


# Load the CIFAR-10 dataset
(x_train, _), (x_test, _) = tf.keras.datasets.cifar10.load_data()
```

```python
# Preprocess the data (normalize, reshape)
x_train = x_train.astype('float32') / 255.
x_test = x_test.astype('float32') / 255.
x_train = x_train.reshape((len(x_train), -1))
x_test = x_test.reshape((len(x_test), -1))

# Define and train the autoencoder model
latent_dim = 2  # Set the desired dimensionality of the latent space
input_dim = x_train.shape[1]

# Define the encoder model
encoder = tf.keras.models.Sequential([
  tf.keras.layers.Dense(512, activation='relu', input_shape=(input_dim,)),
  tf.keras.layers.Dense(256, activation='relu'),
  tf.keras.layers.Dense(latent_dim, activation='linear')
])


# Define the decoder model
decoder = tf.keras.models.Sequential([
  tf.keras.layers.Dense(256, activation='relu', input_shape=(latent_dim,)),
  tf.keras.layers.Dense(512, activation='relu'),
  tf.keras.layers.Dense(input_dim, activation='sigmoid')
])
```

In the following figure, we can see the layers in encoder decode:

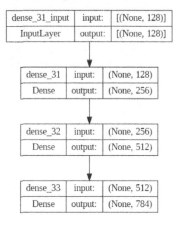

Figure 5.2: Layers in encoder decode

```python
# Combine the encoder and decoder into an autoencoder model
autoencoder = tf.keras.models.Sequential([encoder, decoder])

# Compile and train the autoencoder
autoencoder.compile(optimizer='adam', loss='binary_crossentropy')
autoencoder.fit(x_train,  x_train,  epochs=10,  batch_size=128,  validation_
data=(x_test, x_test))

# Get the latent space representation of the test data
latent_space = encoder.predict(x_test)

# Visualize the latent space
plt.scatter(latent_space[:, 0], latent_space[:, 1], c='b', cmap='tab10')
plt.colorbar()
plt.title('Latent Space Visualization')
plt.xlabel('Latent Dimension 1')
plt.ylabel('Latent Dimension 2')
plt.show()
```

Refer to the following *Figure 5.3*, latent space visualization is shown:

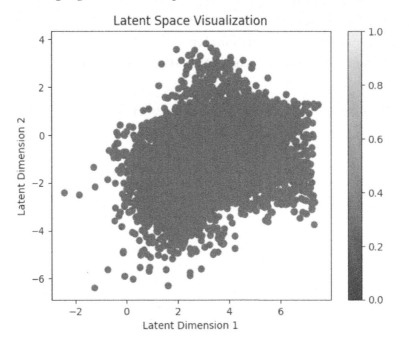

Figure 5.3: Latent space visualization

Difference between GANs latent space and AE latent space

In this code, we first load the CIFAR-10 dataset and normalize the images to the range [-1, 1]. Then, we define the generator model, which takes random latent vectors of size 100 and generates images of size 32x32x3. We generate a batch of random latent vectors and pass them through the generator to obtain generated images.

Finally, we visualize the generated images using matplotlib, where we create a 10x10 grid of subplots and display the generated images. The generated images are rescaled to the **range [0, 1]** before displaying them.

Please note that this is a simplified example to demonstrate the visualization of the latent space using GANs. In a real GAN implementation, you would typically train the generator and discriminator networks together to learn the latent space representation.

Refer to the following code:

```python
import tensorflow as tf
import matplotlib.pyplot as plt


# Load CIFAR-10 dataset
(train_images, _), (_, _) = tf.keras.datasets.cifar10.load_data()
train_images = (train_images - 127.5) / 127.5  # Normalize the images to [-1, 1]


# Generator model
generator = tf.keras.models.Sequential([
  tf.keras.layers.Dense(256, input_dim=100, activation='relu'),
  tf.keras.layers.Dense(512, activation='relu'),
  tf.keras.layers.Dense(1024, activation='relu'),
  tf.keras.layers.Dense(3072, activation='tanh'),
  tf.keras.layers.Reshape((32, 32, 3))
])


# Generate random latent vectors
latent_vectors = tf.random.normal((100, 100))
# Generate images from latent vectors
generated_images = generator.predict(latent_vectors)
```

```
# Visualize the generated images
fig, axes = plt.subplots(10, 10, figsize=(10, 10))
  for i, ax in enumerate(axes.flat):
    ax.imshow((generated_images[i] + 1) / 2)  # Rescale to [0, 1]
  ax.axis('off')
  plt.show()
```

Refer to the following *Figure 5.4*, it shows the generated images:

Figure 5.4: *Visualize the generated images*

Key distinctions with autoencoders latent space

The latent space of **Generative Adversarial Networks (GAN)** and **Autoencoders (AE)** exhibit some fundamental differences in terms of their underlying principles and representations.

- **Training objective:** GANs are trained through a two-player adversarial game, consisting of a generator network and a discriminator network. The generator aims to generate realistic data samples from random noise in the latent space, while the discriminator aims to distinguish between real and generated samples. On the other hand, AEs are trained using an unsupervised learning approach, where the objective is to reconstruct the input data from its latent representation.

- **Data generation vs. data reconstruction:** GANs primarily focus on generating new data samples that resemble the training data distribution. The latent space of GANs is often learned in a way that allows for smooth interpolation and random sampling to generate diverse and novel samples. In contrast, AEs emphasize data reconstruction. The latent space of AEs captures a compressed and meaningful representation of the input data, allowing for effective reconstruction of the original samples.

- **Distribution representation:** GANs typically learn a more complex and flexible latent space distribution. The generator maps random noise to this latent space, and through training, it learns to generate data that closely matches the training distribution. In contrast, AEs tend to learn a more compact and constrained latent space distribution that captures the most salient features of the input data.

- **Interpretability:** The latent space of AEs often exhibits a more interpretable structure. Each dimension in the latent space can correspond to a meaningful feature or attribute of the input data. This makes AEs useful for tasks such as data compression, denoising, and anomaly detection. GANs, on the other hand, may have a less interpretable latent space due to their primary focus on generating realistic samples.

- **Latent space continuity:** GANs typically exhibit smooth and continuous transitions in their latent space. Small changes in the latent vector result in gradual changes in the generated output. This property allows for fine-grained control over the generated samples. AEs, while also having a continuous latent space, may not necessarily exhibit the same level of control and fine-grained transitions since their primary objective is reconstruction rather than generating new samples.

GANs and AEs have different objectives and learning mechanisms, which lead to distinct characteristics in their latent spaces. GANs excel in generating new and diverse data samples, while AEs focus on compactly representing and reconstructing the input data. Understanding these differences is crucial when choosing the appropriate model for specific applications, depending on the desired outcome and usage scenario.

Autoencoders are trained end-to-end with a single loss function. The loss function measures the error between the input data and the output data. The autoencoder is trained to minimize the loss function. The loss function for an autoencoder is typically a mean squared error, but it can also be other loss functions, such as cross-entropy.

While latent spaces in autoencoders can be powerful and useful for various applications, they can also face some challenges. Some of the major issues with latent spaces are:

- **Information loss:** The latent space representation may not capture all the details and nuances of the original input data. Due to the dimensionality reduction involved in the encoding process, some information may be lost, resulting in a compressed representation that may not fully preserve all the characteristics of the input data.

- **Overfitting:** Autoencoders can be prone to overfitting, especially when the model capacity is high or when the training dataset is small. Overfitting occurs when the autoencoder learns to perfectly reconstruct the training data but fails to generalize well to unseen data. This can lead to an overly complex latent space that is not able to generalize to new and diverse inputs.

- **Incomplete or ambiguous representations:** In some cases, the latent space may not capture all the relevant factors of variation in the input data. It may fail to disentangle different factors and mix them in the latent representation. This can result in incomplete or ambiguous representations, making it challenging to manipulate or generate meaningful samples from the latent space.

- **Lack of interpretability:** The latent space of autoencoders is often a high-dimensional, non-linear space that may not have a direct semantic interpretation. While the encoder learns to compress the input data, the resulting latent space dimensions may not correspond to easily interpretable features or concepts. This can make it difficult to understand and interpret the latent representations.

- **Mode collapse:** In some cases, the latent space may suffer from mode collapse, where the autoencoder fails to capture and represent the entire distribution of the input data. This can result in the generation of limited and repetitive samples, as the autoencoder may focus on a few dominant modes of the data distribution and neglect the others.

It is important to consider these issues when working with latent spaces in autoencoders and to carefully design and train the models to address these challenges, ensuring that the latent space captures the desired properties and characteristics of the input data.

Advanced latent space engineering techniques aim to enhance the capabilities and properties of the latent space in autoencoders. Here are some techniques commonly used for advanced latent space engineering:

- **Regularization techniques:** Regularization methods, such as L1 or L2 regularization, can be applied to the latent space to encourage sparsity or smoothness. Regularization helps in promoting meaningful and structured representations in the latent space, reducing noise and irrelevant features.

- **Variational Autoencoders (VAEs):** VAEs are a type of generative model that introduces probabilistic modeling in the latent space. By modeling the latent space with a probability distribution, VAEs enable controlled generation and interpolation of new data samples. VAEs use a specific loss function called the "variational lower bound" to train the model and learn a more structured latent space.

- **Adversarial Autoencoders (AAEs):** AAEs combine autoencoders with GANs. AAEs use an additional discriminator network to distinguish between real and reconstructed samples, encouraging the autoencoder to generate more realistic samples. AAEs can lead to more diverse and realistic latent space representations.

- **Disentangled Representation Learning:** Disentanglement aims to learn latent space representations that separate underlying factors of variation in the data.

Techniques such as β-VAE, FactorVAE, and InfoGAN focus on disentangling different factors, such as identity, pose, style, or attributes, enabling control and manipulation of specific aspects in the latent space.

- **Interpolation and manipulation:** Advanced latent space engineering techniques involve interpolation and manipulation of points in the latent space. By linearly interpolating between two points in the latent space, we can generate new samples that blend the characteristics of the two points. Additionally, manipulating specific dimensions or components of the latent space can lead to controlled transformations or modifications in the generated samples.

- **Transfer learning:** Transfer learning can be applied to the latent space by pre-training the encoder on a large dataset or a related task. The pre-trained encoder can then be fine-tuned or used as a feature extractor for a specific target task or dataset, leveraging the learned representations in the latent space.

These advanced techniques expand the capabilities of autoencoders and offer more control, interpretability, and generative power in latent space. By incorporating these methods, researchers and practitioners can unlock new possibilities for data representation, generation, and manipulation in various applications.

Adding color to a grayscale image using autoencoders

This occurs in the following step-wise manner:

1. The autoencoder is trained on a dataset of grayscale and color images. The autoencoder learns to represent the input data in a lower-dimensional latent space.

2. When a new grayscale image is input to the autoencoder, it is first encoded into the latent space.

3. The latent space representation is then decoded into a color image.

The autoencoder can learn to add color to a grayscale image by learning the relationships between the grayscale and color features of the training data. For example, the autoencoder might learn that the sky is typically blue, the grass is typically green, and the skin is typically a light shade of brown.

The autoencoder can also be used to add color to a grayscale image by using a technique called transfer learning. Transfer learning is a machine learning technique where a model trained on one task is used as a starting point for training a model on a different task. In the case of colorization, a model trained to classify images can be used as a starting point for training an autoencoder to colorize images.

Here are some of the benefits of using an autoencoder to add color to a grayscale image:

- **Accuracy:** Autoencoders can learn to add color to grayscale images with high accuracy.

- **Speed:** Autoencoders can add color to grayscale images quickly.

- **Scalability:** Autoencoders can be scaled to handle large datasets of grayscale and color images.

Here are some of the challenges of using an autoencoder to add color to a grayscale image:

- **Data requirements:** Autoencoders require a large dataset of grayscale and color images to train.

- **Overfitting:** Autoencoders can be prone to overfitting, which can lead to inaccurate colorization.

- **Interpretability:** It can be difficult to interpret the results of autoencoders, which can make it difficult to debug and improve the models.

This code defines a CNN-based autoencoder with convolutional layers for both the encoder and decoder. It uses the MNIST dataset, normalizes the input data, and constructs a grayscale image as input and a colorized image as output. The model is trained using the Adam optimizer and binary cross-entropy loss. After training, it generates colorized output for the test images and visualizes the original and reconstructed colorized images using matplotlib.

One use case where you can use two encoders and one decoder for MNIST, is in the context of semi-supervised learning. Semi-supervised learning aims to leverage both labeled and unlabeled data to improve the performance of a machine learning model.

In the case of MNIST, where you have labeled images of handwritten digits, you can use a traditional encoder-decoder architecture to reconstruct the input images and generate output images that closely resemble the original input. However, by incorporating a second encoder, you can introduce an additional pathway to capture information from unlabeled data.

Here is a high-level overview of how the architecture can be structured:

1. The first encoder takes in the labeled MNIST images and learns to extract meaningful features from them. This encoder aims to capture the discriminative information relevant to the digit labels.

2. The second encoder takes in both labeled and unlabeled MNIST images. It is trained to extract more general and unsupervised features from the images. This encoder aims to capture underlying patterns and variations in the data that are not explicitly tied to the digit labels.

3. The two encoders produce separate latent space representations, which capture different aspects of the input data.

4. The decoder takes the combined latent space representations from the two encoders and reconstructs the input images. The decoder aims to generate high-quality reconstructions that closely resemble the original images.

By training the model with both labeled and unlabeled data, the idea is that the two encoders can collectively learn to extract more informative and robust representations of the MNIST images. This can potentially improve the overall performance of the model, especially when labeled data is limited.

It is worth noting that implementing a model with two encoders and one decoder requires careful design and training strategies to ensure effective information flow and balance between the two encoders. Additionally, proper regularization techniques, such as incorporating labeled data loss and unsupervised loss functions, need to be considered to guide the learning process effectively.

Overall, using two encoders and one decoder in a semi-supervised learning setup for MNIST can potentially enhance the model's ability to capture both labeled and unlabeled data characteristics, leading to improved performance and generalization capabilities.

Refer to the following code:

```
import tensorflow as tf
from tensorflow.keras.datasets import mnist
import numpy as np


# Load MNIST dataset
(x_train, _), (x_test, _) = mnist.load_data()


# Normalize and reshape input data
x_train = x_train.astype('float32') / 255.0
x_test = x_test.astype('float32') / 255.0
x_train = np.expand_dims(x_train, axis=-1)
x_test = np.expand_dims(x_test, axis=-1)


# Define the encoder model
encoder = tf.keras.Sequential([
tf.keras.layers.Conv2D(16, (3, 3), activation='relu', padding='same', input_
shape=(28, 28, 1)),
tf.keras.layers.MaxPooling2D((2, 2), padding='same'),
tf.keras.layers.Conv2D(8, (3, 3), activation='relu', padding='same'),
```

```python
    tf.keras.layers.MaxPooling2D((2, 2), padding='same'),
    tf.keras.layers.Conv2D(4, (3, 3), activation='relu', padding='same'),
    tf.keras.layers.MaxPooling2D((2, 2), padding='same')
])

# Define the decoder model
decoder = tf.keras.Sequential([
  tf.keras.layers.Conv2D(4, (3, 3), activation='relu', padding='same'),
  tf.keras.layers.UpSampling2D((2, 2)),
  tf.keras.layers.Conv2D(8, (3, 3), activation='relu', padding='same'),
  tf.keras.layers.UpSampling2D((2, 2)),
  tf.keras.layers.Conv2D(16, (3, 3), activation='relu'),
  tf.keras.layers.UpSampling2D((2, 2)),
  tf.keras.layers.Conv2D(1, (3, 3), activation='sigmoid', padding='same')
])

# Combine the encoder and decoder
autoencoder = tf.keras.Sequential([encoder, decoder])

# Compile the model
autoencoder.compile(optimizer='adam', loss='binary_crossentropy')

# Train the model
autoencoder.fit(x_train,  x_train,  epochs=10,  batch_size=128,  validation_
data=(x_test, x_test))

# Generate colored output for test images
colored_images = autoencoder.predict(x_test)

# Visualize the original and reconstructed images
import matplotlib.pyplot as plt

n = 10  # Number of images to visualize
plt.figure(figsize=(20, 4))
for i in range(n):
    # Display original MNIST image
```

```
    ax = plt.subplot(2, n, i + 1)
plt.imshow(x_test[i].reshape(28, 28), cmap='gray')
plt.title('Original')
plt.axis('off')

    # Display reconstructed colorized image
    ax = plt.subplot(2, n, i + 1 + n)
plt.imshow(colored_images[i].reshape(28, 28), cmap='jet')
plt.title('Colorized')
plt.axis('off')

plt.show()
```

Refer to the following figure, to see the difference in original black and white and colorized images:

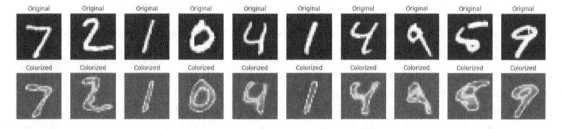

Figure 5.5: *Original black and white and colorized images*[1]

Coding advanced auto encoders

Let us now delve deeper into advanced auto encoders.

Multi modal auto encoders

A multi-modal autoencoder is a type of autoencoder architecture that is designed to handle multi-modal data, where each modality represents a different type of information or feature. Unlike traditional autoencoders that are typically used for single-modal data, multi-modal autoencoders can learn joint representations from multiple input modalities.

In a multi-modal autoencoder, the encoder takes multiple modalities as input, and each modality is processed separately before being combined in the latent space. The latent

---

space representation captures the shared information across modalities. The decoder then reconstructs the input modalities from the latent space representation.

The main advantage of multi-modal autoencoders is their ability to capture complex relationships and dependencies between different modalities. By jointly learning representations across multiple modalities, the autoencoder can uncover complementary information and improve overall performance. Multi-modal autoencoders have been successfully applied in various domains, including computer vision, natural language processing, and audio processing.

The specific architecture and design of a multi-modal autoencoder can vary depending on the characteristics of the data and the desired application. It may involve separate encoders for each modality, followed by fusion or combination layers to merge the representations. Similarly, the decoder may have separate branches for each modality to reconstruct the original inputs.

A multi-modal autoencoder provides a powerful framework for learning meaningful representations from multi-modal data and can be utilized in tasks such as cross-modal retrieval, multimodal fusion, and information fusion in various domains.

Here is a pseudo code of how you can generate multiple modalities from a single dataset using a multimodal autoencoder in TensorFlow.

In this example, we assume that the dataset is loaded and preprocessed beforehand. The number of modalities is set to 2, but you can modify it based on your specific requirements. The encoder model is defined separately for each modality, and the outputs are concatenated to form the latent space representation. The decoder model is also defined for each modality, and the full multimodal autoencoder model is created using multiple inputs and outputs. The model is then compiled and trained using the dataset. Finally, the reconstructed outputs for each modality can be obtained by passing the dataset through the autoencoder.

Refer to the following code:

```
import tensorflow as tf
from tensorflow.keras.layers import Input, Dense
from tensorflow.keras.models import Model

# Load and preprocess your dataset
dataset = …  # Your dataset
# Perform any necessary preprocessing steps

# Define input shape
input_shape = dataset.shape[1:]
```

```python
# Define the number of modalities
num_modalities = 2


# Define the encoder model for each modality
encoder_inputs = [Input(shape=input_shape) for _ in range(num_modalities)]
encoders = [Dense(256, activati'n='r'lu')(input) for input in encoder_inputs]


# Concatenate the encoder outputs to form the latent space representation
combined_latent_space = tf.keras.layers.concatenate(encoders)


# Define the decoder model for each modality
decoder_outputs = [Dense(256, activati'n='r'lu')(combined_latent_space) for
 _ in range(num_modalities)]


# Define the full multimodal autoencoder model
autoencoder = Model(inputs=encoder_inputs, outputs=decoder_outputs)


# Compile the model
autoencoder.compile(optimiz'r='a'am', lo's=''se')


# Train the model
autoencoder.fit([dataset]  *  num_modalities,  [dataset]  *  num_modalities,
epochs=10, batch_size=32)


# Generate reconstructed outputs for each modality
reconstructed_outputs = autoencoder.predict([dataset] * num_modalities)
```

To clarify, in the provided code example, we are utilizing a single autoencoder with multiple modalities. Each modality has its own encoder and decoder, but they share the same latent space representation. The purpose is to learn joint representations across modalities.

In the given code snippet, the encoders and decoders are defined separately for each modality, but they are all part of the same autoencoder model. The encoder takes the input of each modality separately and processes it through the respective encoder layers. The outputs of the encoders are then concatenated to form the latent space representation. Similarly, the decoder takes the combined latent space representation and passes it through the respective decoder layers for each modality.

By training this single autoencoder model on multiple modalities simultaneously, the model can learn to extract shared representations and capture the dependencies between different modalities.

If you intend to use separate autoencoders for each modality, you will need to define multiple independent autoencoder models, each with its own encoder and decoder. This approach treats each modality as a separate entity and does not explicitly learn joint representations across modalities.

One use case where you can use two encoders and one decoder for MNIST is in the context of semi-supervised learning. Semi-supervised learning aims to leverage both labeled and unlabeled data to improve the performance of a machine learning model.

In the case of MNIST, where you have labeled images of handwritten digits, you can use a traditional encoder-decoder architecture to reconstruct the input images and generate output images that closely resemble the original input. However, by incorporating a second encoder, you can introduce an additional pathway to capture information from unlabeled data.

Refer to the following figure, to see the neural network architecture:

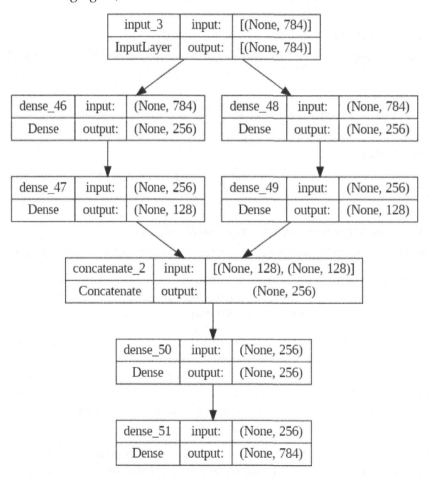

Figure 5.6: Neural network architecture

Here is a high-level overview of how the architecture can be structured:

1. The first encoder takes in the labeled MNIST images and learns to extract meaningful features from them. This encoder aims to capture the discriminative information relevant to the digit labels.

2. The second encoder takes in both labeled and unlabeled MNIST images. It is trained to extract more general and unsupervised features from the images. This encoder aims to capture underlying patterns and variations in the data that are not explicitly tied to the digit labels.

3. The two encoders produce separate latent space representations, which capture different aspects of the input data.

4. The decoder takes the combined latent space representations from the two encoders and reconstructs the input images. The decoder aims to generate high-quality reconstructions that closely resemble the original images.

By training the model with both labeled and unlabeled data, the idea is that the two encoders can collectively learn to extract more informative and robust representations of the MNIST images. This can potentially improve the overall performance of the model, especially when labeled data is limited.

It is worth noting that implementing a model with two encoders and one decoder requires careful design and training strategies to ensure effective information flow and balance between the two encoders. Additionally, proper regularization techniques, such as incorporating labeled data loss and unsupervised loss functions, need to be considered to guide the learning process effectively.

Overall, using two encoders and one decoder in a semi-supervised learning setup for MNIST can potentially enhance the model's ability to capture both labeled and unlabeled data characteristics, leading to improved performance and generalization capabilities.

Refer to the following code:

```
import tensorflow as tf
from tensorflow.keras.layers import Input, Dense
from tensorflow.keras.models import Model
from tensorflow.keras.datasets import mnist
import numpy as np


# Load and preprocess the MNIST dataset
(x_train, _), (x_test, _) = mnist.load_data()
x_train = x_train.astype('float32') / 255.0
x_test = x_test.astype('float32') / 255.0
```

```python
x_train = np.reshape(x_train, (len(x_train), 784))
x_test = np.reshape(x_test, (len(x_test), 784))

# Define input shape
input_shape = (784,)  # MNIST images are 28x28 = 784 pixels

# Define number of classes
num_classes = 10

# Define first encoder model
input_images = Input(shape=input_shape)
encoder1 = Dense(256, activation='relu')(input_images)
latent_space1 = Dense(128, activation='relu')(encoder1)

# Define second encoder model
encoder2 = Dense(256, activation='relu')(input_images)
latent_space2 = Dense(128, activation='relu')(encoder2)

# Concatenate the latent spaces from both encoders
combined_latent_space = tf.keras.layers.concatenate([latent_space1, latent_
space2])

# Define decoder model
decoder = Dense(256, activation='relu')(combined_latent_space)
output_images = Dense(784, activation='sigmoid')(decoder)

# Define the full autoencoder model
autoencoder = Model(inputs=input_images, outputs=output_images)

# Compile the model
autoencoder.compile(optimizer='adam', loss='binary_crossentropy')

# Train the model
autoencoder.fit(x_train, x_train, epochs=10, batch_size=32, validation_
data=(x_test, x_test))

# Generate reconstructed images
reconstructed_images = autoencoder.predict(x_test)
```

```
Epoch 1/10
1875/1875 [==============================] - 10s 4ms/step - loss: 0.1027 -
val_loss: 0.0769
Epoch 2/10
1875/1875 [==============================] - 7s 4ms/step - loss: 0.0744 -
val_loss: 0.0719
Epoch 3/10
1875/1875 [==============================] - 7s 4ms/step - loss: 0.0712 -
val_loss: 0.0707
Epoch 4/10
1875/1875 [==============================] - 7s 4ms/step - loss: 0.0696 -
val_loss: 0.0693
Epoch 5/10
1875/1875 [==============================] - 6s 3ms/step - loss: 0.0687 -
val_loss: 0.0681
Epoch 6/10
1875/1875 [==============================] - 7s 4ms/step - loss: 0.0680 -
val_loss: 0.0677
Epoch 7/10
1875/1875 [==============================] - 7s 4ms/step - loss: 0.0675 -
val_loss: 0.0672
Epoch 8/10
1875/1875 [==============================] - 6s 3ms/step - loss: 0.0671 -
val_loss: 0.0671
Epoch 9/10
1875/1875 [==============================] - 7s 4ms/step - loss: 0.0668 -
val_loss: 0.0666
Epoch 10/10
1875/1875 [==============================] - 7s 4ms/step - loss: 0.0666 -
val_loss: 0.0665
313/313 [==============================] - 1s 3ms/step
```

More complex architectures in autoencoders can offer additional capabilities and improvements in performance but may come at the cost of increased computational complexity. As the architecture becomes more intricate, the number of parameters and computational operations typically increases, resulting in higher computational requirements during training and inference.

Complex autoencoder architectures may include deeper neural networks with more layers, convolutional layers for handling spatial data, recurrent layers for sequential data, or even incorporating advanced techniques like residual connections, attention mechanisms, or variational components. These architectural choices aim to enhance the model's ability to capture intricate patterns and generate higher-quality reconstructions.

However, it is important to consider the computational resources available and the trade-off between model complexity and training time. More complex architectures may require longer training times, larger memory capacity, and more computational power. Therefore, it is crucial to strike a balance between the desired model complexity and the available resources to ensure efficient training and deployment.

Additionally, techniques such as model parallelism, distributed training, or hardware acceleration (for example, GPUs or TPUs) can be employed to mitigate the computational challenges associated with complex autoencoder architectures. These techniques can help leverage parallel processing capabilities and accelerate the training process.

Ultimately, the choice of autoencoder architecture should align with the specific requirements of the task at hand, considering both the desired model capabilities and the available computational resources.

Loss in autoencoders

Autoencoders can use various loss functions depending on the specific task and characteristics of the input data. Here are some commonly used loss functions in autoencoders.

Mean squared error loss

The formula is:

$$MSE = (1/n) * \sum(x - \hat{x})^2$$

The MSE loss measures the average squared difference between the input data (x) and the reconstructed output ($\hat{x}$). It is widely used in autoencoders to ensure that the reconstructed output closely resembles the original input.

Use case: This is commonly used when the input data are continuous and normally distributed. It is particularly suitable for images or any data where the magnitude of the output is important.

Example: Suppose you are working on an image reconstruction task where your input and output are images (like photos or medical images). MSE loss will penalize the model based on the square of the difference between the original and reconstructed images, emphasizing exact pixel value reconstruction.

Binary cross-entropy loss

The formula is:

$$BCE = -(1/n) * \Sigma(x * log(\hat{x}) + (1 - x) * log(1 - \hat{x}))$$

Binary cross-entropy loss is used when the input data is binary or binarized. It compares the similarity between the input data (x) and the reconstructed output $(\hat{x})$ based on the binary representation.

Use Case: This loss function is ideal for binary or grayscale images, where each pixel intensity is between 0 and 1. It's useful when the output of the autoencoder is interpreted as a probability.

Example: If you're training an autoencoder to denoise binary images (like handwritten digits), binary cross-entropy will measure the difference between the binary values of each pixel in the original and reconstructed images.

Categorical cross-entropy loss

The formula is:

$$CCE = -(1/n) * \Sigma(x * log(\hat{x}))$$

Categorical cross-entropy loss is used when the input data is categorical. It measures the dissimilarity between the input data (x) and the reconstructed output $(\hat{x})$ based on their categorical representations.

Use case: Used when the input data can be categorized into multiple classes and the output of the autoencoder represents probabilities of these classes.

Example: If an autoencoder is designed for a multi-label classification task, such as categorizing images into multiple classes, categorical cross-entropy loss would be appropriate.

Kullback-leibler divergence loss

The formula is:

$$KL = - \Sigma(x * log(x/\hat{x}))$$

Kullback-Leibler (KL) divergence loss is used in **variational autoencoders** (**VAEs**) to capture the difference between the learned latent distribution and a prior distribution. It encourages the latent space to follow a specific distribution, typically a Gaussian distribution.

Use Case: Often used in VAEs, where it measures how much one probability distribution (the output of the encoder) diverges from a second, expected probability distribution.

Example: In a VAE, which learns to encode data to a probabilistic latent space, KL divergence can be used to regularize the encoder by penalizing deviations of its outputs from a standard normal distribution.

Huber loss

The formula is:

$$Huber = (1/n) * \sum(0.5 * (x - \hat{x})^2) \text{ if } |x - \hat{x}| <= \delta, otherwise (\delta * |x - \hat{x}|) - (0.5 * \delta^2)$$

Huber loss behaves like MSE for small errors and like **mean absolute error** (**MAE**) for large errors. This characteristic makes it less sensitive to outliers than MSE.

There is a parameter, often denoted as δ (delta), which defines the threshold at which the loss transitions from quadratic to linear.

Use case: Huber loss is valuable in scenarios where you expect your training data to have outliers or be noisy, but you still want a loss function more sensitive than MAE. It strikes a balance between sensitivity to small errors (like MSE) and robustness against outliers (like MAE).

Example: Let's consider an autoencoder used for predicting housing prices, a classic regression problem. In this data, most houses are within a standard price range, but there are a few extreme values (very cheap or very expensive houses). If you use MSE as a loss function, your model might focus too much on these outliers, leading to poor general performance. However, using MAE might not sufficiently capture the nuances in the majority of the data. Huber loss would be a good middle ground, providing sensitivity to the bulk of the data while not being overly influenced by the few extreme values.

Challenges in training auto encoders and mitigation

Here are some of the challenges in training autoencoders:

- **Data scarcity:** Autoencoders require a large amount of data to train effectively. If there is not enough data, the autoencoder may not be able to learn the underlying patterns in the data and may not be able to generalize well to new data.

- **Overfitting:** Autoencoders can be prone to overfitting, which means that they learn the training data too well and are unable to generalize to new data. This can happen if the model is too complex or if the training data is not large enough.

- **Underfitting:** Autoencoders can also be underfitting, which means that they do not learn the training data well enough and are unable to make accurate predictions on new data. This can happen if the model is too simple or if the training data is not diverse enough.

Here are some of the ways to mitigate these challenges:

- **Data augmentation:** Data augmentation is a technique that can be used to increase the amount of data available for training. This can be done by creating new data points from existing data points by applying transformations such as rotations, shifts, and zooms.

- **Regularization:** Regularization is a technique that can be used to prevent overfitting. This can be done by adding terms to the loss function that penalizes the model for being too complex.

- **Early stopping:** Early stopping is a technique that can be used to prevent overfitting by stopping the training process early, before the model has had a chance to overfit the training data.

- **Ensemble learning:** Ensemble learning is a technique that can be used to improve the performance of autoencoders by combining the predictions of multiple autoencoders.

Here are some examples of how these challenges can be mitigated:

- **Data scarcity:** If there is not enough data to train an autoencoder, data augmentation can be used to increase the amount of data available. For example, if you are trying to train an autoencoder to classify images of cats and dogs, you could use data augmentation to create new images of cats and dogs by rotating, shifting, and zooming existing images.

- **Overfitting:** If an autoencoder is overfitting, regularization can be used to prevent overfitting. For example, you could use L2 regularization, which adds a penalty to the loss function that is proportional to the square of the weights of the model.

- **Underfitting:** If an autoencoder is underfitting, you can try to increase the complexity of the model or increase the amount of data available for training. For example, you could add more layers to the autoencoder or train the autoencoder on a larger dataset.

It is important to note that these are just some of the challenges that can be encountered when training autoencoders. There are many other challenges that may arise depending on the specific application.

Here are some additional tips for training autoencoders:

- **Use a good optimizer:** The optimizer used to train the autoencoder can have a big impact on the performance of the model. Some good optimizers for autoencoders include Adam, Adagrad, and RMSProp.

- **Choose the right loss function:** The loss function used to train the autoencoder should be chosen carefully. Some good loss functions for autoencoders include mean squared error and binary cross-entropy.

- **Use a validation set:** A validation set should be used to evaluate the performance of the autoencoder during training. This will help to prevent overfitting.

- **Train for the right amount of time:** The amount of time needed to train an autoencoder will vary depending on the size of the model and the amount of data available. It is important not to train the model for too long, as this can lead to overfitting.

AE vs. VAE

While **Autoencoders (AEs)** and **Variational Autoencoders (VAEs)** are both popular models in generative AI, they have some fundamental differences in their approaches and capabilities. AEs focus on efficient reconstruction of input data, VAEs introduce a probabilistic framework for generative modeling. VAEs enable the generation of new samples, exhibit a structured latent space, and allow for smooth interpolations and controlled generation. However, VAEs come with additional complexity and computational costs compared to AEs. The choice between the two depends on the specific requirements and goals of the generative AI task:

Latent space representation:

- **AE:** AEs learn a fixed and deterministic latent space representation. The encoder maps the input data to a fixed latent code, and the decoder reconstructs the input from this code. However, there is no explicit control over the distribution of latent space.

- **VAE:** VAEs introduce a probabilistic approach to the latent space. Instead of a fixed code, VAEs learn a distribution in the latent space. The encoder maps the input data to the mean and variance of this distribution, and the decoder generates samples from the distribution. This stochastic nature allows VAEs to generate new samples by sampling from the learned latent space.

Generation of new samples:

- **AE:** AEs are primarily focused on reconstruction, aiming to reconstruct the input data with minimal loss. They are not explicitly designed for generating new samples beyond the input distribution.

- **VAE:** VAEs are generative models that can generate new samples by sampling from the latent space distribution. By sampling latent codes and passing them through the decoder, VAEs can generate diverse and novel outputs that resemble the training data.

Latent space continuity and interpolation:

- **AE:** In AEs, the latent space often lacks a meaningful structure, making it challenging to perform smooth interpolations or meaningful manipulations between latent codes.

- **VAE:** VAEs encourage a continuous and structured latent space representation. The latent space distribution allows for smooth interpolations between latent codes, enabling meaningful transformations and controlled generation of new samples.

Conclusion

We examined the concept of latent space in autoencoders, which refers to the compressed and meaningful representation of input data learned by the encoder. Understanding the latent space allows us to leverage the power of autoencoders in various applications, including anomaly detection, data generation, and dimensionality reduction.

We also touched upon advanced topics such as dual input autoencoders, loss functions, optimization techniques, and the comparison between autoencoders and VAEs. These discussions provided insights into the versatility and capabilities of autoencoders in solving complex problems.

Overall, autoencoders offer a powerful framework for unsupervised learning and generative AI. They enable us to extract valuable information from data, reconstruct inputs, detect anomalies, and even generate new samples. With their versatility and wide range of applications, autoencoders continue to be a valuable tool in the field of artificial intelligence and machine learning.

In the next chapter, we will dive into the theory and practice of VAEs, a powerful type of generative model that combines the power of autoencoders with Bayesian inference.

Join our book's Discord space

Join the book's Discord Workspace for Latest updates, Offers, Tech happenings around the world, New Release and Sessions with the Authors:

https://discord.bpbonline.com

CHAPTER 6
Designing Generative Variation Auto Encoder

Introduction

In this chapter, we will dive into the theory and practice of **Variational Autoencoders** (**VAE**s), a powerful type of generative model that combines the power of autoencoders with Bayesian inference. VAEs will emerge as a popular approach for learning latent representations of complex data and generating new samples from those representations. They will offer a principled framework for unsupervised learning and will find applications in a wide range of domains, including image generation, natural language processing, and anomaly detection.

To understand VAEs, we will first explore the fundamental differences between VAEs and traditional **autoencoders** (**AE**). We will examine how VAEs introduce probabilistic modeling into the encoding process, enabling the capture of underlying distributions in the data. This distinction will set VAEs apart from AEs and will make them particularly suitable for generative tasks.

Moving further, we will delve into the network architecture of VAEs. We will discuss the components of the VAE, including the encoder and decoder networks, and examine how they work together to encode input data into a latent representation and decode it back into the original data space.

To understand the inner workings of VAEs, we will then unravel the mathematics behind the architecture. We will introduce the reparameterization trick, a key element of VAEs that allows us to back-propagate through the stochastic sampling process. We will also discuss the **Evidence Lower Bound (ELBO)** objective function, which will serve as the training criterion for VAEs, and explore its components and implications for learning meaningful latent representations.

Finally, we will cover topics related to the interpretation of the learned latent space in VAEs. We will discuss methods for understanding the underlying structure of the latent space and visualizing its representations.

By the end of this chapter, you will have a comprehensive understanding of VAEs, from their basic principles and network architecture to the mathematics behind the training process. You will also be equipped with advanced techniques and insights for working with VAEs in practical applications, enabling you to leverage their generative capabilities effectively. Let us embark on this journey into the world of VAEs and unlock their potential for learning and creativity.

Structure

In this chapter, we will cover the following topics:

- Story of VAE

- VAE vs AE

- Key distinctions with autoencoder latent space

- Importance of the latent space when designing a VAE

- Vanilla VAE architecture

- Challenges in Vanilla VAE

- Types of VAE

Objectives

By the end of this chapter, the reader will be able to understand the fundamental differences between VAEs and traditional AEs. We will also explore the network architecture of VAEs, including the encoder and decoder networks, and their role in learning latent representations. The reader will also gain insight into the mathematical principles underlying VAEs, including the reparameterization trick and the ELBO objective function.

The chapter will then move to advanced techniques in VAEs, such as employing different prior distributions, utilizing various forms of the encoder network, and handling missing or incomplete data. We will also discover methods for interpreting the latent space of a VAE and visualizing its representations, explore the generative capabilities of VAEs by generating novel samples using the decoder network, and lastly, acquire the necessary knowledge and skills to apply VAEs in practical applications, including image generation, natural language processing, and anomaly detection.

By achieving these key objectives, readers will develop a comprehensive understanding of VAEs and be able to leverage their power and flexibility in various domains, ultimately enhancing their ability to learn and generate meaningful representations from complex data.

Story of VAE

Imagine that on the floor in front of you is a pile of all the ingredients you have in your pantry—spices, vegetables, grains, and proteins, all of different types. Your talented chef friend, Sarah, is becoming increasingly frustrated with the time it takes her to find the ingredients she needs, so she comes up with a brilliant plan.

Refer to the following *Figure 6.1*:

Figure 6.1: *Story of Variational Auto Encoder*

She instructs you to organize the ingredients into a pantry that is infinitely stocked and organized (*Figure 6.1*). Whenever you want to request a specific ingredient, all you need to do is tell Sarah its location, and she will magically create the ingredient from scratch using her culinary skills and equipment. It becomes apparent that arranging similar ingredients close to each other is crucial for Sarah to accurately recreate each item based solely on its location.

After several weeks of practice, you and Sarah have developed a seamless understanding of the pantry layout. Now, you can simply communicate the location of any ingredient you desire, and Sarah can expertly recreate it!

This sparks an intriguing thought, what if you gave Sarah a pantry location that was empty? To your astonishment, you discover that Sarah has the ability to generate entirely new dishes that have never been prepared before. By combining her culinary knowledge and creativity, she can create unique and delicious recipes that delight your taste buds.

The empty pantry location becomes a gateway to culinary exploration and innovation. Together with Sarah, you embark on a culinary journey, where you can request new ingredients or combinations of ingredients that have never been tasted before. The pantry becomes a playground for culinary experimentation, allowing you to savor the excitement of trying new flavors and experiencing the artistry of Sarah's creations.

Through this newfound collaboration and the magic of the infinite pantry, you and Sarah discover a whole new world of culinary possibilities. The empty pantry locations that once seemed devoid of potential now hold the key to unlocking novel and extraordinary gastronomic experiences.

Prepare yourself for a delectable adventure as we delve into the limitless potential of the infinite pantry and explore the art of culinary innovation like never before. Get ready to savor the flavors of imagination and embark on a culinary journey that transcends boundaries and redefines the way you experience food.

VAE vs AE

To understand the difference between VAE and AE, we need to understand their latent space.

Refer to the following *Figure 6.2*:

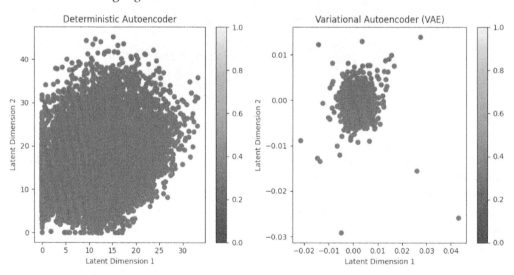

Figure 6.2: *Latent space visualization left side is an AE Latent Space and right side is a VAE latent space*

Now refer to the following *Figure 6.3:*

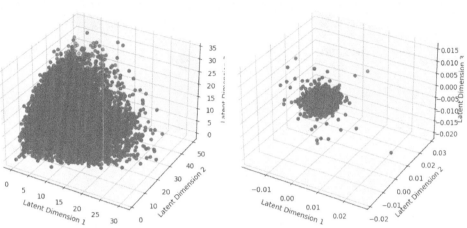

Figure 6.3: 3D Latent space Visualization left side is an AE Latent Space and Right Side is a VAE latent space

An autoencoder is a type of neural network that learns to encode an input into a latent representation, and then decode that representation back into the original input. This can be used for a variety of tasks, such as dimensionality reduction, image compression, and anomaly detection.

A VAE is a type of autoencoder that adds a layer of stochasticity to the latent representation. This allows the VAE to learn a more expressive latent representation, which can be used for tasks such as image generation and image reconstruction.

Figure 6.2 shows the two types of autoencoders side-by-side. The autoencoder on the left is a standard autoencoder, while the VAE on the right is a VA. The two networks are identical up to the latent representation layer. The latent representation layer in the autoencoder is deterministic, while the latent representation layer in the VAE is stochastic.

The text in the figure labels the different parts of the networks. The *encode* blocks represent the encoders, which take the input data and map it to the latent representation. The *decode* blocks represent the decoders, which take the latent representation and map it back to the original input data.

Math behind the latent space

Let us explain the deterministic autoencoder and the stochastic VAE along with the mathematical equations.

Refer to the following *Figure 6.4:*

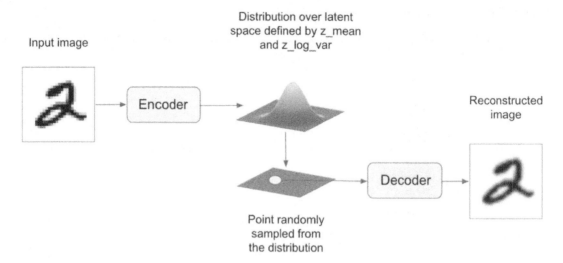

Figure 6.4: Variational autoencoders (VAEs)

Deterministic Autoencoder

A deterministic autoencoder is a type of autoencoder that learns a deterministic mapping from the input data to a fixed-dimensional latent space. It consists of an encoder network that maps the input data to a latent representation and a decoder network that reconstructs the input data from the latent representation.

Mathematically, given an input data point x, the encoder maps it to a latent representation $z\}\backslash)$ as follows:

$$z = \int encoder(x)$$

Where, $\int\_encoder$ represents the encoder function.

The decoder then takes the latent representation z and maps it back to the reconstructed output $\hat{x}$ as follows:

$$\hat{x} = \int encoder(z)$$

Where, represents the decoder function.

The objective of the deterministic autoencoder is to minimize the reconstruction loss, which measures the dissimilarity between the input data x and its reconstructed output $\hat{x}$. The most used reconstruction loss is the **mean squared error (MSE)** loss:

$$L_{reconstruction} = \frac{1}{N}\sum_{i=1}^{n}(x_i - \hat{x}_i)^2$$

Where, N is the number of data points.

Stochastic Variational Autoencoder

VAEs are a type of neural network that can be used to learn latent representations of data. VAEs consist of two parts: an encoder and a decoder. The encoder takes in data and compresses it into a latent representation. The decoder then takes the latent representation and reconstructs the original data.

Figure 6.5 shows the architecture of a VAE and an example of a data sample going through the VAE. The data sample is first compressed by the encoder into mean and standard deviation codings. The coding is then created from the mean and standard deviation codings, with the addition of Gaussian noise. The decoder then uses the codings (or latent variables) to reconstruct the input.

The Gaussian noise added to the codings helps to ensure that the latent representation is not deterministic. This allows the VAE to learn a more expressive latent representation, which can be used for tasks such as image generation and image reconstruction.

The following *Figure 6.5* is based on a graphic by Aurélien Geron:

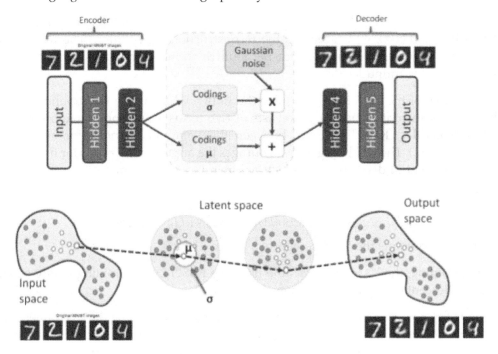

Figure 6.5: *Architecture of a VAE and an example of a data sample going through the VAE*

A stochastic VAE is an extension of the traditional autoencoder that incorporates probabilistic modeling and Bayesian inference. It learns a probabilistic mapping from the input data to a latent space, where each point in the latent space represents a distribution rather than a single point.

The VAE consists of an encoder network that parameterizes the approximate posterior distribution $q\_\phi(z|x)$ and a decoder network that parameterizes the conditional distribution $p\_\theta(x|z)$.

The encoder maps the input data **x** to the parameters of the approximate posterior distribution $q\_\phi(z|x)$, which is typically assumed to be a multivariate Gaussian distribution. The mean vector and the diagonal covariance matrix of the Gaussian distribution are predicted by the encoder:

$$z \sim (z\phi x) = N((x), diag((\sigma(x)))$$

Where, $(\mu\_\phi(x)$ and $\sigma2|\phi(x)$ and are the mean and variance vectors predicted by the encoder.

To generate a latent point z, the VAE employs the reparameterization trick, which introduces a noise variable ε sampled from a standard Gaussian distribution N(0,I):

$$z = \mu\_\phi(x) + \sigma\_\phi(x) \odot \varepsilon$$

Where, $\odot$ represents element-wise multiplication.

The decoder then maps the latent representation z to the parameters of the conditional distribution $p\_\theta(x|z)$, which models the reconstruction distribution. The reconstruction distribution is typically assumed to be a Bernoulli distribution for binary data or a Gaussian distribution for continuous data.

The objective of the VAE is to maximize the ELBO, which is a lower bound on the log-likelihood of the data. The ELBO consists of two terms: the reconstruction loss and the **Kullback-Leibler (KL)** divergence between the approximate posterior and the prior distribution p(**z**). The KL divergence encourages the approximate posterior distribution to be close to the prior distribution and acts as a regularization term.

The ELBO is given by:

$$LELBO = Eq\_\phi(z/x)[log p\_\theta(x/z)] - KL(q\_\phi(z/x)//p(z))$$

Where, KL represents the KL divergence.

During training, the VAE optimizes the negative ELBO by minimizing -using stochastic gradient descent or other optimization algorithms.

By modeling networksroximate posterior distribution and utilizing the reparameterization trick, the VAE enables efficient sampling from the latent space and provides a framework for generating novel samples by sampling from the prior distribution and decoding them using the decoder network.

Key distinctions with autoencoder latent space

In *Table 6.1*, key distinctions with autoencoder latent space are discussed:

Model	Latent space	Deterministic	Stochastic	Training objective
Autoencoder	Deterministic	Yes	No	Reconstruction loss
GAN	Stochastic	No	Yes	Generative adversarial loss
VAE	Stochastic	Yes	Yes	Reconstruction loss + KL divergence

Table 6.1: Key distinctions with autoencoder latent space

Can the VAE Latent space be stochastic as well as deterministic

Yes, the VAE's latent space can be both stochastic and deterministic, depending on the modeling choices and design of the VAE.

In a standard VAE, the latent space is typically stochastic, meaning that each point in the latent space is sampled from a distribution. This stochasticity allows for the generation of diverse and novel samples during the decoding process. The variability in the latent space is typically achieved through the reparameterization trick, where a random noise variable is sampled from a prior distribution (often a standard Gaussian) and combined with the mean and variance predicted by the encoder to generate the latent representation.

However, it is also possible to design a VAE with a deterministic latent space. In such cases, the latent space does not involve sampling from a distribution, and each input is deterministically mapped to a fixed point in the latent space. This can be achieved by modifying the encoder or decoder architecture to remove the stochastic element, such as by removing the reparameterization trick.

Both stochastic and deterministic latent spaces have their advantages and use cases. A stochastic latent space allows for better exploration and generation of diverse samples, while a deterministic latent space may be more suitable for tasks where consistency and fine-grained control over the generated outputs are desired.

Let us understand more.

The latent space of a VAE can be stochastic as well as deterministic. This is because the latent space of a VAE is a probability distribution, and there are two possible distributions that can be used:

- **Normal distribution:** This is the most common distribution used for VAEs. It is a bell-shaped distribution that is centered around a mean value and has a variance.

- **Dirichlet distribution:** This distribution is less common than the normal distribution, but it can be useful for modeling categorical data. It is a distribution that assigns probabilities to a set of discrete values.

The choice of distribution for the latent space of a VAE depends on the application. For example, if the goal is to generate images, then a normal distribution is typically used. However, if the goal is to model categorical data, then a Dirichlet distribution may be a better choice.

It is also possible to use a mixture of distributions for the latent space of a VAE. This can be done by using a hierarchical VAE. A hierarchical VAE is a VAE that has multiple levels of latent variables. The latent variables at each level can be different distributions.

The use of a stochastic latent space in a VAE allows the model to learn a more expressive latent representation. This is because the stochastic latent space allows the model to capture the uncertainty in the data. This uncertainty can be due to noise in the data or to the inherent variability of the data.

The use of a deterministic latent space in a VAE can make the model more interpretable. This is because the deterministic latent space allows the model to learn a latent representation that is directly related to the input data. This can be useful for tasks such as dimensionality reduction and anomaly detection.

The choice of whether to use a stochastic or deterministic latent space in a VAE depends on the specific application. In general, a stochastic latent space is a better choice for tasks that require the model to be able to capture uncertainty. However, a deterministic latent space is a better choice for tasks that require the model to be more interpretable.

Ultimately, the choice between a stochastic or deterministic latent space in a VAE depends on the specific requirements and objectives of the problem at hand.

Dirichlet distribution

The Dirichlet distribution is a probability distribution that models the behavior of random variables representing proportions or compositions. It is a multivariate distribution defined on a simplex, which is a geometric object in a high-dimensional space that represents all possible combinations of proportions that sum to a constant value.

The Dirichlet distribution is inherently stochastic. It is parameterized by a vector of positive values, often denoted as α which determines the shape and concentration of the distribution. Each component of α corresponds to a different dimension of the simplex.

When sampling from a Dirichlet distribution, each draw represents a set of proportions or probabilities that sum to a constant value. The resulting samples are inherently stochastic and subject to variation based on the chosen parameter values.

Mathematically, a Dirichlet distribution with parameter vector α has a probability density function (PDF) given by:

$$f(x;\alpha) = \frac{1}{B(\alpha)} \prod_{i=1}^{K} x_i^{\alpha_i - 1}$$

Where, x is a vector of proportions or probabilities that sums to a constant (for example, $\sum_{i=1}^{K} x_i = 1$), K is the dimensionality of the distribution, α_i are the elements of the parameter vector α and $B(\alpha)$ is the multivariate beta function that normalizes the distribution.

The Dirichlet distribution is commonly used in Bayesian statistics, particularly in applications involving multinomial models, Bayesian inference with categorical data, or as prior distributions in mixture models. It allows for modeling uncertainty and variability in proportions or probabilities.

In summary, the Dirichlet distribution is a stochastic distribution that models proportions or compositions. It characterizes uncertainty and randomness in the distribution of proportions, making it a powerful tool in probabilistic modeling and Bayesian inference.

To sample from a Dirichlet distribution, you can follow these steps:

1. **Specify the parameters:** The Dirichlet distribution is defined by a vector of positive parameters α = [α1, α2,...,αK]where K is the dimensionality of the distribution.

2. **Generate random variables:** Sample K random variables from a gamma distribution with shape parameter αi for each i from 1 to K. These random variables can be denoted as X1,X2,...,XK, where Xi~Gamma(αi,1).

3. **Normalize the variables:** Calculate the sum of the K random variables, denoted S = X1+X2 +...+XK

4. **Calculate the normalized variables:** Obtain the normalized variables by dividing each random variable by the sum: $Y_i = \frac{X_i}{S}$ for each i from 1 to K

The resulting vector **Y**=[Y1,Y2,...,YK] represents a sample from the Dirichlet distribution with parameters α.

It is important to note that the Dirichlet distribution is defined on a simplex, meaning that the resulting sample vector Y will have the property that $\sum_{n=1}^{k} Yi = 1$. This property makes the Dirichlet distribution suitable for modeling proportions or compositions.

Refer to the following *Figure 6.6*:

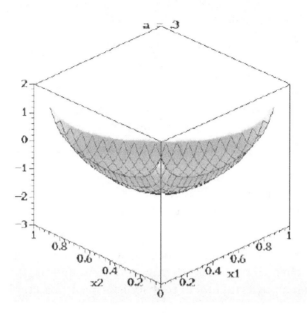

Figure 6.6: Dirichlet distribution

You can use libraries or functions in programming languages like Python to generate samples from the Dirichlet distribution. For example, in Python, you can use the **numpy** library's **random.dirichlet** function to generate samples from the Dirichlet distribution.

Importance of the latent space when designing a VAE

Understanding the latent space is crucial when designing a VAE, because it directly influences the model's generative capabilities, interpretability, and the quality of the learned representations. Here are a few reasons why understanding the latent space is important in VAE design:

- **Generation and sampling:** The latent space serves as a low-dimensional representation of the data distribution. By sampling points from the latent space, you can generate new data samples through the decoder network. Understanding the latent space helps ensure that the generated samples are meaningful, diverse, and aligned with the desired data distribution.

- **Interpolation and manipulation:** The latent space facilitates smooth interpolation between data points. By navigating in the latent space, you can perform operations such as interpolating between two latent representations to generate intermediate samples. Understanding the latent space allows for meaningful and controllable manipulations of generated data, such as morphing between different attributes or classes.

- **Data representation:** The latent space captures the underlying structure and salient features of the data. By examining the latent space, you can gain insights into the data manifold, identify clusters or subgroups, and understand the distribution of the data. Understanding the latent space aids in interpreting and visualizing the learned representations, helping to extract meaningful information from the data.

- **Disentangled representations:** A desirable property of the latent space is disentanglement, where each dimension of the latent space corresponds to a semantically meaningful and independent attribute. Understanding the latent space assists in designing VAE architectures and training strategies that promote disentanglement, allowing for explicit control over specific attributes or factors of variation.

- **Anomaly detection and outlier identification:** The latent space can be leveraged for anomaly detection or outlier identification. By learning a probabilistic representation of the data, the VAE can assign low probability or high reconstruction error to out-of-distribution or anomalous samples. Understanding the latent space helps in setting appropriate thresholds for identifying such instances.

By comprehending the characteristics and properties of the latent space, you can make informed decisions in VAE design, including architecture choices, loss functions, regularization techniques, and interpretability considerations. Understanding the latent space empowers you to create more effective and versatile VAE models for tasks such as generative modeling, data augmentation, data synthesis, and exploratory data analysis.

One benefit of mapping images into a lower-dimensional latent space is that we can perform arithmetic on vectors in this latent space that has a visual analogue when decoded back into the original image domain. This means that we can change the attributes of an image by adding or subtracting vectors in the latent space.

For example, suppose we want to take an image of somebody who looks sad and give them a smile. To do this, we first need to find a vector in the latent space, that points in the direction of increasing smile. We can find this vector by taking the average position of encoded images in the latent space with the attribute Smiling and subtracting the average position of encoded images that do not have the attribute Smiling. This will give us the vector that points in the direction of Smiling, which is exactly what we need.

Conceptually, we are performing the following vector arithmetic in the latent space:

*latent_space_vector = alpha * smile_vector + original_latent_space_vector*

Where, alpha is a factor that determines how much of the smile vector is added or subtracted.

This vector arithmetic can be used to change the attributes of an image in a variety of ways. For example, we could use it to make someone look younger, older, or more attractive. We could also use it to change the color of someone's hair or eyes.

The ability to perform vector arithmetic in the latent space is a powerful tool that can be used to create new and interesting images. It is one of the reasons why Variational Autoencoders are such powerful generative models.

Vanilla VAE architecture

Generative models are a type of machine learning model that can be used to learn the distribution of data. This means that they can be used to generate new data that is similar to the data that they were trained on.

One way to train a generative model is to use a technique called **maximum Likelihood Estimation (MLE)**. MLE works by finding the parameters of the model that maximize the likelihood of the data.

However, MLE can be computationally expensive, especially for large datasets. This is because it requires evaluating the likelihood of the data for all possible values of the parameters.

VAEs are a type of generative model that can be used to avoid the computational expense of MLE. VAEs work by introducing a latent variable into the model. The latent variable is a hidden variable that is not directly observed, but that is used to represent the underlying distribution of the data.

To deal with the problem of generating realistic data points $x \in R\ d$ given a dataset $D = \{x(1), \ldots, x(N)\}$, generative models usually make the assumption that there exists a ground-truth distribution μGT supported on a low dimensional manifold $\chi \subseteq R\ d$ with dimension $k < d$, absolutely continuous with respect to the Hausdorff measure on χ and with density $pgt(x)$. With this assumption, one can rewrite

$$pgt(x) = Z\ Rkpgt(x, z)dz = Z\ Rkpgt(x \mid z)p(z)dz = Ep(z)\ [pgt(x \mid z)]$$

Note: The Hausdorff measure is a measure of the size of a set in a metric space. In the case of VAEs, the metric space is the latent space, and the set is the manifold χ. The Hausdorff measure ensures that the latent variable is distributed over a manifold with a finite volume.

The density $pg(x)$ is the probability density function of the ground-truth distribution. This density function is used to train the decoder distribution, so that it can generate new data that is similar to the data that was used to train the VAE.

Where, $z \in R\ k$ is the latent variable associated with x, distributed with a simple distribution $p(z)$ named prior distribution.

The idea behind generative models is that if we can learn a good approximation of $pgt(x \mid z)$ from the data, then we can use that approximation to generate new samples with ancestral sampling, that is: – *Sample $z \sim p(z)$*. – *Generate $x \sim pgt(x \mid z)$*. For this reason, it is common to define a parametric family of probability distributions $P\theta = \{p\theta(x \mid z) \mid \theta \in R\ s\}$ with a neural network, and to find $\theta*$ such that

$$\theta * = arg\ max\ \theta\ ED[log\ p\theta(x)] = arg\ max\ \theta\ ED\ h\ log\ Z\ Rkp\theta(x \mid z)p(z)dz$$

That is, the Maximum Likelihood Estimation (MLE)

Unfortunately, MLE is usually computationally infeasible. For this reason, VAEs define another probability distribution $q\phi(z|x)$ named encoder distribution which describes the relationship between a data point $x \in \chi$ and its latent variable $z \in R\,k$ and optimizes ϕ and θ such that:

$\theta*, \phi* = arg\ min\ ED[DKL(q\phi(z|x)||p\theta(z|x))]$

Where, $DKL(q\phi(z|x)||p\theta(z|x)) = Eq\phi(z|x)\ [log\ q\phi(z|x)-log\ p\theta(z|x)]$ is the KullbackLeibler divergence between $q\phi(z|x)$ and $p\theta(z|x)$.

The ELBO

Since ELBO is more tractable than MLE, it is used as the cost function for the training of neural network in order to optimize

VAEs are trained to maximize the **Evidence Lower Bound (ELBO)**. The ELBO is a lower bound on the likelihood of the data, and it can be evaluated more efficiently than the likelihood itself, in order to optimize both θ and ϕ:

The ELBO is defined as follows:

$L\theta,\phi(x) := Eq\phi(z|x)\ [log\ p\theta(x|z)] - DKL(q\phi(z|x)||p(z))$

Where:

- $q\phi(z|x)$ is the encoder distribution, which represents the probability of the latent variable given the data

- $p\theta(x|z)$ is the decoder distribution, which represents the probability of the data given the latent variable

- $p(z)$ is the prior distribution, which represents the prior belief about the latent variable

- $DKL(q\phi(z|x)||p(z))$ is the Kullback-Leibler divergence between the encoder distribution and the prior distribution

The ELBO can be interpreted as the difference between the log likelihood of the data and the KL divergence between the encoder distribution and the prior distribution. The KL divergence is a measure of how different two distributions are.

The ELBO is a lower bound on the likelihood of the data because the KL divergence can never be negative. This means that the ELBO is always less than or equal to the likelihood of the data.

VAEs are trained to maximize the ELBO by iteratively updating the parameters of the encoder and decoder distributions. This process is called gradient descent.

The ELBO can be used as a cost function for training VAEs. This means that the VAE is trained to minimize the ELBO.

Since $DKL(q\phi(z|x)||p\theta(z|x)) \geq 0$, which implies that the Left Hand Side of the equation above is a lower bound for the loglikelihood of $p\theta(x)$. For this reason, it is usually called ELBO (Evidence Lower BOund).

The reparameterization trick

The reparameterization trick is a technique used in VAEs to enable the backpropagation of gradients through stochastic operations during training. It is a key component that allows VAEs to efficiently sample from a continuous latent distribution and optimize the model parameters using gradient-based methods.

In other words, the VAE predicts the parameters of a distribution which then is used to generate encoded embeddings. **This process of sampling from a distribution that is parameterized by our model is not differentiable.** If something is not differentiable, that is a problem, at least for gradient-based approaches like ours. So, we need some method of making our predictions separate from the stochastic sampling element.

Refer to the following *Figure 6.7*:

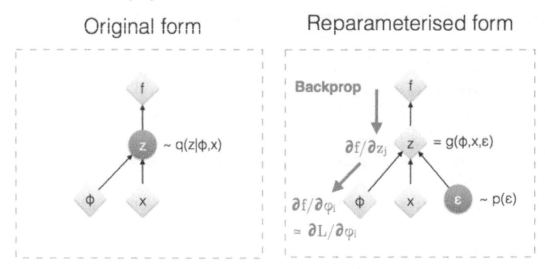

Figure 6.7: *The reparameterization trick*
Source: http://kiwi.bridgeport.edu/cpeg589/CPEG589_Lecture6.pdf

Refer to the following *Figure 6.8*:

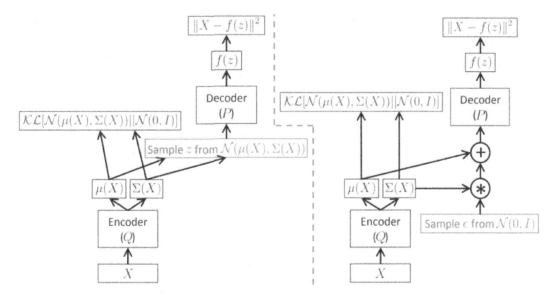

Figure 6.8: *The reparameterization trick network view*
Source: http://kiwi.bridgeport.edu/cpeg589/CPEG589_Lecture6.pdf

In a VAE, the encoder network approximates the posterior distribution $q\varphi(z|x)$ over the latent variables z given the input data x. This posterior is typically assumed to be a multivariate Gaussian distribution with a diagonal covariance matrix.

During training, to sample from the posterior distribution, the reparameterization trick is used to decouple the stochasticity from the parameters of the distribution. This decoupling enables the gradients to flow through the sampling operation and facilitates efficient optimization.

The reparameterization trick can be mathematically defined as follows:

1. First, we sample a random noise variable $\in$ from a fixed distribution, such as a standard Gaussian distribution ($\in$~N(0,1))

2. Next, we transform the sampled noise variable $\in$ using the parameters of the posterior distribution, which are predicted by the encoder network. This transformation is defined as:

   $z = \mu + \sigma \odot \in$

   Where, μ represents the mean and σ represents the standard deviation (or diagonal elements of the covariance matrix) predicted by the encoder network, and $\odot$ denotes element-wise multiplication.

By applying the reparameterization trick, the sampling operation becomes differentiable with respect to the parameters of the encoder network. This allows the gradients to flow through the sampling process, enabling efficient backpropagation and optimization of the model parameters using standard gradient-based methods.

The reparameterization trick is crucial in VAEs because it enables the training of the model through gradient descent optimization. It allows the model to learn meaningful latent representations by mapping the input data to the latent space and back. Moreover, by decoupling the stochasticity from the model parameters, the reparameterization trick facilitates efficient and stable training, enabling VAEs to generate diverse and realistic samples from the learned latent space.

You might wonder if we have the reparameterization trick in AE. The answer is no, the reparameterization trick is specific to VAEs and is not used in traditional AEs. The reparameterization trick is employed in VAEs to enable the sampling of latent variables from a continuous distribution during the training process while allowing for the backpropagation of gradients.

In VAEs, the latent variables are typically modeled as continuous random variables, such as a multivariate Gaussian distribution. The reparameterization trick decouples the stochasticity in the sampling process from the model parameters, making it differentiable and allowing for the efficient optimization of the VAE through gradient descent.

On the other hand, traditional AEs do not involve probabilistic modeling or the sampling of latent variables. AEs aim to reconstruct the input data faithfully without explicitly modeling a probability distribution in the latent space. Therefore, the reparameterization trick is not applicable or necessary in the context of traditional autoencoders.

Let us understand in terms of code:

```python
import numpy as np
import matplotlib.pyplot as plt
from tensorflow import keras
from tensorflow.keras.datasets import mnist
from tensorflow.keras.models import Model
from tensorflow.keras.layers import Input, Dense, Lambda
from tensorflow.keras import backend as K


# Load MNIST dataset
(x_train, _), (x_test, _) = mnist.load_data()
```

Following figure shows original MNIST images:

Figure 6.9: *Original MNIST images*

```python
# Normalize and flatten images
x_train = x_train.astype('float32') / 255.
```

```
x_test = x_test.astype('float32') / 255.
x_train = x_train.reshape((len(x_train), np.prod(x_train.shape[1:])))
x_test = x_test.reshape((len(x_test), np.prod(x_test.shape[1:])))

# Deterministic Autoencoder
input_dim = x_train.shape[1]
latent_dim = 2  # 2-dimensional latent space

# Encoder
input_img = Input(shape=(input_dim,))
encoded = Dense(latent_dim, activation='relu')(input_img)

# Decoder
decoded = Dense(input_dim, activation='sigmoid')(encoded)

# Define autoencoder model
autoencoder = Model(input_img, decoded)

# Compile and train the autoencoder
autoencoder.compile(optimizer='adam', loss='binary_crossentropy')
autoencoder.fit(x_train, x_train, epochs=10, batch_size=256, shuffle=True,
validation_data=(x_test, x_test))

# Extract the encoder model
encoder = Model(input_img, encoded)

# Generate latent space points using deterministic autoencoder
latent_points_deterministic = encoder.predict(x_test)

# Variational Autoencoder (VAE)
# Reparameterization trick
def sampling(args):
z_mean, z_log_var = args
   epsilon = K.random_normal(shape=(K.shape(z_mean)[0], latent_dim), mean=0.,
stddev=1.0)
    return z_mean + K.exp(0.5 * z_log_var) * epsilon

# Encoder
input_img = Input(shape=(input_dim,))
```

```python
z_mean = Dense(latent_dim)(input_img)
z_log_var = Dense(latent_dim)(input_img)
z = Lambda(sampling)([z_mean, z_log_var])

# Decoder
decoded = Dense(input_dim, activation='sigmoid')(z)

# Define VAE model
vae = Model(input_img, decoded)

# Compute VAE loss
reconstruction_loss = keras.losses.binary_crossentropy(input_img, decoded)
kl_loss = -0.5 * K.sum(1 + z_log_var - K.square(z_mean) - K.exp(z_log_var),
axis=-1)
vae_loss = K.mean(reconstruction_loss + kl_loss)

# Compile and train the VAE
vae.add_loss(vae_loss)
vae.compile(optimizer='adam')
vae.fit(x_train, epochs=10, batch_size=256, shuffle=True, validation_data=(x_
test, None))

# Extract the encoder model
encoder = Model(input_img, z_mean)

# Generate latent space points using VAE
latent_points_vae = encoder.predict(x_test)

# Visualize the latent space
plt.figure(figsize=(10, 5))
plt.subplot(1, 2, 1)
plt.scatter(latent_points_deterministic[:,0], latent_points_deterministic[:,
1], c='b', cmap='rainbow')
plt.title('Deterministic Autoencoder')

plt.xlabel('Latent Dimension 1')
plt.ylabel('Latent Dimension 2')
plt.colorbar()
```

Following figure shows autoencoder output:

Figure 6.10: autoencoder output

```
plt.subplot(1, 2, 2)
plt.scatter(latent_points_vae[:,  0],  latent_points_vae[:,  1],  c='b',
cmap='rainbow')
plt.title('Variational Autoencoder (VAE)')

plt.xlabel('Latent Dimension 1')
plt.ylabel('Latent Dimension 2')
plt.colorbar()

plt.tight_layout()
plt.show()
```

In the following figure variational autoencoder is shown:

Figure 6.11: Variational Autoencoder (VAE) output

Challenges in Vanilla VAE

Vanilla VAEs, while effective in many scenarios, do face some challenges. Here are some of the major challenges associated with vanilla VAEs:

- **Posterior collapse:** Vanilla VAEs can suffer from posterior collapse, where the approximate posterior distribution collapses to a point mass, resulting in an uninformative latent space. This occurs when the model ignores the input data and relies solely on the prior distribution. Posterior collapse limits the diversity and quality of the generated samples.

- **Blurry reconstructions:** Vanilla VAEs often produce blurry reconstructions of the input data. This blurriness is due to the choice of the pixel-wise binary cross-entropy loss, which prioritizes overall similarity rather than capturing fine-grained details. The use of continuous data likelihoods, such as Gaussian or Bernoulli distributions, can result in improved reconstructions.

- **Limited disentanglement:** While VAEs aim to learn disentangled representations, vanilla VAEs may struggle to achieve complete disentanglement. Factors of variation in the data may be entangled in the latent space, making it challenging to independently control specific attributes or features.

- **Sensitive to hyperparameters:** The performance of vanilla VAEs is sensitive to the choice of hyperparameters, including the dimensionality of the latent space and the weight assigned to the KL divergence term in the loss function. Selecting appropriate hyperparameters is crucial to ensure a good trade-off between reconstruction accuracy and latent space regularization.

- **Difficulty handling large and complex datasets:** Vanilla VAEs may encounter difficulties when applied to large and complex datasets. Training VAEs on such datasets can be computationally expensive and may require careful optimization techniques or architectural modifications to achieve satisfactory results.

- **Limited sequential modeling:** Vanilla VAEs are primarily designed for modeling static data and may not be well-suited for sequential or time-series data. Capturing temporal dependencies or modeling high-dimensional sequential data can be challenging within the VAE framework.

Addressing these challenges has led to the development of various extensions and modifications to the vanilla VAE, such as incorporating different loss functions, introducing regularization techniques, or adopting more complex architectures. These advancements aim to overcome the limitations and enhance the capabilities of VAEs in modeling and generating data.

Types of VAE

The various types of VAE are as follows:

- **Standard VAE:** It is the most basic type of VAE that uses a simple Gaussian distribution as the prior and posterior.

- **Regularized VAE (RAE):** One of the most interesting variations of vanilla VAE is the work of *Partha Ghos*h and *Mehdi S. M. Sajjadi*, where the authors tried to solve all the problems related to the classical VAE by completely changing the way of approaching the problem. They pointed out that, in their typical implementation, VAEs can be seen as a regularized Autoencoder with Additive Gaussian Noise on the decoder input. In their work, the authors argued that noise injection in decoders input can be seen as a form of regularization, since it implicitly helps to smooth the function learnt by the network.

- **Conditional VAE:** It is used when there is additional information available about the data that can be used to improve the quality of the generated samples.

- **Adversarial Autoencoder (AAE):** It uses adversarial training to improve the quality of generated samples.

- **Ladder VAE:** It is used when there are multiple levels of abstraction in the data[5].

- **Semi-Supervised VAE:** It is used when there are only a few labeled examples available.

- β-VAE: β-VAE introduces a hyperparameter β to balance the importance of the reconstruction loss and the KL divergence term in the ELBO objective. By tuning β, it allows for explicit control over the disentanglement of factors of variation in the latent space.

- **InfoVAE:** InfoVAE incorporates an additional term in the loss function to maximize the mutual information between the input data and the latent variables. This encourages the VAE to learn informative and meaningful representations in the latent space.

- **DIP-VAE:** DIP-VAE incorporates a specific regularizer called the "DIP term" to promote the independence of individual dimensions in the latent space. This helps to disentangle different factors of variation in the data.

- **Cyclical Annealing VAE:** This type of VAE uses cyclical annealing schedules for the KL divergence term, gradually increasing its weight during training. It can help to mitigate issues like posterior collapse, where the posterior distribution becomes uninformative or collapses to a single point.

- **Joint VAE:** Joint VAE is designed for learning from multiple modalities or data sources simultaneously. It can handle datasets with multiple types of inputs, such as images and text, by jointly modeling the shared and private latent spaces for each modality.

- **Two-Stage VAE**: To address the mismatch of aggregate posterior versus the expected prior, Bin Dai and David Wipf introduced the Two-Stage VAEs.

- **Hierarchical Variational Autoencoder**: A **Hierarchical Variational Autoencoder (HVAE)** is an extension of the traditional VAE that introduces a hierarchical structure in the latent space. The HVAE architecture aims to capture hierarchical representations of data by organizing the latent space into multiple levels or layers, allowing for more structured and expressive modeling.

In a **Conditional Variational Autoencoder (CVAE)**, the latent space is conditioned on additional input variables, typically referred to as the *conditioning variables* or *class labels*. This allows the CVAE to generate samples conditioned on specific attributes or classes.

The latent space of a CVAE consists of two components: the shared latent variables and the conditioning variables. The shared latent variables capture the underlying structure of the data and are shared across all instances in the dataset. The conditioning variables encode the specific attributes or classes that the generated samples should possess.

Mathematically, in a CVAE, the encoder network maps the input data x and the conditioning variables y to the parameters of the approximate posterior distribution $q\varphi(\mathbf{z}|\mathbf{x},\mathbf{y})$ over the latent variables z The approximate posterior distribution is typically assumed to be a multivariate Gaussian distribution.

During training, the encoder network is optimized to infer the parameters of the approximate posterior distribution that best explains the given input data and conditioning variables. The reparameterization trick is then used to sample latent variables from the approximate posterior distribution.

The decoder network maps the sampled latent variables z and the conditioning variables y to the parameters of the conditional distribution $q\varphi(z|x,y)$ over the reconstructed data x.

The objective of the CVAE is to maximize the ELBO, which consists of the reconstruction loss and the KL divergence between the approximate posterior and the prior distribution over the latent variables. The KL divergence term encourages the approximate posterior to be close to the prior distribution and acts as a regularization term.

The latent space of a CVAE allows for conditional generation of samples by providing specific conditioning variables. By manipulating the conditioning variables, the CVAE can generate samples with different attributes or classes while preserving the underlying structure captured in the shared latent variables.

The latent space of a conditional variational autoencoder incorporates both the shared latent variables and the conditioning variables, enabling the generation of samples conditioned on specific attributes or classes.

Conclusion

Throughout the chapter, we explored various aspects of VAEs and their extensions. We began by understanding the fundamental concepts of VAEs, including the difference between VAEs and autoencoders, the network architecture, and the mathematics behind the encoder-decoder framework. We also delved into advanced techniques such as the reparameterization trick and ELBO objective function.

We then expanded our knowledge to different types of VAEs. We learned about conditional VAEs, which incorporate additional information to improve generated samples.

Additionally, we discussed the importance of understanding the latent space in VAE design. The latent space plays a crucial role in generation, interpolation, data representation, and disentanglement of factors of variation. We examined the stochastic nature of VAEs' latent space and how it facilitates sampling and exploration.

Lastly, we touched upon challenges faced by vanilla VAEs, such as posterior collapse, blurry reconstructions, limited disentanglement, sensitivity to hyperparameters, and difficulty with large and complex datasets. Overall, our discussion provided a comprehensive understanding of VAEs and their variations, the significance of the latent space, and the challenges associated with vanilla VAEs. This knowledge equips us with a strong foundation to explore and apply VAEs in various domains, including generative modeling, data synthesis, anomaly detection, and more.

In the next chapter, we will also explore various architectural choices, such as using convolutional or recurrent networks as the encoder or decoder, to handle different types of data and capture complex dependencies. We will explore KL divergence and why it is important.

We will explore advanced techniques in VAEs. We will examine the use of different prior distributions and their impact on the generative process. We will investigate alternative forms of the encoder network, such as convolutional or recurrent networks, to handle specific data modalities effectively. Additionally, we will tackle the challenge of dealing with missing or incomplete data within the VAE framework. We will start with training a VAE on the MNIST dataset for 100 epochs and then visualize the learned latent space along with samples generated from a Dirichlet distribution compare it will normal distribution VAE. Furthermore, we will focus on Loss functions to be probable issues during training and optimization.

Join our book's Discord space

Join the book's Discord Workspace for Latest updates, Offers, Tech happenings around the world, New Release and Sessions with the Authors:

https://discord.bpbonline.com

CHAPTER 7

Building Variational Autoencoders for Generative AI

Introduction

In the previous chapters, we delved into the foundational principles of **Variational Autoencoders** (**VAE**s) and explored their potential in generating high-quality data representations. We learned about the essential components of a VAE, such as the encoder and decoder networks, the reparameterization trick, and the role of the latent space in capturing meaningful data representations.

In this next chapter, we will take our understanding of VAEs to a higher level and investigate various advanced techniques that can enhance their capabilities. Specifically, we will explore the architectural choices we can make in the encoder and decoder networks, tailoring them to handle different types of data and capture complex dependencies effectively.

One key aspect that we will delve into is the use of convolutional or non-convolution networks as the encoder or decoder. These choices can greatly impact the performance of VAEs, especially when dealing with data modalities like images or sequential data.

Another crucial concept we will explore is the **Kullback-Leibler** (**KL**) divergence and its importance in VAEs. Understanding how KL divergence is utilized to measure the similarity between the learned latent space and the prior distribution will shed light on the model's ability to generate diverse and meaningful data samples.

Moving forward, we will investigate alternative forms of the encoder network to address specific data modalities more effectively. Convolutional or encoder architectures can significantly improve VAE performance when dealing with images or sequences.

An intriguing challenge we will tackle is the treatment of missing or incomplete data within the VAE framework. Dealing with such scenarios can be critical in real-world applications, and we will explore strategies to effectively handle such cases and still generate meaningful data representations.

To illustrate these concepts in practice, we will begin by training a VAE on the well-known MNIST dataset for 100 epochs. Through this process, we will visualize the learned latent space and compare samples generated from a Dirichlet distribution with those generated from a standard normal distribution VAE. This comparison will provide us with valuable insights into the impact of different prior distributions on the generative process.

Furthermore, we will focus on loss functions and potential issues that may arise during training. Understanding the intricacies of VAE training is essential to ensure stable convergence and high-quality generative performance.

In summary, this chapter will be an exciting journey into the advanced techniques in Variational Autoencoders. By the end of this chapter, you will have a comprehensive understanding of how-to tailor VAEs to specific data modalities, handle missing data, and utilize various prior distributions for improved generative capabilities.

Structure

In this chapter, we will go over the following topics:

- Key focus areas in VAE research
- Building a VAE with Dirichlet distribution: Non-CNN
- Building a VAE with Dirichlet distribution: CNN
- VAE with non-Dirichlet distribution
- KL divergence
- Common Loss function sin VAE
- Common issues and possible solutions while training VAE
- Missing data handling during generation
- Optimization techniques

Objectives

By the end of this chapter, the reader will have explored various architectural choices, including convolutional or Non convolution networks, to handle complex dependencies in VAEs. We will also investigate the impact of KL divergence and different prior distributions on the generative process of VAEs, and develop strategies to effectively handle missing or incomplete data within the VAE framework. The reader will also understand the role of loss functions and address potential issues during training to ensure stable convergence, as well as optimize VAE performance and generative capabilities for diverse data modalities.

By achieving these key objectives, readers will develop a comprehensive understanding of VAEs and be able to leverage their power and flexibility in various domains, ultimately enhancing their ability to learn and generate meaningful representations from complex data.

Key focus areas in VAE research

Previously, we had a comprehensive exploration of VAEs, starting with training on a specific dataset, understanding the latent space, comparing different prior distributions, addressing loss function challenges, and optimizing the model for better performance. The following sequence of tasks and areas of focus will be addressed in the study related to VAEs:

- **Training a VAE on the MNIST dataset for 100 epochs:** The first step involves training a VAE (a type of generative model) using the MNIST dataset, which consists of images of handwritten digits. Training will occur over multiple iterations or epochs, allowing the model to learn and improve its representations over time.

- **Visualizing the learned latent space:** The latent space is the lower-dimensional representation of data learned by the VAE. After training, the study will visualize this latent space to observe how the VAE is representing the input data in a more compressed form.

- **Generating samples from a Dirichlet distribution and comparing with a normal distribution VAE:** During this part of the study, the VAE will be used to generate new data samples. However, there will be two different approaches: one using a Dirichlet distribution and the other using a normal distribution. By comparing the generated samples from both distributions, the researchers can observe how the choice of prior distribution impacts the quality and diversity of generated data.

- **Focus on loss functions and probable issues during training:** Loss functions play a crucial role in training VAEs. They quantify the difference between the generated data and the original data, guiding the model towards improved representations. The study will explore various loss functions and identify potential challenges that may arise during the training process.

- **Optimization:** Optimization in the context of VAEs refers to fine-tuning the model and its parameters to achieve better performance, convergence, and generative abilities. The study will investigate optimization techniques to improve the VAE's overall effectiveness in generating high-quality data samples.

Building a VAE with Dirichlet distribution: Non-CNN Approach

The Dirichlet distribution is a continuous probability distribution that is commonly used in statistics and machine learning, particularly in applications related to Bayesian inference and probability modeling. It is named after the French mathematician *Peter Gustav Lejeune Dirichlet*.

The Dirichlet distribution is primarily used to model data that consists of multiple proportions or percentages that sum up to a constant value, typically 1.0. It is a multivariate distribution, meaning it can handle multiple variables simultaneously. In the context of the Dirichlet distribution, these variables represent the proportions or probabilities of different categories or outcomes within a dataset.

A **Variational Autoencoder (VAE)** with a Dirichlet distribution is a specialized type of VAE that utilizes the Dirichlet distribution as a probabilistic model for capturing latent variable distributions. In a traditional VAE, Gaussian distributions are commonly used for encoding and decoding latent representations. However, in certain applications where data exhibits a more categorical or discrete nature, the Dirichlet distribution can be a more suitable choice.

The Dirichlet distribution is particularly useful when dealing with data that can be represented as probability distributions over multiple categories or dimensions. It can model the uncertainty and relationships among these categories effectively.

Building a VAE with a Dirichlet distribution involves modifying the VAE architecture to incorporate Dirichlet parameters in the encoder and decoder networks. This allows the model to generate samples that represent the underlying probability distributions within the data.

Applications of VAEs with Dirichlet distributions can be found in various domains, including natural language processing, where documents can be represented as probability distributions over topics, and in any scenario where capturing complex, multivariate categorical data is essential. This approach provides a powerful tool for learning and generating data that adheres to categorical distributions, making it a valuable addition to the VAE family.

Building a VAE with a Dirichlet distribution, using a non-**Convolutional Neural Network (CNN)** approach, is an innovative endeavor. Instead of relying on convolutional layers, this approach leverages fully connected layers to model the latent space and decode data. The Dirichlet distribution introduces a probabilistic element, allowing the VAE to capture complex data distributions effectively. By adopting this non-CNN approach, you can achieve remarkable results in applications like topic modeling, document analysis, and more, providing a versatile alternative to CNN-based VAEs for scenarios where fully connected architectures and probabilistic modeling are advantageous.

Refer to the following code:

```python
import numpy as np
import matplotlib.pyplot as plt
from tensorflow import keras
from tensorflow.keras.datasets import mnist
from tensorflow.keras.models import Model
from tensorflow.keras.layers import Input, Dense, Lambda
from tensorflow.keras import backend as K

# Load MNIST dataset
(x_train, _), (x_test, _) = mnist.load_data()

# Normalize and flatten images
x_train = x_train.astype('float32') / 255.
x_test = x_test.astype('float32') / 255.
x_train = x_train.reshape((len(x_train), np.prod(x_train.shape[1:])))
x_test = x_test.reshape((len(x_test), np.prod(x_test.shape[1:])))

# Define VAE architecture
input_dim = x_train.shape[1]
latent_dim = 2  # 2-dimensional latent space

# Encoder
input_img = Input(shape=(input_dim,))
encoded = Dense(256, activation='relu')(input_img)
z_mean = Dense(latent_dim)(encoded)
z_log_var = Dense(latent_dim)(encoded)

# Reparameterization trick
def sampling(args):
    z_mean, z_log_var = args
  epsilon = K.random_normal(shape=(K.shape(z_mean)[0], latent_dim), mean=0.,
```

```python
stddev=1.0)
    return z_mean + K.exp(0.5 * z_log_var) * epsilon

z = Lambda(sampling)([z_mean, z_log_var])

# Decoder
decoder_input = Input(shape=(latent_dim,))
decoded = Dense(256, activation='relu')(decoder_input)
output_img = Dense(input_dim, activation='sigmoid')(decoded)

# Define VAE model
encoder = Model(input_img, z_mean)
decoder = Model(decoder_input, output_img)

# VAE model
vae_output = decoder(z)
vae = Model(input_img, vae_output)

# Compute VAE loss
reconstruction_loss  =  keras.losses.binary_crossentropy(input_img, vae_output)
kl_loss = -0.5 * K.sum(1 + z_log_var - K.square(z_mean) - K.exp(z_log_var), axis=-1)
vae_loss = K.mean(reconstruction_loss + kl_loss)

vae.add_loss(vae_loss)
vae.compile(optimizer='adam')
vae.summary()

# Train the VAE
epochs = 100
batch_size = 128
history = vae.fit(x_train, epochs=epochs, batch_size=batch_size, validation_data=(x_test, None))

# Generate latent space points using VAE
latent_points_vae = encoder.predict(x_test)

# Generate samples from Dirichlet distribution
samples = np.random.dirichlet(np.ones(latent_dim), size=10)
```

```python
# Visualize the latent space after 100 epochs
plt.figure(figsize=(6, 6))
plt.subplot(1, 2, 1)
plt.scatter(latent_points_vae[:,  0],   latent_points_vae[:,  1],   c='b',
cmap='rainbow')
plt.title('Latent Space Visualization (VAE)')
plt.xlabel('Latent Dimension 1')
plt.ylabel('Latent Dimension 2')

# Generate and visualize samples from the VAE after 100 epochs
decoded_samples = decoder.predict(samples)
decoded_samples = decoded_samples.reshape(-1, 28, 28)

plt.subplot(1, 2, 2)
for i in range(10):
    plt.imshow(decoded_samples[i], cmap='gray')
    plt.xticks([])
    plt.yticks([])
    plt.title('Generated Samples (VAE)')
    plt.tight_layout()
plt.show()
```

In the following figure, VAE output with Latent Space Visualization is shown:

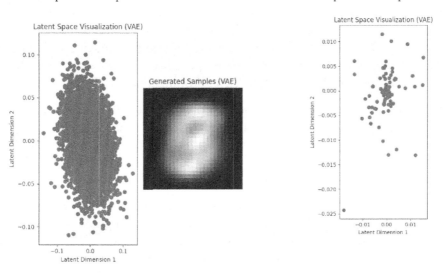

Figure 7.1: VAE output with Latent Space Visualization

Refer to the following figure, it shows the generated samples:

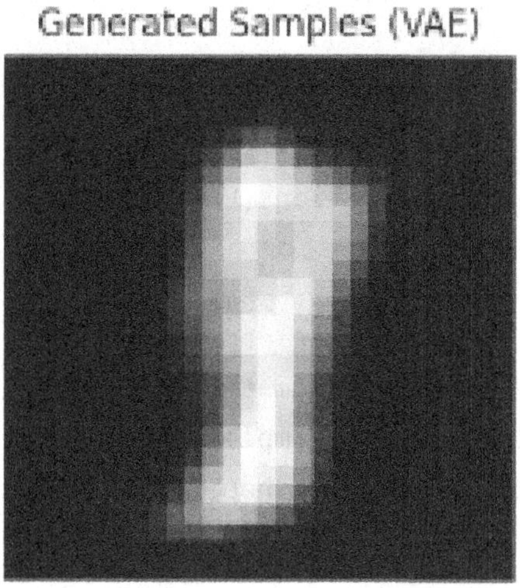

Figure 7.2: *Generated Samples (VAE)*

Building a VAE with Dirichlet distribution: CNN Approach

The Dirichlet distribution is particularly useful in modeling categorical uncertainties in CNNs due to its properties as a multivariate generalization of the beta distribution. It is often used in the context of Bayesian neural networks, where the uncertainty in the model's predictions is explicitly accounted for.

In a CNN used for classification, the final layer typically outputs a set of probabilities for each class using a softmax function. These probabilities reflect the model's confidence in its predictions. However, they do not capture the model's uncertainty about the data itself, which can be critical in decision-making processes, especially in areas like medical diagnosis or autonomous driving where the cost of mistakes is high.

By placing a Dirichlet distribution over the class probabilities, we can model the uncertainty in these predictions. The parameters of the Dirichlet distribution, called concentration parameters, control the variance of the probability vectors, thus expressing the model's confidence in its predictions. A higher concentration indicates more certainty, while a lower concentration indicates more uncertainty.

This approach allows a CNN not only to make predictions but also to provide a measure of its confidence in those predictions. It becomes possible to distinguish between cases where the model is uncertain due to lack of knowledge (for example, ambiguous or previously unseen data) versus cases where it is making a strong prediction based on the learned data distribution. As a result, the Dirichlet distribution enhances CNNs with a more nuanced understanding of categorical uncertainties, enabling more robust and informed decision-making in practice.

klConstructing a VAE with a Dirichlet distribution using a **Convolutional Neural Network (CNN)** approach is a cutting-edge strategy in deep learning. By integrating CNN layers into the VAE architecture, this model can efficiently handle complex image data. The Dirichlet distribution introduces probabilistic modeling to capture intricate relationships within categorical data. This approach excels in applications like image generation, where the spatial information in images is crucial. By combining CNN's ability to extract features and the Dirichlet distribution's capacity to model categorical uncertainty, this VAE variant offers a powerful solution for image-based generative tasks, enabling the synthesis of diverse and realistic visual content, refer to the following code:

```
import numpy as np
import matplotlib.pyplot as plt
from tensorflow import keras
from tensorflow.keras.datasets import mnist
from tensorflow.keras.models import Model
from tensorflow.keras.layers import Input, Dense, Reshape, Flatten, Conv2D,
Conv2DTranspose, Lambda
from tensorflow.keras import backend as K


# Load MNIST dataset
(x_train, _), (x_test, _) = mnist.load_data()


# Normalize and reshape images
x_train = x_train.astype('float32') / 255.
x_test = x_test.astype('float32') / 255.
x_train = np.expand_dims(x_train, axis=-1)
x_test = np.expand_dims(x_test, axis=-1)


# Define VAE architecture
input_shape = x_train.shape[1:]
latent_dim = 2  # 2-dimensional latent space


# Encoder
inputs = Input(shape=input_shape)
x = Conv2D(32, 3, activation='relu', strides=2, padding='same')(inputs)
x = Conv2D(64, 3, activation='relu', strides=2, padding='same')(x)
```

```python
x = Flatten()(x)
z_mean = Dense(latent_dim)(x)
z_log_var = Dense(latent_dim)(x)

# Reparameterization trick
def sampling(args):
    z_mean, z_log_var = args
  epsilon = K.random_normal(shape=(K.shape(z_mean)[0], latent_dim), mean=0.,
stddev=1.0)
    return z_mean + K.exp(0.5 * z_log_var) * epsilon

z = Lambda(sampling)([z_mean, z_log_var])

# Decoder
decoder_inputs = Input(shape=(latent_dim,))
x = Dense(7 * 7 * 64, activation='relu')(decoder_inputs)
x = Reshape((7, 7, 64))(x)
x = Conv2DTranspose(64, 3, activation='relu', strides=2, padding='same')(x)
x = Conv2DTranspose(32, 3, activation='relu', strides=2, padding='same')(x)
outputs = Conv2DTranspose(1, 3, activation='sigmoid', padding='same')(x)

# Define VAE model
encoder = Model(inputs, z_mean)
decoder = Model(decoder_inputs, outputs)
vae_inputs = inputs
vae_outputs = decoder(encoder(vae_inputs))
vae = Model(vae_inputs, vae_outputs)

# Compute VAE loss
reconstruction_loss = keras.losses.binary_crossentropy(K.flatten(vae_inputs),
K.flatten(vae_outputs))
reconstruction_loss *= input_shape[0] * input_shape[1]
kl_loss = -0.5 * K.sum(1 + z_log_var - K.square(z_mean) - K.exp(z_log_var),
axis=-1)
vae_loss = K.mean(reconstruction_loss + kl_loss)

vae.add_loss(vae_loss)
```

```
vae.compile(optimizer='adam')
vae.summary()


# Train the VAE
epochs = 100
batch_size = 128
history = vae.fit(x_train, epochs=epochs, batch_size=batch_size, validation_
data=(x_test, None))


# Generate latent space points using VAE
latent_points_vae = encoder.predict(x_test)


# Generate samples from Dirichlet distribution
samples = np.random.dirichlet(np.ones(latent_dim), size=10)


# Visualize the latent space after 100 epochs
plt.figure(figsize=(6, 6))
plt.subplot(1, 2, 1)
plt.scatter(latent_points_vae[:,   0],   latent_points_vae[:,   1],   c='b',
cmap='rainbow')
plt.title('Latent Space Visualization (VAE)')
plt.xlabel('Latent Dimension 1')
plt.ylabel('Latent Dimension 2')


# Generate and visualize samples from the VAE after 100 epochs
decoded_samples = decoder.predict(samples)
decoded_samples = decoded_samples.reshape(-1, 28, 28)


plt.subplot(1, 2, 2)
for i in range(10):
    plt.imshow(decoded_samples[i], cmap='gray')
    plt.xticks([])
    plt.yticks([])
    plt.title('Generated Samples (VAE)')
plt.tight_layout()
plt.show()
```

Refer to the following figure, it shows improved VAE output with Latent Space Visualization:

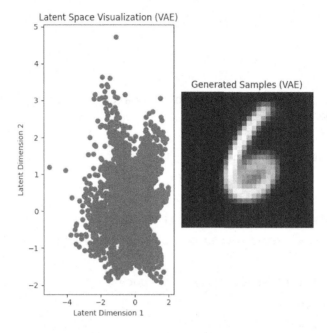

Figure 7.3: *Improved VAE output with Latent Space visualization*

Difference between two networks

The key differences between the Dirichlet distribution approach with a CNN and the non-CNN approach in building a VAE lie in the architecture and the type of data they are suited for:

- **Architectural differences**:

  o **CNN approach**: In the CNN approach, Convolutional Neural Networks are used as part of the VAE architecture. CNNs are highly effective at capturing spatial relationships in data, making them well-suited for tasks involving images or other structured grid-like data. The convolutional layers in a CNN extract hierarchical features from the input data, allowing the model to capture patterns and structures.

  o **Non-CNN approach**: In the non-CNN approach, fully connected layers are typically used. This approach may be more suitable for data that doesn't have a grid-like structure, such as tabular data or sequences. Fully connected layers can capture complex relationships between variables but may struggle with spatial data.

- **Data type**:

  o **CNN approach**: Suited for data with a spatial or grid-like structure, such as images or 2D data grids. CNNs are excellent at capturing local and global patterns in such data, making them ideal for tasks like image generation and computer vision.

  o **Non-CNN approach**: More versatile and can be used for a broader range of data types, including tabular data, time series, and text. It may be preferred when data lacks a clear spatial arrangement.

- **Dirichlet distribution**:

  o **CNN approach**: The Dirichlet distribution can be used to model categorical or probability distributions over learned features extracted by the CNN. This is especially useful when dealing with image data where the VAE needs to capture complex relationships among categories.

  o **Non-CNN approach**: The Dirichlet distribution can be applied directly to model the uncertainty and relationships among categorical data, making it suitable for scenarios where data itself represents categorical distributions.

The choice between the CNN and non-CNN approach for building a VAE with a Dirichlet distribution depends on the nature of the data you are working with. CNNs are well-suited for structured grid-like data like images, while the non-CNN approach is more versatile and can be used for various data types. The Dirichlet distribution, in both cases, is valuable for modeling categorical data or probability distributions over latent variables. The second network clearly shows better output when trained till 100 epochs.

The first network shows:

```
# Define VAE architecture
input_dim = x_train.shape[1]
latent_dim = 2  # 2-dimensional latent space


# Encoder
input_img = Input(shape=(input_dim,))
encoded = Dense(256, activation='relu')(input_img)
z_mean = Dense(latent_dim)(encoded)
z_log_var = Dense(latent_dim)(encoded)


# Reparameterization trick
defsampling(args):
    z_mean,z_log_var = args
```

```
            epsilon  =  K.random_normal(shape=(K.shape(z_mean)[0],latent_dim),
mean=0.,stddev=1.0)
    returnz_mean + K.exp(0.5 * z_log_var) * epsilon


z = Lambda(sampling)([z_mean,z_log_var])


# Decoder
decoder_input = Input(shape=(latent_dim,))
decoded = Dense(256, activation='relu')(decoder_input)
output_img = Dense(input_dim, activation='sigmoid')(decoded)
```

The preceding VAE architecture effectively learns a compressed and meaningful representation of the input data in the lower-dimensional latent space. It can then use this representation to generate new data samples by sampling from the learned distribution in the latent space.

Let us break down the different components of the VAE:

- **Input and Latent Space Dimensions:** The VAE takes input data of dimension **input_dim**. In this case, **x_train.shape[1]** determines the input dimensionality. The VAE compresses the input data into a lower-dimensional latent space of **latent_dim**, which is set to 2 in this example.

- **Encoder:** The encoder part of the VAE aims to map the input data into the latent space. In this architecture, the encoder consists of a single Dense layer with 256 units and **relu** activation function (**Dense(256, activation='relu')**). This layer learns to extract meaningful representations from the input data and project it into the higher-dimensional space. The output of this layer, denoted as **encoded**, is then split into two branches: **z_mean** and **z_log_var**, which represent the mean and logarithm of the variance of the distribution of the latent space, respectively.

- **Reparameterization Trick:** The reparameterization trick is a critical component in VAEs, enabling the model to generate samples from the learned latent space distribution. The *sampling* function takes the **z_mean** and **z_log_var** as inputs and generates a random sample (*epsilon*) from a standard normal distribution. The function then combines this sample with the mean and variance using a linear transformation, producing a sample (**z**) from the learned latent space.

- **Decoder:** The decoder part of the VAE aims to reconstruct the original input data from the samples in the latent space. It takes the **z** (sampled from the latent space) as input. In this architecture, the decoder consists of two Dense layers. The first Dense layer (**Dense(256, activation='relu')**) processes the latent sample **z**, allowing the model to gradually upsample and reconstruct the data. The final Dense layer (**Dense(input_dim, activation='sigmoid')**) produces the output image, reconstructing the original input data with **input_dim** dimensions and using a *sigmoid* activation function.

This following VAE architecture allows for the encoding of the input data into a lower-dimensional latent space representation and then decoding it back to the original data space. By training the VAE on a dataset, it can learn meaningful representations and generate new data samples by sampling from the learned latent space distribution.

The architecture consists of an encoder, a reparameterization trick, and a decoder.

- **Encoder:** The encoder takes the input data and gradually reduces its dimensionality to capture the important features. In this case, convolutional layers are used for feature extraction. The input data is passed through two Conv2D layers with increasing filters (32 and 64), using the **relu** activation function. The strides of 2 are used to downsample the data, and padding is set to *same* to maintain spatial dimensions. The output is then flattened, and two Dense layers are applied to obtain the mean and logarithm of the variance of the latent space distribution (**z_mean** and **z_log_var**).

- **Reparameterization Trick:** The reparameterization trick allows the model to sample from the latent space distribution using a differentiable function, enabling the use of backpropagation for training. The sampling function takes the mean (**z_mean**) and logarithm of the variance (**z_log_var**) from the encoder as inputs. It generates a random sample (*epsilon*) from a standard normal distribution and combines it with the mean and variance to produce a sample from the latent space.

- **Decoder:** The decoder takes the latent space representation (**z**) as input and aims to reconstruct the original data. The decoder begins with a Dense layer, followed by a reshape operation to convert the flat representation into a 3D tensor. Then, two Conv2DTranspose layers are used to upsample the data, increasing its spatial dimensions. The number of filters decreases with each layer (64 and 32), and the **relu** activation function is used. Finally, a Conv2DTranspose layer with one filter and a *sigmoid* activation function is applied to reconstruct the output data.

Refer to the following code:

```
# Define VAE architecture
input_shape = x_train.shape[1:]
latent_dim = 2  # 2-dimensional latent space


# Encoder
inputs = Input(shape=input_shape)
x = Conv2D(32,3, activation='relu', strides=2, padding='same')(inputs)
x = Conv2D(64,3, activation='relu', strides=2, padding='same')(x)
x = Flatten()(x)
```

```
z_mean = Dense(latent_dim)(x)
z_log_var = Dense(latent_dim)(x)


# Reparameterization trick
defsampling(args):
    z_mean,z_log_var = args
        epsilon  =  K.random_normal(shape=(K.shape(z_mean)[0],latent_dim),
mean=0.,stddev=1.0)
    returnz_mean + K.exp(0.5 * z_log_var) * epsilon


z = Lambda(sampling)([z_mean,z_log_var])


# Decoder
decoder_inputs = Input(shape=(latent_dim,))
x = Dense(7 * 7 * 64, activation='relu')(decoder_inputs)
x = Reshape((7,7,64))(x)
x = Conv2DTranspose(64,3, activation='relu', strides=2, padding='same')(x)
x = Conv2DTranspose(32,3, activation='relu', strides=2, padding='same')(x)
outputs = Conv2DTranspose(1,3, activation='sigmoid', padding='same')(x)
```

The two networks are both **Variational Autoencoders (VAE**s) but differ in their architecture and the types of layers used. Let us highlight the key differences:

- **Input Shape:** The first network uses a **Convolutional Neural Network (CNN)** based architecture and expects input data in the form of images with spatial dimensions (such as, height and width), as represented by **input_shape**. On the other hand, the second network uses a fully connected or Dense layer-based architecture and takes one-dimensional input data with **input_dim**, which means it is designed for tabular or sequential data.

- **Encoder:** In the first network (Convolutional VAE), the encoder includes two Conv2D layers for feature extraction from images. In contrast, the second network (Dense VAE) has a simpler encoder with just one Dense layer.

- **Decoder:** Similarly, the first network (Convolutional VAE) employs Conv2DTranspose layers for upsampling and reconstructing the image. In contrast, the second network (Dense VAE) uses Dense layers for decoding and reconstructing the one-dimensional input data.

- **Architecture Complexity:** The Convolutional VAE tends to have more parameters and a more complex architecture due to the use of convolutional and transpose convolutional layers. On the other hand, the Dense VAE has a simpler architecture, as it mainly consists of fully connected Dense layers.

- **Applicability:** The choice between these architectures depends on the type of data and the specific task at hand. Convolutional VAEs are well-suited for image-related tasks, where spatial relationships are crucial. Dense VAEs, on the other hand, are better suited for tabular or sequential data, such as time series or text data.

- **Performance:** The performance and effectiveness of each architecture will depend on the characteristics of the dataset and the complexity of the task. Convolutional VAEs are known for their ability to capture spatial features and patterns, making them popular for image generation tasks. Dense VAEs may perform better on certain tabular or sequential data types, where spatial information is not as important.

So, the choice between the two VAE architectures should be based on the nature of the data and the specific requirements of the task. Convolutional VAEs are ideal for image-related tasks, while Dense VAEs are more suitable for tabular or sequential data.

VAE with Non Dirichlet distribution

Let us build a Model with MNIST Fashion dataset with Non Dirichlet distribution:

```
import tensorflow as tf
import numpy as np
import matplotlib.pyplot as plt

# Load Fashion MNIST dataset
(train_images, _), (test_images, _) = tf.keras.datasets.fashion_mnist.load_
data()

# Normalize and reshape data
train_images = train_images.astype('float32') / 255.0
train_images = np.reshape(train_images, (-1, 28, 28, 1))

# Define Conv2D VAE architecture
latent_dim = 2

class Sampling(tf.keras.layers.Layer):
    def call(self, inputs):
        z_mean, z_log_var = inputs
        batch = tf.shape(z_mean)[0]
        dim = tf.shape(z_mean)[1]
        epsilon = tf.random.normal(shape=(batch, dim), mean=0.0, stddev=1.0)
        return z_mean + tf.exp(0.5 * z_log_var) * epsilon
```

```python
encoder_inputs = tf.keras.Input(shape=(28, 28, 1))
x = tf.keras.layers.Conv2D(32, 3, activation='relu', strides=2, padding='same')
(encoder_inputs)
x = tf.keras.layers.Conv2D(64, 3, activation='relu', strides=2, padding='same')
(x)
x = tf.keras.layers.Flatten()(x)
z_mean = tf.keras.layers.Dense(latent_dim)(x)
z_log_var = tf.keras.layers.Dense(latent_dim)(x)
z = Sampling()([z_mean, z_log_var])
encoder   =   tf.keras.Model(encoder_inputs,   [z_mean,   z_log_var,   z],
name='encoder')


decoder_inputs = tf.keras.Input(shape=(latent_dim,))
x = tf.keras.layers.Dense(7 * 7 * 64, activation='relu')(decoder_inputs)
x = tf.keras.layers.Reshape((7, 7, 64))(x)
x = tf.keras.layers.Conv2DTranspose(64, 3, activation='relu', strides=2,
padding='same')(x)
x = tf.keras.layers.Conv2DTranspose(32, 3, activation='relu', strides=2,
padding='same')(x)
decoder_outputs = tf.keras.layers.Conv2DTranspose(1, 3, activation='sigmoid',
padding='same')(x)
decoder = tf.keras.Model(decoder_inputs, decoder_outputs, name='decoder')


# Create VAE model
vae_inputs = encoder_inputs
vae_outputs = decoder(encoder(encoder_inputs)[2])
vae_model = tf.keras.Model(vae_inputs, vae_outputs, name='vae')


def loss_func(encoder_mu, encoder_log_variance):
    def vae_reconstruction_loss(y_true, y_predict):
        reconstruction_loss_factor = 1000
      reconstruction_loss = tf.keras.backend.mean(tf.keras.backend.square(y_
true-y_predict), axis=[1, 2, 3])
        return reconstruction_loss_factor * reconstruction_loss


    def vae_kl_loss(encoder_mu, encoder_log_variance):
        kl_loss = -0.5 * tf.keras.backend.sum(1.0 + encoder_log_variance
- tf.keras.backend.square(encoder_mu) - tf.keras.backend.exp(encoder_log_
variance), axis=1)
```

```
        return kl_loss

    def vae_kl_loss_metric(y_true, y_predict):
        kl_loss = -0.5 * tf.keras.backend.sum(1.0 + encoder_log_variance
- tf.keras.backend.square(encoder_mu)  -  tf.keras.backend.exp(encoder_log_
variance), axis=1)
        return kl_loss

    def vae_loss(y_true, y_predict):
        reconstruction_loss = vae_reconstruction_loss(y_true, y_predict)
        kl_loss = vae_kl_loss(y_true, y_predict)

        loss = reconstruction_loss + kl_loss
        return loss

    return vae_loss

# Compile the model
vae_model.compile(optimizer='adam', loss=loss_func(z_mean, z_log_var))
#vae.compile(optimizer=tensorflow.keras.optimizers.Adam(lr=0.0005),
loss=loss_func(encoder_mu, encoder_log_variance))
# Training the model
 #vae_model.fit(train_images, train_images, epochs=30, batch_size=128)
history = vae_model.fit(train_images, train_images, epochs=20, batch_size=32,
shuffle=True)
# Plot the loss curve
plt.plot(history.history['loss'])
plt.title('VAE Loss')
plt.xlabel('Epoch')
plt.ylabel('Loss')
plt.show()

# Generate samples of "Trouser" and "Shirt" classes
num_samples = 10

# Generate "Trouser" samples
z_samples_trouser = np.random.normal(size=(num_samples, latent_dim))
generated_images_trouser = decoder.predict(z_samples_trouser)
```

```
# Generate "Shirt" samples
z_samples_shirt = np.random.normal(size=(num_samples, latent_dim))
generated_images_shirt = decoder.predict(z_samples_shirt)

# Plot generated samples
plt.figure(figsize=(15, 4))
for i in range(num_samples):
    plt.subplot(2, num_samples, i + 1)
    plt.imshow(generated_images_trouser[i].reshape(28, 28), cmap='gray')
    plt.title('Trouser')
    plt.axis('off')

    plt.subplot(2, num_samples, num_samples + i + 1)
    plt.imshow(generated_images_shirt[i].reshape(28, 28), cmap='gray')
    plt.title('Shirt')
    plt.axis('off')

plt.show()
```

Refer to the following figure, it shows the loss after 20 epoch:

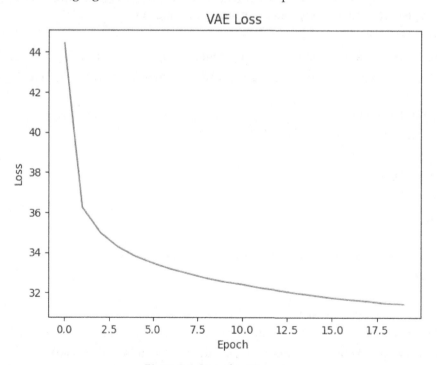

Figure 7.4: Loss after 20 epoch

Refer to the following figure, it shows the output after 20 epochs:

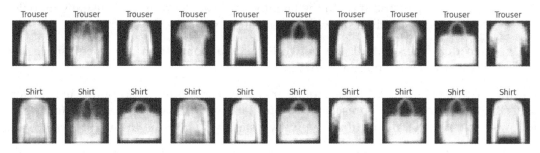

Figure 7.5: *Output after 20 epochs*

An autoencoder is a type of neural network that learns to encode an input into a latent representation, and then decode that representation back into the original input. This can be used for a variety of tasks, such as dimensionality reduction, image compression, and anomaly detection.

KL divergence

KL divergence, short for Kullback-Leibler divergence, is a measure of how one probability distribution differs from another. It is often used in information theory and statistics to quantify the difference between two probability distributions. In the context of VAE, KL divergence plays a crucial role in the training process and ensures that the latent space generated by the VAE follows a desired probability distribution.

Refer to the following figure:

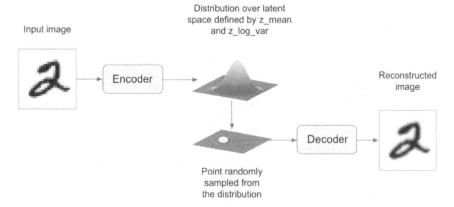

Figure 7.6: *Variational autoencoders (VAEs)*

In a VAE, the objective is to learn a probabilistic mapping between the input data and a latent space, where each point in the latent space represents a meaningful encoding of the data. The VAE consists of two main components:

- **Encoder:** This part of the network maps the input data (for example, an image) to a probability distribution in the latent space. The distribution is usually modeled as a Gaussian distribution with a mean and a variance.

- **Decoder:** This part of the network takes a point from the latent space and reconstructs the input data from it.

During the training of the VAE, the model aims to find an optimal distribution in the latent space that can accurately represent the input data while ensuring that the latent space follows a specific prior distribution, typically a standard Gaussian (mean=0, variance=1).

This is where the KL divergence comes into play. The KL divergence loss term in the VAE objective function encourages the learned distribution in the latent space to match the desired prior distribution. By minimizing the KL divergence between the learned distribution and the target distribution (the prior Gaussian), the VAE ensures that the latent space remains regularized and has desirable properties.

Mathematically, the KL divergence between two distributions P and Q is defined as:

$$KL(P \mid\mid Q) = \int P(x) \, log(P(x) \, / \, Q(x)) \, dx$$

In the context of VAE, the KL divergence term in the loss function is calculated as the KL divergence between the learned distribution from the encoder (usually Gaussian) and the target Gaussian distribution (prior). The VAE objective function is a combination of the reconstruction loss (how well the input data is reconstructed) and the KL divergence loss (how well the latent space adheres to the prior distribution). By jointly optimizing these two components, the VAE learns to represent the input data efficiently in the latent space and generates meaningful samples during the generation process.

The **Evidence Lower Bound (ELBO)** is a key concept in variational inference and is closely related to the KL divergence. In the context of VAE, the ELBO is used as an objective function to train the model efficiently.

Let us explore the relationship between ELBO and KL divergence:

- In a VAE, the goal is to maximize the log-likelihood of the data, which is intractable due to the complex nature of the generative model. Instead, the VAE uses variational inference to approximate the posterior distribution over the latent variables.

- The ELBO is derived using the concept of evidence (or marginal) likelihood, which represents the likelihood of the data integrated over the latent variables. The ELBO is an inequality that relates the log-likelihood of the data (**log p(x)**) to the expected lower bound of the log-joint probability of the data and the latent variables (**log p(x, z)**) under a variational distribution **q(z|x)** over the latent space:

$$ELBO = E[log \, p(x, z) - log \, q(z \mid x)]$$

Where:

E[.] denotes the expectation over the samples drawn from the variational distribution **q(z|x)**.

log p(x, z) is the log-joint probability of the data and the latent variables (prior distribution **p(z)** multiplied by the likelihood **p(x|z)**).

log q(z|x) is the log-probability of the latent variables given the data, which is the variational distribution that the encoder of the VAE outputs (typically a Gaussian distribution).

Now, let us expand the ELBO using the properties of logarithms:

$$ELBO = E[log\ p(x, z) - log\ q(z\,|\,x)]$$

$$= E[log\ p(x\,|\,z) + log\ p(z) - log\ q(z\,|\,x)]$$

At this point, you might recognize the terms **log p(x|z)** and **log q(z|x)** as the reconstruction loss and the negative KL divergence, respectively. The reconstruction loss measures how well the VAE can reconstruct the input data given a sampled latent variable, while the negative KL divergence ensures that the learned distribution in the latent space (**q(z|x)**) approximates the prior distribution (**p(z)**).

So, the ELBO can be further written as:

$$ELBO = E[log\ p(x\,|\,z) + log\ p(z) - log\ q(z\,|\,x)]$$

$$= E[log\ p(x\,|\,z)] - KL(q(z\,|\,x)\ |\ |\ p(z))$$

Maximizing the ELBO is equivalent to minimizing the KL divergence between the variational distribution **q(z|x)** and the prior distribution **p(z)**.

In practice, the ELBO is often maximized using an iterative optimization procedure. This procedure starts with an initial guess for the variational distribution **q(z|x)**, and then it iteratively updates **q(z|x)** to minimize the KL divergence. The optimization procedure is terminated when the ELBO converges to a maximum value.

This is why during the training of a VAE, the objective is to maximize the ELBO, which encourages the model to learn a good approximation of the true posterior distribution and effectively regularizes the latent space to follow the desired prior distribution.

Common loss function sin VAE

Let us go over the following:

- **Reconstruction loss:** This loss function measures how well the VAE can reconstruct the input data. It is typically a measure of the distance between the input data and the reconstructed data. Some common reconstruction losses include the **Mean Squared Error** (**MSE**) and the binary cross-entropy loss.

- **KL divergence loss:** This loss function measures how close the variational distribution **q(z|x)** is to the prior distribution **p(z)**. The KL divergence is always non-negative, so minimizing it will always increase the ELBO. Some common KL divergence losses include the Kullback-Leibler divergence and the Wasserstein distance.

- **Total loss:** The total loss is the sum of the reconstruction loss and the KL divergence loss. This is the loss function that is minimized during the training of the VAE.

Here are some of the specific loss functions that are commonly used in VAEs:

- **MSE loss:** The MSE loss is the most common reconstruction loss used in VAEs. It is defined as the mean squared difference between the input data and the reconstructed data.

- **Binary cross-entropy loss:** The binary cross-entropy loss is a common reconstruction loss used for binary data. It is defined as the cross-entropy between the ground truth labels and the predicted probabilities.

- **Kullback-Leibler divergence:** The Kullback-Leibler divergence is a common KL divergence loss used in VAEs. It is defined as the difference between the two probability distributions.

- **Wasserstein distance:** The Wasserstein distance is a common KL divergence loss used in VAEs. It is a metric that measures the distance between two probability distributions.

The choice of loss function depends on the specific application of the VAE. For example, if the VAE is being used for image generation, then the MSE loss may be a good choice. However, if the VAE is being used for classification, then the binary cross-entropy loss may be a better choice.

Common issues and possible solutions while training VAE

Training a VAE can be challenging, and several common issues can arise during the training process. Here are some of the most common problems and their potential solutions.

- **Vanishing or Exploding Gradients:** The ELBO objective in VAE involves computing the KL divergence between two probability distributions, which can lead to gradients that vanish or explode during backpropagation. This can result in slow convergence or training instability.

  o **Solution:** Use techniques like gradient clipping or normalizing gradients to prevent exploding gradients. Additionally, consider using alternative divergence metrics that have more stable gradients, such as the Wasserstein distance or the Jensen-Shannon divergence.

- **Mode Collapse:** Mode collapse occurs when the VAE fails to capture the full diversity of the input data and generates only a limited subset of possible samples.

o **Solution:** Implement regularization techniques to encourage diversity in the latent space, such as adding an entropy term to the ELBO or using techniques like **Annealed Importance Sampling (AIS)** or **Minimum Description Length (MDL)** to improve the model's ability to explore different modes.

- **Poor Reconstruction Quality:** The VAE may struggle to accurately reconstruct the input data, resulting in blurry or distorted output.

  o **Solution:** Adjust the architecture and capacity of the VAE, including increasing the number of hidden units or layers in the encoder and decoder. You can also try using more complex latent space distributions (for example, hierarchical VAEs) or using convolutional layers for image data to improve reconstruction quality.

- **Latent Space Overcompression:** Sometimes, the VAE may overcompress the information into the latent space, leading to a loss of important features and poor generative performance.

  o **Solution:** Increase the dimensionality of the latent space or adjust the prior distribution to better match the complexity of the data. A more flexible prior distribution, such as a mixture of Gaussians, can be used to better capture multimodal data distributions.

- **Posterior Collapse:** In some cases, the VAE may ignore the input data and collapse the posterior distribution to the prior, leading to low variability in generated samples.

  o **Solution:** Use warm-up strategies during training, gradually increasing the weight of the KL divergence term in the loss function. This encourages the model to focus more on the reconstruction initially and then prioritize the regularization of the latent space as training progresses.

- **Lack of Data Diversity:** Insufficient diversity in the training data can lead to a biased latent space representation and limit the VAE's ability to generate diverse samples.

  o **Solution:** Augment the training data or collect more diverse samples to better represent the underlying data distribution. Data augmentation techniques such as rotation, scaling, and translation can help increase the diversity of the training set.

- **Uninformative Latent Space:** The learned latent space may not exhibit meaningful semantic features or smooth transitions between samples.

  o **Solution:** Implement techniques like variational autoencoder loss annealing or beta-VAE, which introduce hyperparameters to control the trade-off between the reconstruction and regularization objectives, allowing for a more interpretable and informative latent space.

- **Computational Complexity:** VAEs can be computationally intensive, especially for large datasets or complex architectures.

  - o **Solution:** Use techniques like **Stochastic Gradient Variational Bayes (SGVB)** or amortized inference to efficiently estimate the gradients. Additionally, consider using distributed training or hardware accelerators (for example, GPUs or TPUs) to speed up the training process.

Addressing these common issues while training a VAE can significantly improve the model's performance and generative capabilities. It is essential to experiment with different hyperparameters, loss functions, and regularization techniques to find the best configuration for your specific dataset and task.

Missing data handling during generation

Handling missing data during generation in a VAE is a challenging task, as traditional VAEs are designed to work with complete data. However, there are several tricks and techniques that can be used to deal with missing data during the generation process. Here are some common approaches:

- **Imputation with mean or mode:** One simple technique is to impute missing data with either the mean or mode of the corresponding feature in the training dataset. While straightforward, this method may not fully capture the underlying data distribution and could lead to biased imputations.

- **Masking the input:** During generation, you can mask out the missing features by setting them to a placeholder value (for example, zero or a specific value that indicates missingness). The VAE will then generate samples without considering the masked features.

- **Conditional VAE (CVAE):** CVAE extends the traditional VAE to handle conditional data, including scenarios with missing data. During generation, the CVAE takes both the complete and incomplete data as input, allowing it to generate samples conditioned on the observed features and generate missing features accordingly.

- **Multiple imputations:** This technique involves generating multiple imputed versions of the incomplete data and then averaging the predictions across these imputed datasets. Each imputed dataset can be generated using different methods, such as mean imputation, mode imputation, or imputations from a conditional VAE.

- **Bayesian VAE (B-VAE):** Bayesian VAEs incorporate Bayesian techniques to handle missing data. By modeling the missing data as additional latent variables, B-VAEs can capture the uncertainty associated with the missingness during generation.

- **Autoencoder with GAN (GAN-AE):** GAN-AEs combine the traditional VAE with **Generative Adversarial Networks (GAN)**. GANs can help improve the generation process by capturing complex data distributions, even with missing data.

- **Data augmentation:** Data augmentation techniques can be used to artificially introduce missing data during training. This can help the VAE learn to generate plausible samples even in the presence of missing data during the generation phase.

- **Transformer-based VAEs:** Transformer-based VAE architectures, such as VQ-VAE-2 or TransVAE, can effectively handle missing data by using self-attention mechanisms to capture dependencies between features. These models are capable of filling in the missing values effectively during the generation process.

- **Joint VAE (JVAE):** JVAEs are designed to handle multiple datasets with shared latent spaces. This can be useful when dealing with missing data in different parts of the dataset, allowing the model to capture correlations between the features.

Each of these tricks has its strengths and limitations, and the choice of method will depend on the specific characteristics of your data and the problem you are trying to solve. It is essential to carefully consider the trade-offs and test different techniques to determine the most suitable approach for handling missing data in your VAE-based models.

Optimization techniques

Optimization techniques are crucial for training VAEs effectively. Here are some optimization techniques commonly used in VAE training:

- **Gradient clipping:** Gradient clipping is a technique used to prevent exploding gradients during backpropagation. It involves scaling down gradients if their norm exceeds a specified threshold.

- **Learning rate scheduling:** Instead of using a fixed learning rate throughout training, learning rate scheduling adjusts the learning rate over time. Common scheduling strategies include reducing the learning rate gradually or based on certain conditions, such as a plateau in the validation loss.

- **Adam optimizer:** The Adam optimizer is an adaptive learning rate optimization algorithm that combines the benefits of AdaGrad and RMSprop. It is commonly used for training VAEs due to its efficiency and adaptability to different datasets.

- **RMSprop optimizer:** RMSprop is an adaptive learning rate optimization algorithm that uses a moving average of squared gradients to adjust the learning rate. It helps stabilize training and prevent rapid oscillations in the learning process.

- **Variational inference with Monte Carlo (MC) Sampling:** Since the KL divergence term in the VAE loss involves an expectation, it is often approximated using MC sampling. MC sampling involves drawing multiple samples from the encoder's distribution to estimate the expectation more accurately.

- **Reparameterization trick:** The reparameterization trick is a key component of training VAEs. It involves transforming the random samples from the encoder's distribution using a differentiable function. This allows backpropagation to be performed through the sampling process, making it possible to train the model end-to-end using gradient-based optimization.

- **Importance weighting:** Importance weighting is a technique used to address the mismatch between the true posterior and the approximated posterior. It involves reweighting the KL divergence term to account for the discrepancy between the true posterior and the variational distribution.

- **Early stopping:** Early stopping involves monitoring the validation loss during training and stopping the training process when the validation loss stops improving. This prevents overfitting and helps find the optimal model with good generalization performance.

- **Regularization techniques:** Various regularization techniques can be applied to the loss function, such as weight decay (L2 regularization) or dropout. Regularization helps prevent overfitting and improve the generalization ability of the VAE.

- **Beta-VAE:** Beta-VAE introduces a hyperparameter beta that controls the trade-off between the reconstruction loss and the KL divergence term in the ELBO. This allows the model to focus more on the reconstruction or the regularization objective, influencing the interpretability and expressiveness of the learned latent space.

Remember that the effectiveness of these optimization techniques may vary depending on the specific VAE architecture, dataset, and training settings. Experimenting with different combinations of these techniques can help find the best configuration for your particular use case.

Conclusion

In the previous chapters, we laid the groundwork for understanding VAEs and their role in generating data representations. Throughout this chapter, we explored advanced techniques that elevated the capabilities of VAEs, delving into architectural choices such as convolutional or recurrent networks for effective handling of different data types. Emphasis was placed on the significance of **Kullback-Leibler** (**KL**) divergence in measuring latent space and prior distribution similarity. Additionally, we addressed the crucial challenge of dealing with missing data in VAEs. Through hands-on training on the MNIST Fashion and MNIST dataset, we visualized latent spaces and studied the impact of prior distributions on generative processes. As a result, we mastered advanced VAE techniques, unlocking their full potential.

In the next chapter, we will learn about fundamentals of designing new age generative vision transformers.

## CHAPTER 8

Fundamental of Designing New Age Generative Vision Transformer

Introduction

In this chapter, we delve into the world of transformers, a class of neural networks that have revolutionized the field of natural language processing and are now making significant strides in computer vision. We start by exploring the basic concepts and principles of transformers, including self-attention mechanisms and the transformer architecture. We then move on to discuss generative transformers and the key differences between them and regular transformers.

Next, we cover different types of attention, including self-attention, cross attention, and Multi headed Attention, and their specific applications in Image processing. We also explore the math behind the transformer architecture, including positional encoding.

Structure

In this chapter, we will go over the following topics:

- The evolution
- Difference between VAE, GANs and Transformers
- Vision Transformer

- Understanding self-attention

- NLP vs vision

- Architectural attention

- When to use which architectural attention

- Functional attention

- When to use which functional attention

Objectives

By the end of this chapter, readers will have a solid understanding of transformers, their underlying principles, and their various applications in natural language processing and computer vision. They will also have the necessary knowledge to build, train, and fine-tune transformer models for their own use cases. The readers will gain a comprehensive introduction to transformers as a class of neural networks. This includes explaining their significance in revolutionizing natural language processing and their current applications in computer vision. Then, we will explore fundamental transformer concepts, delve into the basic principles and key components of transformers, such as self-attention mechanisms and the transformer architecture. This chapter will cover generative transformers and highlight the main differences between regular transformers and those designed for generative tasks. Apart from this, the reader will also be able to analyze different types of attention, such as self-attention, cross-attention, and multi-headed attention, and elucidate their specific applications in image processing.

Lastly, we will explore transformer math and positional encoding.

The evolution

The Transformer model, initially designed for language translation, uses an encoder to process input language sequences into embeddings and a decoder to generate translated output sequences by considering previous outputs with a right shift. The model's training relies on ground-truth output sequences without the right shift, refer to the following figure:

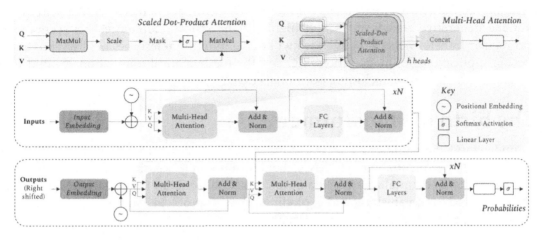

Figure 8.1: *Architecture and building blocks of the Transformer Model*
Source: https://arxiv.org/pdf/2101.01169.pdf

In the rapidly evolving field of artificial intelligence, there are pivotal moments when groundbreaking technologies redefine the landscape of machine learning. One such transformative innovation is the advent of transformers, a class of neural networks that has revolutionized the way we process and understand natural language. Originally introduced by *Vaswani* et al. in 2017, transformers have since become the cornerstone of numerous state-of-the-art language models, propelling the field of **Natural Language Processing (NLP)** to new heights.

The primary motivation behind the development of transformers was to address the limitations of traditional **Recurrent Neural Networks (RNN)** and **Convolutional Neural Networks (CNN)** when dealing with sequential data, such as text. Traditional models faced challenges in capturing long-range dependencies and contextual information efficiently, leading to difficulties in handling complex language tasks. The emergence of transformers marked a paradigm shift, leveraging self-attention mechanisms to process sequences in parallel, allowing for global context awareness and more robust representations of the input data.

Over the years, transformers have demonstrated exceptional performance in various NLP tasks, including machine translation, sentiment analysis, question-answering, language modeling, and more. The immense success of transformer-based models, such as **Bidirectional Encoder Representations from Transformers (BERT)** and **Generative Pre-trained Transformer (GPT)**, has become the driving force behind state-of-the-art NLP systems. However, the impact of transformers extends beyond NLP, making significant strides in computer vision and other fields as well.

This chapter delves into the world of transformers, aiming to unravel their inner workings, discuss their key components and principles, and explore their applications in both NLP and computer vision. We begin by explaining the basic concepts of transformers, including self-attention mechanisms and the transformer architecture. We will then examine generative transformers and highlight the crucial differences between them and regular transformers. Moreover, we will delve into different types of attention, their specific applications in image processing, and the mathematical foundations behind the transformer architecture, including positional encoding.

The birth of transformers

To understand the significance of transformers, it is essential to revisit the challenges faced by earlier sequential models. RNNs held promise in processing sequential data due to their ability to maintain hidden states and pass information through time. However, RNNs suffered from vanishing and exploding gradient problems, limiting their ability to capture long-range dependencies effectively.

CNNs, on the other hand, were highly successful in computer vision tasks due to their ability to exploit local patterns in data. However, they were not naturally suited to sequential data processing and lacked the contextual understanding required for complex language tasks. As a result, researchers sought to develop a novel architecture that would overcome these limitations and unlock the potential of sequential data processing.

The breakthrough came in the form of "Attention Is All You Need," a seminal paper by Vaswani et al., which introduced the transformer architecture. Transformers replaced recurrent connections with self-attention mechanisms, enabling the model to attend to all positions in the input sequence simultaneously. This marked a significant departure from RNNs, allowing for parallel processing and more efficient information flow, making it particularly well-suited for long-range dependencies in sequential data.

Overview of transformer architectures

At the heart of the transformer architecture, lies the concept of self-attention, which forms the core building block of transformer models. Self-attention allows the model to weigh the significance of different elements within the input sequence concerning each other, producing contextualized representations that capture dependencies across the entire sequence. This mechanism enables transformers to process input data in parallel, making them highly scalable and efficient.

The transformer architecture consists of an encoder-decoder framework, where each component comprises multiple layers of self-attention and feed-forward neural networks. The encoder processes the input sequence, generating rich contextual embeddings, while the decoder leverages these embeddings to generate the output sequence, one step at a time. This architecture facilitates a wide range of tasks, from language translation to text generation, all within the same unified framework.

Natural Language Processing (NLP) transformers are composed of several key components:

- **Input embeddings**: They convert tokens (words or subwords) into vectors of continuous values that represent the starting point for processing language.

- **Positional encodings**: Since transformers do not have an inherent sense of order or sequence, positional encodings are added to input embeddings to give the model information about the position of each token within the sequence.

- **Encoder layers**: Each encoder layer consists of two sub-layers: a multi-head self-attention mechanism and a position-wise fully connected feed-forward network. Layer normalization is applied before and after each sub-layer, with residual connections around each of the two sub-layers.

- **Multi-head self-attention**: This mechanism allows the transformer to focus on different parts of the input sequence when processing each token. It does this multiple times in parallel, allowing the model to capture a variety of relationships between tokens.

- **Feed-forward networks**: These networks apply transformations to the output of the attention mechanism and are the same across different positions but use different parameters from layer to layer.

- **Output layer**: In a decoder, the output layer typically generates probabilities over the target vocabulary, often using a softmax function. For models that only have an encoder (like BERT), the output layer can vary depending on the task (e.g., classification, entity recognition).

- **Decoder layers** (for encoder-decoder models like the original Transformer): Each decoder layer has an additional sub-layer for cross-attention, where the decoder attends to the encoder's output.

- **Vision Transformers (ViTs)** represent a class of models adapting the principles of transformers, originally conceived for NLP, to the domain of computer vision. Here are the core components:

  o **Patch embedding:** ViTs begin by dividing an input image into fixed-size patches. These patches are then flattened and linearly projected into embeddings, akin to tokens in NLP. This process converts the 2D spatial image data into a sequence of 1D tokens suitable for processing by a transformer.

  o **Positional encoding:** To retain the positional information lost during patch embedding, ViTs add positional encodings to the patch embeddings. This step ensures the model can account for the location of each patch within the image.

  o **Transformer encoder:** This consists of alternating layers of multi-head self-attention and feed-forward neural networks. The self-attention mechanism allows the model to weigh the importance of different patches relative to one another, capturing both local and global relationships.

o **Multi-head self-attention:** The transformer encoder uses multi-head self-attention to allow the model to focus on different parts of the image simultaneously, enabling it to capture a diverse range of features.

o **Feed-forward neural networks:** Positioned between self-attention layers, these networks apply further transformations to the sequence of patch embeddings.

o **Layer normalization:** Normalization techniques are employed within the encoder to stabilize learning and improve convergence.

o **Classification head:** At the top of the transformer, a classification head (often a simple linear layer) is used to make predictions based on the encoded image representations.

Together, these components allow ViTs to process images in a manner that parallels how transformers process sequential data, leveraging the power of self-attention to model complex dependencies and relationships within visual data.

The scaled dot-product attention is a key component within the multi-head self-attention mechanism of transformers, including ViTs. It operates on the principle of mapping a query (Q) against a set of keys (K) and values (V), which in the context of ViTs are derived from the patch embeddings.

Here is how it works:

- **Dot product**: Each query is compared to all keys by computing the dot product between them. This step measures the similarity between each query and all the keys, resulting in a score that reflects how much focus to place on corresponding values.

- **Scaling**: The dot product scores are scaled down by the square root of the dimension of the keys. This scaling factor prevents the softmax function, which comes next, from having extremely small gradients when the dimensionality of the keys is large, which would make learning inefficient.

- **Softmax**: The scaled scores are then passed through a softmax function, which converts them into a probability distribution. The result is a set of weights that sum to one, reflecting the relative importance of each value as dictated by the query-key similarity.

- **Output**: Finally, the softmax weights are used to take a weighted sum of the values. The output of this operation represents the input sequence with attention applied, where each element is now a composition of information from other parts of the sequence weighted by their relevance.

Applications in NLP

Transformers quickly gained traction in the NLP community due to their exceptional performance on a multitude of language tasks. Pre-trained transformer models like BERT,

GPT, and RoBERTa have achieved groundbreaking results on benchmarks, surpassing traditional methods by a wide margin. The concept of transfer learning, wherein a model is pre-trained on a vast corpus of data and then fine-tuned for specific tasks, proved to be a game-changer in NLP. By leveraging the pre-trained language representations, transformers achieved state-of-the-art results with minimal task-specific fine-tuning.

The success of transformers in NLP can be attributed to their ability to capture deep contextual relationships between words, resulting in more informative and contextually grounded embeddings. This capability significantly enhanced the model's understanding of the underlying semantics of language, enabling better performance on tasks like sentiment analysis, text classification, and named entity recognition.

Generative transformers and language modeling

Generative transformers expanded the scope of transformer applications to language generation tasks, such as text completion, machine translation, and text summarization. These models leveraged the transformer architecture in an autoregressive manner, where the model generates output tokens one at a time, conditioned on the previously generated tokens. This approach made it possible to generate coherent and contextually relevant sequences of text, giving rise to impressive language models.

GPT models, in particular, sparked significant interest in language modeling. By pre-training on a vast corpus of text data and then fine-tuning for specific tasks, GPT models achieved remarkable performance on various language generation benchmarks. The concept of *attention masking* played a crucial role in the success of generative transformers, ensuring that the model attends only to the relevant context while generating each token in the sequence.

Transformer in computer vision

While transformers initially gained prominence in NLP, researchers soon realized their potential in computer vision tasks as well. CNNs had long been the go-to architecture for image processing, but transformers offered a fresh perspective, allowing for more extensive global context awareness and long-range dependencies.

One of the key advancements in applying transformers to computer vision was the introduction of the ViT by *Dosovitskiy et al*. ViT demonstrated that transformers could effectively process images by treating them as sequences of patches, leveraging the same self-attention mechanisms that had revolutionized NLP.

The success of ViT opened the door to various applications of transformers in computer vision, including image classification, object detection, and semantic segmentation. Researchers also explored hybrid architectures that combined CNNs and transformers, capitalizing on the strengths of both approaches to achieve even better performance.

The introduction of transformers has undoubtedly transformed the landscape of natural language processing and computer vision. Their ability to capture complex dependencies, process input in parallel, and leverage pre-trained representations has led to groundbreaking performance on a wide range of tasks. From machine translation to image classification, transformers have proven their versatility and efficiency, earning their place as one of the most influential advancements in the field of artificial intelligence.

In this chapter, we have set out to explore the fascinating world of transformers. We have examined the architecture, the critical concepts behind self-attention mechanisms, and the applications of transformers in both NLP and computer vision. Furthermore, we have touched upon the emergence of generative transformers and their impact on language modeling tasks. By delving into the math and positional encoding, we have attempted to provide a comprehensive understanding and building a VAE with Dirichlet distribution Non-CNN

Difference between VAE, GANs, and Transformers

Transformers, GAN, and VAE are all powerful generative models that have been significant breakthroughs in the field of artificial intelligence. Each model operates differently and has distinct characteristics. In this explanation, we will delve into the differences between transformers, GANs, and VAEs, and highlight their respective strengths and limitations.

Transformers

Transformers are a class of neural networks that excel at sequence-to-sequence tasks, such as natural language processing and language translation. They were introduced by Vaswani et al. in the paper *Attention Is All You Need* in 2017. The transformer architecture employs self-attention mechanisms to capture long-range dependencies and build context-aware embeddings of the input sequence. It comprises an encoder-decoder framework with multiple layers of self-attention and feed-forward neural networks.

The key components of transformers are:

- **Self-attention mechanism:** The self-attention mechanism allows each element in the input sequence to attend to all other elements, producing weighted context-aware representations. The attention score for each pair of elements is calculated using three learned matrices - Query (Q), Key (K), and Value (V). The output of self-attention is obtained by summing the values weighted by the attention scores.

- **Transformer architecture:** The transformer architecture employs a stack of encoder and decoder layers. The encoder processes the input sequence, while the decoder generates the output sequence, conditioned on the encoder's representations. Each layer contains a combination of self-attention and feed-forward neural networks.

- **Positional encoding:** Since transformers process input sequences in parallel, they lack inherent positional information present in sequential data. To address this, positional encoding is added to the input embeddings, providing the model with the sequence order information.

The training of transformers typically involves two stages: pre-training and fine-tuning. In pre-training, the model is trained on a large corpus of text data to learn rich language representations. These pre-trained representations can then be fine-tuned on specific downstream tasks, achieving state-of-the-art performance on various NLP tasks.

Generative Adversarial Networks

Generative Adversarial Networks (GANs), introduced by *Ian Goodfellow* in 2014, are a class of generative models that involve two neural networks in a game-like setting. The generator network takes random noise as input and attempts to generate synthetic samples that resemble real data. On the other hand, the discriminator network tries to distinguish between real data and the synthetic data produced by the generator.

The key components of GANs are:

- **Generator network:** The generator network takes random noise as input and transforms it into synthetic data. The goal of the generator is to produce samples that are indistinguishable from real data.

- **Discriminator network:** The discriminator network is a binary classifier that distinguishes between real data from the training set and synthetic data generated by the generator. It is trained to maximize its ability to correctly classify real and fake data.

- **Adversarial training:** The training process of GANs involves a minimax game. The generator tries to minimize the discriminator's ability to distinguish between real and fake data, while the discriminator tries to maximize its accuracy in classifying real and fake data.

The training of GANs can be challenging and unstable due to the adversarial nature of the process. Achieving a Nash Equilibrium, where the generator produces realistic samples and the discriminator cannot differentiate between real and fake data, is the desired outcome.

Variational autoencoders

Variational Autoencoders (VAEs), introduced by Kingma and Welling in 2013, are generative models that utilize a probabilistic approach to learn a latent representation of the input data. VAEs are a type of autoencoder where the encoder network maps the input data to a probabilistic distribution in the latent space, and the decoder network reconstructs the input data from the latent space.

The key components of VAEs are:

- **Encoder network:** The encoder network maps the input data to a probability distribution in the latent space. It computes the mean and variance vectors, which are then used to sample latent vectors from a Gaussian distribution.

- **Latent space:** The latent space represents the low-dimensional space where the data is encoded. The latent vectors are sampled from the Gaussian distribution defined by the mean and variance vectors obtained from the encoder.

- **Decoder network:** The decoder network takes the sampled latent vectors as input and reconstructs the data back into the original input space. The decoder is trained to generate data that is as close as possible to the original input.

- **Variational loss:** VAEs use a variational loss function that encourages the latent space to follow a specific prior distribution, typically a standard Gaussian. This regularization ensures that the latent space is continuous and smooth, allowing for meaningful interpolation between data points.

The training of VAEs involves optimizing the variational lower bound, also known as the **Evidence Lower Bound** (**ELBO**), which is a combination of the reconstruction loss (measuring how well the decoder can reconstruct the input) and the **Kullback-Leibler** (**KL**) divergence (measuring how closely the encoder's distribution matches the prior distribution).

Differences and applications

Let us now go over the differences and applications.

- **Data type and applications:** Transformers are primarily designed for sequential data, such as natural language text, and excel in NLP tasks like machine translation and text generation. GANs and VAEs, on the other hand, are versatile and can be applied to a wide range of data types, including images, audio, and video.

- **Generative capability:** GANs are known for their ability to generate highly realistic and diverse samples, making them popular for tasks like image synthesis and style transfer. VAEs prioritize the reconstruction and representation of input data and often produce less diverse but more structured and interpretable outputs. Transformers can also generate text but require specific architectures, such as autoregressive transformers.

- **Training mechanism:** Transformers are typically trained in a supervised manner with large amounts of labeled data, followed by fine-tuning on specific tasks. GANs and VAEs, on the other hand, are trained in an unsupervised manner and do not require labeled data during the training phase.

- **Latent space:** Transformers do not explicitly learn a latent space representation of the data. GANs and VAEs, on the other hand, explicitly learn a continuous and probabilistic latent space, which allows for interpolation and smooth exploration of data in the latent space.

Vision Transformer

The **Vision Transformers (ViT)** are a groundbreaking architecture that extends the transformer model's success in natural language processing to the domain of computer vision. Introduced by *Dosovitskiy* et al. in the paper *An Image is Worth 16x16 Words: Transformers for Image Recognition at Scale* in 2020, vision transformers have rapidly become a key technique in image classification and other computer vision tasks.

Traditionally, CNNs have been the dominant architecture in computer vision due to their effectiveness in capturing local patterns and spatial hierarchies in images. However, transformers offer a fresh perspective by leveraging the self-attention mechanism to capture global context and long-range dependencies in images. By adopting transformers, vision transformers aim to address the limitations of CNNs and achieve better performance on image recognition tasks.

The key characteristics of vision transformers are as follows:

- **Patch embedding:** Unlike CNNs that process images with small local receptive fields (typically 3x3 or 5x5), vision transformers divide the input image into fixed-size non-overlapping patches. Each patch is then linearly transformed into a lower-dimensional vector, forming the initial embeddings. This patch-based approach enables transformers to process images as sequences of 1D data, making them computationally efficient and scalable.

- **Positional embedding:** As with natural language processing, transformers require information about the sequence order to process data effectively. In vision transformers, positional embeddings are added to the patch embeddings to provide the model with spatial information about the image. These positional embeddings allow the transformer to understand the relative position of different patches and capture the spatial layout of the image.

- **Transformer encoder:** The core of the vision transformer is the transformer encoder, which comprises multiple layers of self-attention and feed-forward neural networks. The self-attention mechanism allows the model to capture the relationships between patches in the image, capturing both local and global context information. This enables vision transformers to reason about complex structures and long-range dependencies in images.

- **Classification head:** Similar to traditional CNN-based models, vision transformers incorporate a classification head, typically a simple feed-forward neural network, to make predictions based on the encoded image representations. The model is trained using standard supervised learning with labeled data.

The success of vision transformers in image classification tasks has been impressive, often rivaling or surpassing state-of-the-art performance achieved by CNN-based models. Vision transformers have demonstrated strong generalization capabilities, even with fewer labeled training samples, making them highly attractive in scenarios with limited annotated data.

However, vision transformers have certain limitations as well. They require substantial computational resources, especially when processing high-resolution images, due to their quadratic complexity with respect to the number of patches. Moreover, vision transformers may not perform optimally on tasks that require detailed spatial reasoning, such as object detection or instance segmentation, where CNNs are still widely used.

To address some of the limitations and to leverage the strengths of both architectures, researchers have also explored hybrid models that combine the power of CNNs and vision transformers. These hybrid approaches aim to benefit from the strong local feature extraction capabilities of CNNs while integrating the global context understanding of transformers.

Vision transformers represent a significant advancement in computer vision, leveraging the transformer architecture's ability to capture global context and long-range dependencies in images. They have shown promising results in image classification tasks and opened up new possibilities for applying transformers in computer vision domains. As research in this area continues, we can expect further refinements and innovative applications of vision transformers in various computer vision tasks.

Understanding self-attention

Understanding self-attention is crucial to comprehending transformers fully because self-attention is the fundamental building block of the transformer model. Transformers rely on self-attention mechanisms to capture long-range dependencies and build context-aware representations of input sequences, be it natural language text in NLP or image patches in computer vision. Self-attention is what allows transformers to process sequences in parallel, resulting in more efficient and scalable models compared to traditional sequential architectures like RNNs.

Here are several key reasons why understanding self-attention is vital to understanding transformers:

- **Core mechanism:** Self-attention is at the core of the transformer architecture. It enables the model to attend to all positions in the input sequence simultaneously and weigh the importance of each element concerning all other elements. This mechanism allows the transformer to build a global context representation, facilitating more informed decisions and capturing dependencies over long distances.

- **Context-aware representations:** Through self-attention, the transformer generates context-aware representations for each element in the sequence. The attention mechanism computes weights for different elements, emphasizing more relevant information and de-emphasizing less relevant information. This contextual understanding is essential in various tasks, such as understanding the context of a word in a sentence or capturing relationships between image patches.

- **Parallel processing:** Unlike traditional sequential models, which process data one element at a time, self-attention allows transformers to operate in parallel. This parallel processing is more computationally efficient and accelerates training and inference, making transformers more scalable and suitable for large-scale applications.

- **Long-range dependencies:** Capturing long-range dependencies is a significant challenge in sequential tasks, such as language translation or image understanding. Self-attention addresses this issue by allowing the model to attend to any position in the sequence, irrespective of distance. This property is particularly valuable for modeling complex relationships in sequences.

- **Interpretability:** Self-attention is inherently interpretable since the attention scores indicate how much each element depends on or influences other elements. This level of interpretability is advantageous in understanding the model's decision-making process and identifying the salient parts of the input sequence that contribute most to the output.

- **Generalization:** The ability of transformers to capture long-range dependencies and context has led to their impressive generalization capabilities. Transformers can learn rich representations from large amounts of data and transfer this knowledge effectively to new tasks with minimal fine-tuning.

- **Multi-modal applications:** Understanding self-attention in transformers is valuable beyond just NLP or computer vision. Self-attention can be applied in multi-modal scenarios where information from different modalities, such as text, image, and audio, needs to be fused effectively. The self-attention mechanism allows transformers to capture inter-modal relationships, making them suitable for multimodal tasks.

Self-attention is the core mechanism that empowers transformers to revolutionize natural language processing, computer vision, and other sequential data tasks. It enables transformers to process data in parallel, capture long-range dependencies, build context-aware representations, and generalize effectively. By grasping the concept of self-attention, one can gain deeper insights into the workings of transformers and appreciate their significance in advancing the state-of-the-art in AI applications.

NLP vs vision

Let us now understand the NLP Transformer and Vision Transformer using equations.

ViTs and NLP Transformers share the same foundational architecture but are adapted to different types of data: images for ViTs and text for NLP Transformers. The main differences lie in the input preparation and the nature of the data they are designed to process:

- **Input representation**: In NLP, words or subwords are tokenized and represented as vectors, while in ViTs, images are split into patches and each patch is flattened and linearly projected into a vector (patch embedding). Positional encodings are added to maintain sequence information in NLP Transformers, while in ViTs, they preserve spatial information.

- **Data nature**: Text data in NLP is inherently sequential, with a clear order among the tokens. ViTs must impose a sequence structure on image data, which is naturally 2D and spatial. Thus, ViTs must learn both the local structure within individual patches and the global structure of how patches relate to each other to understand the image.

- **Attention scope**: In NLP Transformers, the self-attention mechanism models relationships between words regardless of their position, suitable for capturing linguistic structure. ViTs must learn to apply attention across a 2D space projected into a sequence, capturing the visual patterns that emerge from the arrangement and features within image patches.

Despite these differences, both models utilize the transformer's self-attention mechanism to weigh the importance of different parts of the input, allowing for dynamic feature extraction based on the context within the data—whether it be words in a sentence or patches in an image

NLP transformer

The NLP transformer, originally introduced in the paper *"Attention Is All You Need"* by *Vaswani* et al. in 2017, is a revolutionary model for natural language processing tasks, such as machine translation, language modeling, and sentiment analysis. It utilizes self-attention mechanisms to process sequential data efficiently and capture long-range dependencies. The main components of the NLP Transformer are the self-attention mechanism and the feed-forward neural networks.

Self-attention mechanism

The self-attention mechanism allows the model to weigh the importance of different words in the input sequence concerning each other. The attention scores are computed by comparing the similarity of each word to every other word in the sequence. The weighted sum of the values (representations) of the words, based on their attention scores, produces context-aware word representations.

The self-attention mechanism can be formulated as follows:

Given an input sequence of length N, represented as a set of word embeddings:

$$X = \{x_1, x_2, ..., x_n\}$$

To compute the attention scores (α) for each word in the sequence, we calculate the dot product between the Query (Q), Key (K), and Value (V) matrices:

$$Q = XW\_q$$
$$K = XW\_k$$
$$V = XW\_v$$

Where, W_q, W_k, and W_v are learnable weight matrices.

The attention scores (α) are computed using the scaled dot product attention mechanism:

$$\alpha = softmax(QK^T / \sqrt{d\_k})$$

Where, d_k is the dimension of the Query and Key matrices.

To get the context-aware word representations, we calculate the weighted sum of the Value (V) matrix:

$$context = \alpha V$$

Feed-forward neural networks

After obtaining the context-aware word representations, they are passed through a feed-forward neural network to further refine the features and learn complex patterns in the data.

The feed-forward neural network can be represented as:

$$FFN\_output = ReLU(contextW\_1 + b\_1)W\_2 + b\_2$$

Where, W_1, b_1, W_2, and b_2 are learnable weight matrices and bias terms, and ReLU is the activation function.

The NLP Transformer comprises multiple layers of self-attention and feed-forward neural networks, enabling the model to process the input sequence in parallel, efficiently capturing long-range dependencies, and building context-aware representations.

Vision transformer

The ViT extends the transformer model to computer vision tasks. Instead of processing images with traditional convolutional layers, ViT divides the image into fixed-size patches and processes them as a sequence using transformers. The main components of the Vision Transformer are patch embeddings, positional embeddings, and the transformer encoder.

Patch embeddings

The input image is divided into non-overlapping fixed-size patches, and each patch is linearly transformed into a lower-dimensional vector to form the initial embeddings. These patch embeddings are then fed into the transformer model.

The patch embedding process can be formulated as:

Given an input image I of size $H \times W$, divided into $P \times P$ non-overlapping patches:

$$P = \{p_1, p_2, ..., p_p\}$$

Where, p_i is the embedding vector for the i-th patch:

Figure 8.2: Visualizing Image patches

Positional embeddings

To provide spatial information to the model, positional embeddings are added to the patch embeddings. These positional embeddings help the transformer understand the relative positions of different patches in the image.

The positional embedding process can be represented as:

$$X = P + PE$$

Where, X is the input sequence with positional embeddings, P is the patch embeddings, and PE is the positional encoding.

Transformer encoder

The transformer encoder processes the input sequence with self-attention and feed-forward neural networks to capture global context and relationships between patches in the image.

The transformer encoder can be formulated similar to the NLP Transformer:

Given the input sequence X:

$$context = SelfAttention(X) + FFN(X)$$

Where, *SelfAttention(X)* is the self-attention mechanism to calculate attention scores and context-aware representations, and *FFN(X)* is the feed-forward neural network to refine the features.

The Vision Transformer can achieve impressive results in image classification tasks, demonstrating the ability of transformers to handle computer vision data effectively by capturing long-range dependencies and global context.

Architectural attention

Attention mechanisms play a crucial role in various machine learning models, especially in sequence-to-sequence tasks like natural language processing and computer vision. Here are four types of attention mechanisms commonly used, along with their equations.

Dot product attention

The dot product attention is the most basic and commonly used attention mechanism. Given a query vector (q) and a set of key vectors (k), the attention score between the query and each key is computed as the dot product between them.

Attention Score (α) for each key (k_i) is calculated as:

$$\alpha_i = q \cdot k_i$$

Where, denotes the dot product.

Scaled dot product attention

Scaled dot product attention is an improvement over the dot product attention to address issues with vanishing/exploding gradients. It scales the dot product by dividing it by the square root of the dimension of the key vectors (d_k).

Attention Score (α) for each key (k_i) is calculated as:

$\alpha_i = (q \cdot k_i) / \sqrt{d\_k}$

where, d_k is the dimension of the key vectors.

Additive attention

Additive attention computes the attention scores by passing the query and key vectors through separate learnable feed-forward neural networks. The attention score is then obtained by combining the results of these neural networks.

Attention Score (α) for each key (k_i) is calculated as:

$$\alpha_i = softmax(v^T \cdot tanh(W\_q \cdot q + W\_k \cdot k_i))$$

Where, W_q and W_k are learnable weight matrices, and v is a learnable vector.

Multi-head attention

Multi-head attention is an extension of the attention mechanism that uses multiple sets of learnable weight matrices to compute attention scores in parallel. It helps the model to capture different types of information and increase its representational capacity.

Multi-head attention is calculated as:

$$MultiHead(q, k, v) = Concat(head\_1, head\_2, ..., head\_h) \cdot W\_o$$

Where, $head\_i = Attention(q\ W\_\{qi\}, k \cdot W\_\{ki\}, v \cdot W\_\{vi\})$

W_o, $W\_\{qi\}$, $W\_\{ki\}$, and $W\_\{vi\}$ are learnable weight matrices.

In the preceding equations, q represents the query vector, k represents the set of key vectors, v represents the set of value vectors, and α represents the attention scores. The attention scores are further normalized using the softmax function to ensure that the model allocates appropriate attention weights to each element in the input sequence.

These attention mechanisms are at the core of transformer-based models and have contributed significantly to their success in various sequence-to-sequence tasks, such as machine translation, language modeling, and image processing.

Cross attention

Cross-attention is a type of attention mechanism used in transformer-based models, particularly in sequence-to-sequence tasks, where the model needs to attend to different sets of information between the encoder and decoder components. In such tasks, the encoder processes the input sequence and generates context-aware representations, while the decoder uses these representations to generate the output sequence. Cross-attention allows the decoder to selectively attend to specific parts of the input sequence (encoder outputs) relevant to each step of the decoding process.

The cross-attention mechanism is an extension of the self-attention mechanism, where the query vectors come from the decoder, the key vectors come from the encoder, and the value vectors also come from the encoder. This allows the decoder to focus on different parts of the input sequence based on the context of the generated output.

Mathematically, cross-attention is computed as follows:

Given:

- Decoder query vector (*q_dec*) for a specific decoding step.

- Encoder key vectors (*k_enc*) and value vectors (*v_enc*) representing the context-aware representations of the input sequence.

Compute attention scores

The attention scores (α) for each element in the input sequence (*k_enc*) are calculated by taking the dot product between the decoder query vector (*q_dec*) and the encoder key vectors (*k_enc*).

$$\alpha = softmax(q\_dec \cdot k\_enc^T)$$

Compute cross-attention output

The cross-attention output for the specific decoding step is obtained by the weighted sum of the encoder value vectors (*v_enc*) using the attention scores (*α*) as weights.

$$cross\_attention\_output = \alpha \cdot v\_enc$$

The `cross_attention_output` is then used in the decoder to generate the output for the current decoding step.

In the transformer-based models, cross-attention is applied in the decoder during each decoding step to incorporate the relevant context from the input sequence. This allows the model to generate output sequences that are contextually informed and coherent with respect to the input. By leveraging cross-attention, transformers excel in various sequence-to-sequence tasks, such as machine translation, summarization, and question-answering, where both input and output sequences have variable lengths and require complex dependencies between elements.

When to use which architectural attention

The choice of which attention mechanism to use depends on the specific requirements and characteristics of the task at hand. Different attention mechanisms have distinct strengths and are more suitable for certain scenarios. Here are some guidelines on when to use each type of attention:

- **Self-attention**
  - o Use self-attention in tasks where the input sequence has dependencies within itself, and each element needs to consider the relationships with other elements in the same sequence.
  - o Self-attention is particularly effective in natural language processing tasks, such as language modeling, machine translation, sentiment analysis, and text classification, where the context of each word in a sentence is crucial to understanding the overall meaning.
  - o Also applicable in tasks with sequential data where elements exhibit complex interactions and dependencies.

- **Scaled dot product attention:**
  - o Scaled dot product attention is a commonly used variant of self-attention, and it is generally preferred due to its stability and better handling of vanishing/exploding gradients.
  - o It is suitable for a wide range of tasks where self-attention is required, particularly in transformer-based models.

- **Additive attention:**
  - o Use additive attention when there is a need to model complex interactions and dependencies between elements in the sequence.
  - o It can be a good choice in tasks where simple dot product attention may not sufficiently capture the relationships between elements.
  - o Additive attention is useful in cases where the task's requirements go beyond the capabilities of self-attention mechanisms.

- **Multi-head attention:**
  - o Multi-head attention is useful when the model needs to capture different types of information or attend to different aspects of the input sequence.
  - o It is commonly used in transformer-based models, allowing the model to learn diverse attention patterns and increase representational capacity.
  - o Especially valuable in tasks with multiple subtasks or different levels of granularity in the input data.

- **Cross-attention:**
  - o Use cross-attention in sequence-to-sequence tasks, where the decoder requires access to different parts of the input sequence (encoder outputs) for each decoding step.

o Cross-attention is prevalent in machine translation, summarization, and question-answering tasks, where the decoder needs to align with relevant parts of the input to generate coherent and contextually informed outputs.

o It enables the model to capture the interdependencies between input and output sequences, making it suitable for tasks involving variable-length sequences.

In practice, the choice of attention mechanism often comes down to experimentation and task-specific considerations. It is essential to assess the model's performance and interpretability, taking into account the complexity of the task and the nature of the data. Transformers, with their flexibility in attention mechanisms, have demonstrated outstanding performance across various tasks, and the specific attention mechanism used often plays a crucial role in achieving state-of-the-art results.

Functional attention

In the context of vision, attention mechanisms can be categorized into four types: hard attention, soft attention, global attention, and local attention. These attention mechanisms are used in vision tasks, such as image classification, object detection, and image captioning, to selectively focus on specific regions or patches of the input image.

Hard attention

Hard attention refers to attention mechanisms that perform a discrete and non-differentiable selection of regions or patches from the input image. In hard attention, the model chooses one or a few specific regions to attend to, while ignoring the rest. The selection process is typically based on learned probabilities or through a sampling mechanism. Hard attention can be computationally expensive and challenging to train due to its non-differentiable nature.

Equation: Sampling-based hard attention

Suppose we have an input image represented by a set of feature vectors $F = \{f_1, f_2, ..., f\_n\}$, where n is the number of regions or patches in the image. To perform hard attention, the model selects a specific region (for example, f_i) with the highest probability (or through sampling) and ignores the other regions.

Soft attention

Soft attention, also known as soft spatial attention, is a continuous and differentiable version of attention. It generates a weighted average of the input image features, where each feature's weight is determined by learned attention scores. Soft attention allows the model to attend to all regions simultaneously, with varying degrees of emphasis on each region based on its relevance to the task.

Equation: Soft attention

Given an input image represented by feature vectors $F = \{f_1, f_2, ..., f\_n\}$, and a query vector Q (for example, from the decoder in a sequence-to-sequence task):

Attention Scores (α) are calculated as follows:

$$\alpha\_i = softmax(Q \cdot f\_i)$$

The soft attention output is obtained as the weighted sum of the feature vectors:

$$Soft\_Attention\_Output = \Sigma(\alpha\_i * f\_i)$$

Global attention

Global attention refers to an attention mechanism that attends to all regions or patches in the input image equally. In other words, each feature vector receives the same attention score, effectively giving equal importance to all regions of the image.

Equation: Global attention

Given an input image represented by feature vectors $F = \{f_1, f_2, ..., f\_n\}$, and a query vector Q:

In global attention, all attention scores (α) are set to a constant value, typically $1/n$:

$\alpha\_i = 1/n$, where n is the number of regions or patches in the image.

The global attention output is obtained as the simple average of all feature vectors:

```
Global_Attention_Output = (1/n) * Σf_i
```

Local attention

Local attention focuses on a specific region or a small subset of regions in the input image rather than considering the entire image. Local attention mechanisms are used to handle long-range dependencies efficiently and are particularly useful when dealing with large images.

Equation: local attention

Given an input image represented by feature vectors $F = \{f_1, f_2, ..., f\_n\}$, and a query vector Q:

In local attention, attention scores (α) are computed based on the similarity between the query vector Q and the feature vectors within a defined neighborhood or window around the query vector.

Local_Attention_Output = $\Sigma(\alpha\_i * f\_i)$, where the attention scores (α_i) are calculated based on the similarity between Q and the feature vectors within a local window.

Local attention can be computationally efficient compared to global attention, as it allows the model to focus on a smaller subset of the input image, reducing the number of computations.

Attention mechanisms, such as hard attention, soft attention, global attention, and local attention, provide different ways for models to selectively focus on specific regions or patches in the input image. Each type of attention has its advantages and applications in vision tasks, depending on the specific requirements of the task and the complexity of the input data.

Note: The attentions you mentioned (cross, self, multi-head, and dot) are specifically related to the attention mechanisms used in the transformer architecture. While they share some common principles with hard attention, soft attention, global attention, and local attention, they have distinct characteristics and functions within the context of transformers.

When to use which functional attention

Each type of attention mechanism: hard attention, soft attention, global attention, and local attention, has its specific advantages and applications in vision tasks. The choice of which attention mechanism to use depends on the characteristics of the task, the size and complexity of the input data, and the desired interpretability and computational efficiency. Here are the applications and considerations for each type of attention:

Hard attention

Refer to the following:

- **Applications:**
  - **Image captioning:** Hard attention can be used to selectively attend to specific regions in an image when generating captions. The model can focus on the most relevant parts of the image for describing the content accurately.
  - **Object localization:** Hard attention can be applied in object detection tasks to choose the most salient regions in an image containing the objects of interest.
- **Considerations:**
  - **Computationally expensive:** Hard attention requires a non-differentiable selection process, which can be computationally expensive and difficult to train.

o **Interpretability:** Hard attention provides a clear indication of the selected regions but may not be suitable when the model needs to consider all regions of the image simultaneously.

Soft attention

Refer to the following:

- **Applications:**

  o **Image classification:** Soft attention can be used to assign varying importance to different regions of the image during the classification process. The model can focus on relevant regions to make accurate predictions.

  o **Image captioning:** Soft attention is widely used in image captioning tasks to generate captions by attending to different parts of the image.

- **Considerations:**

  o **Continuous and differentiable:** Soft attention is continuous and differentiable, making it easier to train compared to hard attention.

  o **Global context:** Soft attention allows the model to consider the global context of the image by attending to all regions simultaneously.

Global attention

Refer to the following:

- **Applications:**

  o **Image classification:** Global attention can be used when all regions of the image carry equal importance for the classification task.

  o **Image compression:** Global attention can be used in image compression tasks to summarize the entire image in a single representation.

- **Considerations:**

  o **Equal importance:** Global attention treats all regions of the image equally, which might not be suitable for tasks where specific regions are more informative.

Local attention

Refer to the following:

- **Applications:**

  o **Image segmentation:** Local attention can be applied in image segmentation tasks to focus on specific regions for accurate pixel-wise classification.

o **Image translation:** Local attention can be used in tasks like image-to-image translation, where the model needs to focus on local details to generate realistic outputs.

- **Considerations:**

  o **Efficiency:** Local attention reduces the computational burden by focusing on a smaller subset of the input image.

  o **Handling long-range dependencies:** Local attention is useful when dealing with long-range dependencies in large images without considering the entire image at once.

The choice of attention mechanism depends on the specific requirements of the vision task. Soft attention is the most commonly used and versatile attention mechanism, providing a balance between interpretability, efficiency, and effectiveness. Global attention is suitable when all regions of the image have equal importance, while local attention is efficient for handling long-range dependencies in large images. Hard attention may be useful in specific scenarios requiring discrete selection of regions, but it can be more challenging to train and computationally expensive. As with many machine learning decisions, experimentation and evaluation on the specific task and dataset are crucial to determining the most appropriate attention mechanism.

Conclusion

In this chapter, we explored the transformative impact of transformers in both NLP and computer vision domains. Transformers, powered by self-attention mechanisms, have revolutionized NLP with their ability to capture long-range dependencies and build context-aware representations of sequential data. These models have become the foundation of various language tasks, from machine translation to sentiment analysis, owing to their efficiency in parallel processing and impressive generalization capabilities.

Building on the success of transformers in NLP, researchers extended the concept to ViTs for computer vision tasks. Vision transformers divide input images into fixed-size patches, enabling them to process images as sequences and use self-attention to capture global context. ViTs have showcased remarkable performance in image classification and other vision tasks, rivaling traditional convolutional neural networks. However, researchers have also explored hybrid models that combine the strengths of CNNs and transformers for tasks requiring spatial reasoning.

In conclusion, transformers, fueled by self-attention, have redefined the landscape of NLP and brought powerful advancements to computer vision. Their ability to process sequences efficiently, capture long-range dependencies, and build context-aware representations makes them a versatile and potent tool for various AI applications. By understanding different attention mechanisms and their applications, researchers and practitioners can leverage transformers to tackle diverse tasks and continue advancing the boundaries of artificial intelligence.

In the next chapter, we will delve into a fascinating topic combining AEs and VAEs with transformers to model the STL dataset. Autoencoders are unsupervised learning models used for feature learning and data compression, while VAEs add a probabilistic aspect to AEs, enabling better data generation and exploration of the latent space. Combining these techniques with transformers presents exciting possibilities for image generation, compression, and reconstruction.

Join our book's Discord space

Join the book's Discord Workspace for Latest updates, Offers, Tech happenings around the world, New Release and Sessions with the Authors:

https://discord.bpbonline.com

CHAPTER 9

Implementing Generative Vision Transformer

Introduction

In the rapidly evolving landscape of machine learning and artificial intelligence, the realm of image generation has witnessed remarkable advancements, thanks to novel architectures like Generative Transformers. These cutting-edge models, with their roots in the foundational Transformer architecture, have pushed the boundaries of creative synthesis. This chapter embarks on a journey to explore the nuanced differences between Generative Transformers and conventional Transformers, unraveling their distinctive roles in generating compelling images.

Our exploration begins by delving into the world of **Variational Autoencoders (VAE)** and their application to the intricate STL dataset. VAEs, renowned for their latent feature extraction prowess, provide a stepping stone to understanding the core principles of image generation. We will guide readers through the intricate process of constructing VAE models, emphasizing the fusion of encoder and decoder networks along with loss functions that enable the creation of meaningful latent spaces.

As we traverse the terrain of image synthesis, our chapter takes a transformative turn as we venture to merge the VAE architecture with the transformative power of Generative Transformers. This innovative fusion introduces a paradigm shift, allowing for the learning of complex contextual relationships within latent spaces through the incorporation of self-attention mechanisms and positional encodings. Through this convergence, we illuminate the potential of crafting images that encapsulate both diversity and coherence.

Throughout the chapter, our objective is to provide readers with a comprehensive understanding of the evolution from conventional Transformers to Generative Transformers, equipped with the skills to construct VAE models, and empowered to adapt and refine these models for unparalleled image generation. By the end, readers will not only comprehend the theoretical underpinnings but also wield practical insights into applying these models across a spectrum of real-world applications.

Structure

In this chapter, we will go over the following topics:

- STL dataset
- Developing a VAE model on STL dataset
- Implementation of VAE architecture with TensorFlow
- Pytorch
- Transition from VAE to Generative Transformer Model: Keras Vit Library
- Implementing a Vit model from scratch
- Implementing a Vit model pre trained with ViT model
- Training Pretrained ViT vs ViT scratch
- Examining the Loss Curve
- Optimization for ViT models

Objectives

In this chapter, our primary objective is to explore and understand the fundamental distinctions between Generative Transformers and conventional Transformers, highlighting their key differences and applications within the realm of image generation. We will then delve into VAE models and their application to the STL dataset, emphasizing their capability to capture latent features and generate images. Building upon this foundation, our objective further extends to the conversion of a VAE model into a Generative Transformer model, showcasing the integration of these two powerful architectures to enhance image synthesis.

Throughout the chapter, we will compare Generative Transformers and Transformers. We will thoroughly dissect the distinctions between Generative Transformers and traditional Transformers in terms of architecture, training methodologies, and their respective strengths and weaknesses. We'll construct VAEs for the STL dataset, then transition to Generative Transformer models, adapting VAE components to fit Transformer's self-attention and positional encodings. Our comprehensive evaluation will compare image quality, diversity, and speed against traditional models. We'll also explore real-world applications, demonstrating the model's capability to produce diverse, contextually coherent images. Ultimately, this chapter aims to deepen understanding of Generative Transformers versus traditional models, guide in VAE construction, and reveal the innovative transition to Generative Transformer architecture.

STL dataset

The STL-10 dataset is a widely used benchmark dataset in computer vision and machine learning. It was introduced by *Adam Coates, Honglak Lee*, and *Andrew Ng* in their 2011 paper titled *An Analysis of Single-Layer Networks in Unsupervised Feature Learning*.

The STL-10 dataset is derived from the larger CIFAR-10 dataset, which contains 60,000 32x32 color images belonging to 10 different classes. However, the STL-10 dataset contains a reduced subset of this data, with only 5,000 labeled training images and 8,000 test images. Additionally, the STL-10 dataset includes an unlabeled dataset with 100,000 images that can be used for unsupervised learning tasks.

Key features of the STL-10 dataset

The key features of the STL-10 dataset are as follows:

- **Image dimensions:** Each image in the dataset has a resolution of 96x96 pixels and is in RGB format, meaning it has three color channels (red, green, and blue).

- **Classes:** The STL-10 dataset includes a total of 10 classes, similar to CIFAR-10. However, the labels for the classes are provided only for the training set, while the test set remains unlabeled.

- **Labeled vs. unlabeled data:** The dataset is split into labeled and unlabeled parts. The labeled set contains 5,000 images with class labels for supervised learning tasks. The unlabeled set consists of 100,000 images, which can be used for self-supervised or unsupervised learning approaches.

- **Image diversity:** The dataset is known for its diversity in terms of object appearances, background, and lighting conditions. It poses significant challenges for computer vision models to handle variations in object shapes and sizes.

The STL-10 dataset has been widely used for various research tasks, such as image classification, object recognition, unsupervised learning, self-supervised learning, transfer learning, and few-shot learning. Its popularity stems from the fact that it offers a more challenging and realistic scenario compared to some other datasets due to its higher resolution images and unlabeled data, which encourages the development of more robust and generalized machine learning models.

Developing a VAE model on STL dataset

Creating a VAE from scratch is a complex task that involves designing and training multiple components. Following is a step-by-step guide on building a better VAE model for the STL10 dataset, which consists of 32x32 color images with ten classes (for example, airplane, bird, cat, and so on):

1. **Data preprocessing**

   a. Download and preprocess the STL10 dataset. You can use the torchvision library in Python to do this.

2. **Model architecture**

   a. **Define the encoder architecture:** The encoder will map the input images to a latent space. You can use convolutional layers to capture spatial features.

   b. **Define the decoder architecture:** The decoder will map the latent space back to the original image space. Mirror the encoder's architecture using transpose convolutions (also known as deconvolutions or upsampling layers).

   c. **Define the latent space:** Choose the dimensionality of the latent space (for example, 32, 64, or more). A smaller latent space can lead to more compressed representations but may lose some information.

3. **Loss function:**

   a. Define the VAE loss, which consists of two parts:

      i. **Reconstruction Loss:** Measures the difference between the input and the reconstructed output. Commonly, the **mean squared error** (**MSE**) or binary cross-entropy is used for image data.

      ii. **KL Divergence Loss:** Measures the divergence between the learned latent distribution and the standard normal distribution. This term encourages the latent space to be approximately normally distributed, aiding in better sampling.

4. **Training:**

   a. Combine the encoder and decoder into a single VAE model.

   b. Define an optimizer (for example, Adam) and an appropriate learning rate.

   c. Iterate over the dataset and update the model's weights using backpropagation.

5. **Sampling and Generation:**

   a. After training the VAE, you can sample from the learned latent space and use the decoder to generate new images.

Implementation of VAE architecture with TensorFlow

Here is an implementation of the VAE architecture with TensorFlow:

VAE architecture:

```
import tensorflow as tf
from tensorflow.keras.layers import Input, Conv2D, Flatten, Dense,
Conv2DTranspose, Reshape
from tensorflow.keras.models import Model
import numpy as np
import matplotlib.pyplot as plt
import os
import urllib.request
import tarfile

# Download STL-10 dataset
url = 'http://ai.stanford.edu/~acoates/stl10/stl10_binary.tar.gz'
file_name = 'stl10_binary.tar.gz'

if not os.path.exists(file_name):
    urllib.request.urlretrieve(url, file_name)

# Extract the dataset
tar = tarfile.open(file_name, "r:gz")
tar.extractall()
tar.close()

# Load the dataset
data_dir = 'stl10_binary'
file_names = ['train_X.bin', 'train_y.bin', 'test_X.bin', 'test_y.bin']

x_train_path = os.path.join(data_dir, file_names[0])
y_train_path = os.path.join(data_dir, file_names[1])
x_test_path = os.path.join(data_dir, file_names[2])
y_test_path = os.path.join(data_dir, file_names[3])

x_train = np.fromfile(x_train_path, dtype=np.uint8).reshape(-1, 3, 96, 96).
transpose(0, 2, 3, 1)
```

```python
y_train = np.fromfile(y_train_path, dtype=np.uint8) - 1  # Class labels range
from 1 to 10, so subtract 1
x_test = np.fromfile(x_test_path, dtype=np.uint8).reshape(-1, 3, 96, 96).
transpose(0, 2, 3, 1)
y_test = np.fromfile(y_test_path, dtype=np.uint8) - 1  # Class labels range
from 1 to 10, so subtract 1

# Preprocessing: normalize the data
x_train = x_train.astype('float32') / 255.0
x_test = x_test.astype('float32') / 255.0

# Define the VAE architecture
latent_dim = 128

# Encoder
inputs = Input(shape=(96, 96, 3))
x = Conv2D(32, (3, 3), activation='relu', strides=(2, 2), padding='same')
(inputs)
x = Conv2D(64, (3, 3), activation='relu', strides=(2, 2), padding='same')(x)
x = Flatten()(x)
x = Dense(256, activation='relu')(x)

# Latent space
z_mean = Dense(latent_dim)(x)
z_log_var = Dense(latent_dim)(x)

# Reparameterization trick

def sampling(args):
    z_mean, z_log_var = args
    epsilon = tf.random.normal(shape=(tf.shape(z_mean)[0], latent_dim))
    return z_mean + tf.exp(0.5 * z_log_var) * epsilon

z = tf.keras.layers.Lambda(sampling)([z_mean, z_log_var])

# Decoder
decoder_inputs = Input(shape=(latent_dim,))
x = Dense(6 * 6 * 64, activation='relu')(decoder_inputs)
x = Reshape((6, 6, 64))(x)
x = Conv2DTranspose(64, (3, 3), activation='relu', strides=(2, 2),
padding='same')(x)
```

```
x = Conv2DTranspose(32, (3, 3), activation='relu', strides=(2, 2),
padding='same')(x)
outputs = Conv2DTranspose(3, (3, 3), activation='sigmoid', padding='same')
(x)

# VAE model
encoder = Model(inputs, z_mean)
decoder = Model(decoder_inputs, outputs)
vae_output = decoder(z)
vae = Model(inputs, vae_output)

# Reshape inputs and outputs

inputs_reshaped = tf.image.resize(inputs, (24, 24))
vae_output_reshaped = tf.image.resize(vae_output, (24, 24))

# Define the loss function
reconstruction_loss = tf.keras.losses.binary_crossentropy(tf.reshape(inputs_
reshaped, (-1, 24 * 24 * 3)),

                                                    tf.reshape(vae_
output_reshaped, (-1, 24 * 24 * 3)))

reconstruction_loss *= 24 * 24 * 3
kl_loss = 1 + z_log_var - tf.square(z_mean) - tf.exp(z_log_var)
kl_loss = tf.reduce_mean(kl_loss, axis=-1)
kl_loss *= -0.5

vae_loss = tf.reduce_mean(reconstruction_loss + kl_loss)

# Compile the model
vae.add_loss(vae_loss)
vae.compile(optimizer='adam')

# Train the model
epochs = 100
batch_size = 128
history = vae.fit(x_train, epochs=epochs, batch_size=batch_size, validation_
data=(x_test, None))

# Store the training and validation loss (reconstruction loss) in the history
object
```

```
history.history['train_reconstruction_loss'] = history.history['loss']
history.history['val_reconstruction_loss'] = history.history['val_loss']
```

Note: Please note that the provided implementation is a basic VAE architecture. Depending on your specific requirements and the complexity of the dataset, you may want to experiment with different hyperparameters, architectures, and training strategies to improve the model's performance.

Also, you may consider additional techniques such as:

- Using deeper encoder and decoder networks.

- Using a more advanced loss function like the Beta-VAE loss or adversarial loss (VAE-GAN).

- Applying data augmentation during training.

- Trying different learning rates, batch sizes, and numbers of training epochs.

Additionally, using a higher-dimensional latent space (for example, 128 or 256) may improve the expressiveness of the model but might also require more data and computational resources. Experimentation and tuning are key to achieving the best results for your specific use case.

Outputs

The models clearly over Fits with no reconstruction, as shown in the following *Figure 9.1:*

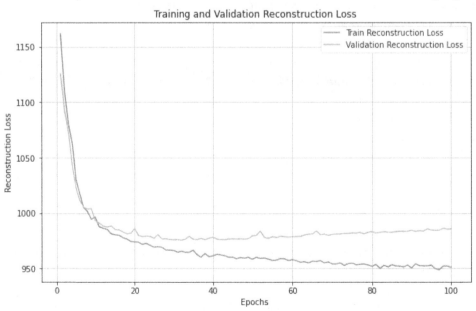

Figure 9.1: Training and validation loss over time

Let us ascertain whether switching the library to PyTorch can effectively address the issue of overfitting. This segment of the code serves as an experimental endeavor, and it is imperative for the reader to possess a profound comprehension of PyTorch before engaging in the practical implementation.

Pytorch

Here is a implementation of the VAE architecture:

```python
import torch
import torch.nn as nn
import torch.optim as optim
import torchvision
import torchvision.transforms as transforms
from torch.utils.data import DataLoader, random_split
import matplotlib.pyplot as plt

# Step 1: Data Preprocessing
transform = transforms.Compose([
  transforms.ToTensor(),
  transforms.Resize((32, 32)),  # Resize the images to 32x32
    transforms.Normalize(mean=[0.5, 0.5, 0.5], std=[0.5, 0.5, 0.5]),  #
Normalize the data
])

stl10_dataset = torchvision.datasets.STL10(root='./data', split='train',
download=True, transform=transform)

# Divide data into training and validation sets
train_size = int(0.8 * len(stl10_dataset))
val_size = len(stl10_dataset) - train_size
train_dataset, val_dataset = random_split(stl10_dataset, [train_size, val_
size])

trainloader = DataLoader(train_dataset, batch_size=64, shuffle=True)
valloader = DataLoader(val_dataset, batch_size=64, shuffle=False)

# Step 2: Model Architecture
class VAE(nn.Module):
    def __init__(self, latent_dim=64):
```

```python
        super(VAE, self).__init__()
self.latent_dim = latent_dim

        # Encoder layers
self.encoder = nn.Sequential(
            nn.Conv2d(3, 32, kernel_size=4, stride=2, padding=1), nn.ReLU(),
           nn.Conv2d(32, 64, kernel_size=4, stride=2, padding=1), nn.ReLU(),
          nn.Conv2d(64, 128, kernel_size=4, stride=2, padding=1), nn.ReLU(),
         nn.Conv2d(128, 256, kernel_size=4, stride=2, padding=1), nn.ReLU(),
            nn.Flatten(),
            nn.Linear(256 * 2 * 2, 1024),
            nn.ReLU(),
            nn.Linear(1024, self.latent_dim * 2),
        )

        # Decoder layers
self.decoder = nn.Sequential(
nn.Linear(self.latent_dim, 1024),
nn.ReLU(),
nn.Linear(1024, 256 * 2 * 2),
nn.ReLU(),
nn.Unflatten(1, (256, 2, 2)),
            nn.ConvTranspose2d(256, 128, kernel_size=4, stride=2, padding=1),
nn.ReLU(),
            nn.ConvTranspose2d(128, 64, kernel_size=4, stride=2, padding=1),
nn.ReLU(),
            nn.ConvTranspose2d(64, 32, kernel_size=4, stride=2, padding=1),
nn.ReLU(),
            nn.ConvTranspose2d(32, 3, kernel_size=4, stride=2, padding=1),
nn.Tanh(),  # To map output to [-1, 1] range for images with normalized data
        )

    def encode(self, x):
        x = self.encoder(x)
        mu = x[:, :self.latent_dim]
logvar = x[:, self.latent_dim:]
        return mu, logvar
```

```python
    def reparameterize(self, mu, logvar):
        std = torch.exp(0.5 * logvar)
        eps = torch.randn_like(std)
        z = mu + eps * std
        return z

    def decode(self, z):
        return self.decoder(z)

    def forward(self, x):
        mu, logvar = self.encode(x)
        z = self.reparameterize(mu, logvar)
        return self.decode(z), mu, logvar

# Step 3: Loss Function with Regularizer (KL Divergence)
def vae_loss(recon_x, x, mu, logvar):
    # Reconstruction Loss (MSE for images)
reconstruction_loss = nn.MSELoss()(recon_x, x)
    # KL Divergence Loss (Regularizer)
kl_divergence_loss = -0.5 * torch.sum(1 + logvar - mu.pow(2) - logvar.exp())
    return reconstruction_loss + kl_divergence_loss

# Step 4: Training with Weight Decay and Learning Rate Scheduler
def train_vae(model, trainloader, valloader, optimizer, num_epochs=10):
model.train()
    losses = []
val_losses = []

    for epoch in range(num_epochs):
running_loss = 0.0
        for i, data in enumerate(trainloader, 0):
            inputs, _ = data
            inputs = inputs.to(device)

optimizer.zero_grad()

recon_batch, mu, logvar = model(inputs)
            loss = vae_loss(recon_batch, inputs, mu, logvar)
```

```python
loss.backward()
optimizer.step()

running_loss += loss.item()

epoch_loss = running_loss / len(trainloader)
losses.append(epoch_loss)

        # Validation loss
model.eval()
        with torch.no_grad():
val_loss = 0.0
            for data in valloader:
                inputs, _ = data
                inputs = inputs.to(device)
recon_batch, mu, logvar = model(inputs)
val_loss += vae_loss(recon_batch, inputs, mu, logvar).item()

val_loss /= len(valloader)
val_losses.append(val_loss)

model.train()

        print(f"Epoch {epoch + 1}/{num_epochs}, Loss: {epoch_loss}, Val Loss:
{val_loss}")

    return losses, val_losses

# Step 5: Sampling and Generation
def generate_images(model, num_images=10):
model.eval()
    with torch.no_grad():
        z = torch.randn(num_images, model.latent_dim).to(device)
generated_images = model.decode(z).cpu()
        return generated_images

def plot_generated_vs_original(generated_images, original_images):
    fig, axes = plt.subplots(2, len(generated_images), figsize=(15, 5))
```

```python
    for i, img in enumerate(generated_images):
img_gen = img.permute(1, 2, 0)  # Transpose to (H, W, C)
img_gen = (img_gen + 1) / 2.0  # De-normalize from [-1, 1] to [0, 1]
        axes[0, i].imshow(img_gen)
        axes[0, i].axis('off')

    for i, img in enumerate(original_images[:len(generated_images)]):
img_orig = img.permute(1, 2, 0)  # Transpose to (H, W, C)
img_orig = (img_orig + 1) / 2.0  # De-normalize from [-1, 1] to [0, 1]
        axes[1, i].imshow(img_orig)
        axes[1, i].axis('off')

    axes[0, 0].set_title('Generated Images')
    axes[1, 0].set_title('Original Images')
plt.show()

# Main
device = torch.device("cuda" if torch.cuda.is_available() else "cpu")

vae_model = VAE(latent_dim=64).to(device)
optimizer = optim.Adam(vae_model.parameters(), lr=0.001, weight_decay=1e-5)
scheduler = optim.lr_scheduler.StepLR(optimizer, step_size=5, gamma=0.5)  #
Learning rate scheduler

# Train VAE with losses recorded
train_losses, val_losses = train_vae(vae_model, trainloader, valloader,
optimizer, num_epochs=10)

# Plot the learning curve
def plot_learning_curve(train_losses, val_losses):
plt.figure()
    epochs = range(1, len(train_losses) + 1)
plt.plot(epochs, train_losses, '-o', label='Train Loss')
plt.plot(epochs, val_losses, '-o', label='Val Loss')
plt.xlabel('Epoch')
plt.ylabel('Loss')
plt.legend()
plt.title('Variational Autoencoder Learning Curve')
```

```
plt.show()

plot_learning_curve(train_losses, val_losses)

# Generate and display images
generated_images = generate_images(vae_model, num_images=10)
original_images = []
for i, data in enumerate(valloader, 0):
    inputs, _ = data
original_images.append(inputs[0])
    if i>= 9:  # Display 10 original images
        break


plot_generated_vs_original(generated_images, original_images)
```

Refer to the following *Figure 9.2*:

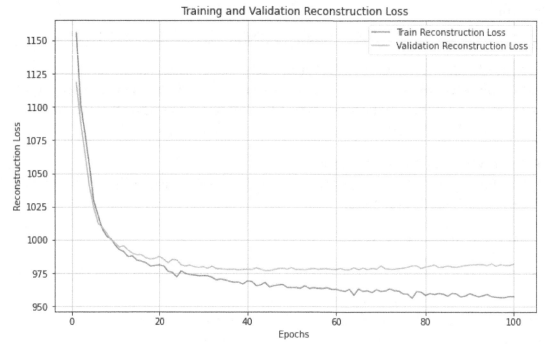

Figure 9.2: *Training and validation loss over time*

Refer to the following *Figure 9.3*:

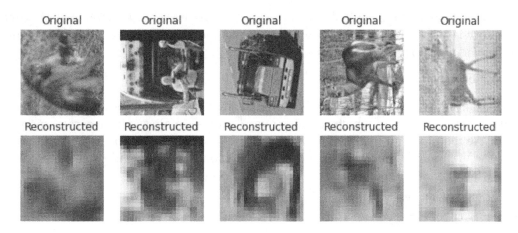

Figure 9.3: *Original and reconstructed images form the model*

Transition from VAE to Generative Transformer Model: Keras Vit Library

The GitHub repository **https://github.com/faustomorales/vit-keras** is a project that provides a Keras implementation of the **Vision Transformer** (**ViT**) model. ViT is a powerful image recognition model that is based on the transformer architecture, which is commonly used for natural language processing tasks.

The **vit-keras** repository provides a variety of features for using ViT models, including:

- The ability to load pre-trained ViT models, which can be used for image classification tasks without any further training.

- The ability to fine-tune ViT models on your own dataset.

- The ability to visualize the attention maps of ViT models, which can help you to understand how the model is making its predictions.

The **vit-keras** repository is maintained by *Fausto Morales*, a software engineer at Google. The repository is open source and licensed under the Apache License 2.0.

Here are some of the benefits of using the **vit-keras** repository:

- It is a well-maintained and actively developed project.

- It is open source and licensed under a permissive license.

- It provides a variety of features for using ViT models.

- It is easy to use and has a well-documented API.

If you are interested in using ViT models for image recognition tasks, then the **vit-keras** repository is a great resource. It provides a simple and easy-to-use API for loading, fine-tuning, and visualizing ViT models.

https://libraries.io/pypi/vit-keras

In this example, we load a pre-trained ViT model called vit_b16. This model has been trained on the ImageNet dataset, which contains over 1 million images and their corresponding labels. We then load an image of a Granny Smith apple from Wikipedia and preprocess it for the ViT model. Finally, we make a prediction on the image and print the predicted class, which is *Granny smith*. Refer to the following code:

```python
import numpy as np
import matplotlib.pyplot as plt
from vit_keras import vit, utils


# Load the ViT model
image_size = 384
classes = utils.get_imagenet_classes()
model = vit.vit_b16(image_size=image_size, pretrained=True, include_top=True,
pretrained_top=True)


# Load an image
url    =    'https://upload.wikimedia.org/wikipedia/commons/d/d7/Granny_smith_
and_cross_section.jpg'
image = utils.read(url, image_size)


# Preprocess the image
X = vit.preprocess_inputs(image).reshape(1, image_size, image_size, 3)


# Make a prediction
y = model.predict(X)


# Print the predicted class
print(classes[y[0].argmax()])
```

The **vit-keras** library is a powerful tool for image recognition tasks. It provides a simple and easy-to-use API for loading, fine-tuning, and visualizing ViT models. If you are interested in using ViT models for your own image recognition projects, then the **vit-keras** library is a great resource.

Implementing a ViT model from scratch

Refer to the following code:

```
!pip install tensorflow-addons
!pip install vit_keras


# Load the dataset
x_train_path = os.path.join(data_dir, file_names[0])
y_train_path = os.path.join(data_dir, file_names[1])
x_test_path = os.path.join(data_dir, file_names[2])
y_test_path = os.path.join(data_dir, file_names[3])


x_train = np.fromfile(x_train_path, dtype=np.uint8).reshape(-1, 3, 96, 96).
transpose(0, 2, 3, 1)
y_train = np.fromfile(y_train_path, dtype=np.uint8) - 1
x_test = np.fromfile(x_test_path, dtype=np.uint8).reshape(-1, 3, 96, 96).
transpose(0, 2, 3, 1)
y_test = np.fromfile(y_test_path, dtype=np.uint8) - 1


# Preprocessing: normalize the data
x_train = x_train.astype('float32') / 255.0
x_test = x_test.astype('float32') / 255.0


# Define the VIT Autoencoder architecture
latent_dim = 128


# Encoder (Vision Transformer)
inputs = Input(shape=(96, 96, 3))
x = vit.vit_l32(image_size=96, activation='gelu', pretrained=False, include_
top=False, pretrained_top=False)(inputs)
x = Reshape((-1, x.shape[-1]))(x)  # Flatten the sequence of patches
x = tf.keras.layers.GlobalAveragePooling1D()(x)   # Reduce sequence to a
single vector
latent_space = Dense(latent_dim, activation='relu')(x)  # Dense layer for the
latent representation


# Decoder
decoder_inputs = Input(shape=(latent_dim,))
```

```python
x = Dense(6 * 6 * 32, activation='relu')(decoder_inputs)
x = Reshape((6, 6, 32))(x)
x = Conv2DTranspose(32, (3, 3), activation='relu', strides=(2, 2),
padding='same')(x)
x = Conv2DTranspose(16, (3, 3), activation='relu', strides=(2, 2),
padding='same')(x)
outputs = Conv2DTranspose(3, (3, 3), activation='sigmoid', padding='same')
(x)


# VAE model
encoder = Model(inputs, latent_space)
decoder = Model(decoder_inputs, outputs)


# Create the autoencoder by connecting the encoder and decoder
autoencoder_output = decoder(encoder(inputs))
autoencoder = Model(inputs, autoencoder_output)


# Reshape inputs and outputs
inputs_reshaped = tf.image.resize(inputs, (24, 24))
autoencoder_output_reshaped = tf.image.resize(autoencoder_output, (24, 24))


# Define the loss function (Autoencoder loss)
reconstruction_loss = tf.keras.losses.mean_squared_error(tf.reshape(inputs_
reshaped, (-1, 24 * 24 * 3)),

                                        tf.reshape(autoencoder_
output_reshaped, (-1, 24 * 24 * 3)))


autoencoder_loss = tf.reduce_mean(reconstruction_loss)


# Compile the model
autoencoder.add_loss(autoencoder_loss)
autoencoder.compile(optimizer='adam')


# Train the model
epochs = 100
batch_size = 128
history = autoencoder.fit(x_train, epochs=epochs, batch_size=batch_size,
validation_data=(x_test, None))
```

```
# Plot the learning curves for loss
plt.figure(figsize=(10, 6))
plt.plot(history.history['loss'], label='Train Loss')
plt.plot(history.history['val_loss'], label='Validation Loss')
plt.xlabel('Epochs')
plt.ylabel('Loss')
plt.title('Training and Validation Loss')
plt.legend()
plt.grid()
plt.show()

# Generate and plot some reconstructed images using the VIT Autoencoder
num_samples = 5
random_indices = np.random.randint(0, len(x_test), num_samples)
sample_images = x_test[random_indices]
reconstructed_images = autoencoder.predict(sample_images)

plt.figure(figsize=(10, 4))

for i in range(num_samples):
    plt.subplot(2, num_samples, i + 1)
    plt.imshow(sample_images[i])
    plt.title("Original")
    plt.axis('off')

    plt.subplot(2, num_samples, num_samples + i + 1)
    plt.imshow(reconstructed_images[i])
    plt.title("Reconstructed")
    plt.axis('off')

plt.show()
```

Outputs

The models clearly over Fits with no reconstruction, as shown in the following *Figure 9.4:*

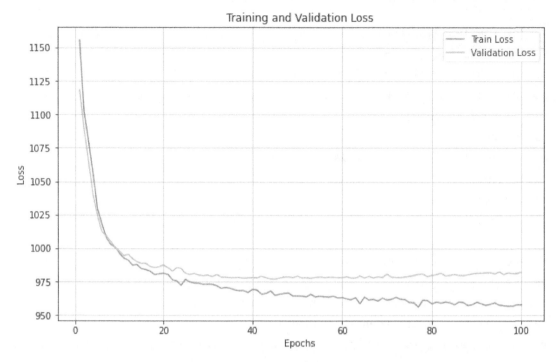

Figure 9.4: *Training and validation loss over time*

Refer to the following *Figure 9.5*, original and reconstructed images from the model are shown:

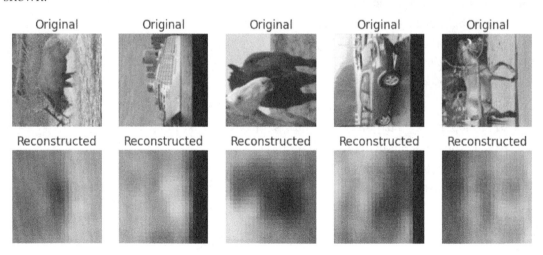

Figure 9.5: *Original and reconstructed images from the model*

Implementing a ViT model pre trained with ViT model

Refer to the following code:

```python
# Variational Autoencoder (VAE) using a Vision Transformer (ViT) as the
encoder
# Variational Autoencoder (VAE) using a Vision Transformer (ViT) as the
encoder
import tensorflow as tf
from tensorflow.keras.layers import Input, Conv2D, Flatten, Dense,
Conv2DTranspose, Reshape, LayerNormalization
from tensorflow.keras.models import Model
import numpy as np
import matplotlib.pyplot as plt
import os
import urllib.request
import tarfile
import shutil
from vit_keras import vit

# Download STL-10 dataset (if not already downloaded)
url = 'http://ai.stanford.edu/~acoates/stl10/stl10_binary.tar.gz'
file_name = 'stl10_binary.tar.gz'

if not os.path.exists(file_name):
    urllib.request.urlretrieve(url, file_name)

# Extract the dataset (if not already extracted)
data_dir = 'stl10_binary'
file_names = ['train_X.bin', 'train_y.bin', 'test_X.bin', 'test_y.bin']

if os.path.exists(data_dir):
    shutil.rmtree(data_dir)  # Delete the existing folder if it exists

tar = tarfile.open(file_name, "r:gz")
tar.extractall()
tar.close()
```

```python
# Load the dataset
x_train_path = os.path.join(data_dir, file_names[0])
y_train_path = os.path.join(data_dir, file_names[1])
x_test_path = os.path.join(data_dir, file_names[2])
y_test_path = os.path.join(data_dir, file_names[3])

x_train = np.fromfile(x_train_path, dtype=np.uint8).reshape(-1, 3, 96, 96).
transpose(0, 2, 3, 1)
y_train = np.fromfile(y_train_path, dtype=np.uint8) - 1
x_test = np.fromfile(x_test_path, dtype=np.uint8).reshape(-1, 3, 96, 96).
transpose(0, 2, 3, 1)
y_test = np.fromfile(y_test_path, dtype=np.uint8) - 1

# Preprocessing: normalize the data
x_train = x_train.astype('float32') / 255.0
x_test = x_test.astype('float32') / 255.0

# Define the VAE architecture with Vision Transformer
latent_dim = 128

# Load the pre-trained Vision Transformer model weights
vit_weights_path = 'ViT-L_32_imagenet21k+imagenet2012.npz'

# Encoder
inputs = Input(shape=(96, 96, 3))
x = vit.vit_l32(image_size=96, activation='relu', pretrained=False, include_
top=False, pretrained_top=False)(inputs)
x = LayerNormalization(epsilon=1e-6)(x)
x = Flatten()(x)
x = Dense(256, activation='relu')(x)
# Latent space
z_mean = Dense(latent_dim)(x)
z_log_var = Dense(latent_dim)(x)

# Reparameterization trick
def sampling(args):
    z_mean, z_log_var = args
```

```python
    epsilon = tf.random.normal(shape=(tf.shape(z_mean)[0], latent_dim))
    return z_mean + tf.exp(0.5 * z_log_var) * epsilon


z = tf.keras.layers.Lambda(sampling)([z_mean, z_log_var])


# Decoder
decoder_inputs = Input(shape=(latent_dim,))
x = Dense(6 * 6 * 32, activation='relu')(decoder_inputs)
x = Reshape((6, 6, 32))(x)
x = Conv2DTranspose(32, (3, 3), activation='relu', strides=(2, 2),
padding='same')(x)
x = Conv2DTranspose(16, (3, 3), activation='relu', strides=(2, 2),
padding='same')(x)
outputs = Conv2DTranspose(3, (3, 3), activation='sigmoid', padding='same')
(x)


# VAE model
encoder = Model(inputs, z_mean)
decoder = Model(decoder_inputs, outputs)
vae_output = decoder(z)
vae = Model(inputs, vae_output)


# Reshape inputs and outputs
inputs_reshaped = tf.image.resize(inputs, (24, 24))
vae_output_reshaped = tf.image.resize(vae_output, (24, 24))


# Define the loss function
reconstruction_loss = tf.keras.losses.binary_crossentropy(tf.reshape(inputs_
reshaped, (-1, 24 * 24 * 3)),
                                                    tf.reshape(vae_
output_reshaped, (-1, 24 * 24 * 3)))


reconstruction_loss *= 24 * 24 * 3
kl_loss = 1 + z_log_var - tf.square(z_mean) - tf.exp(z_log_var)
kl_loss = tf.reduce_mean(kl_loss, axis=-1)
kl_loss *= -0.5
```

```
vae_loss = tf.reduce_mean(reconstruction_loss + kl_loss)

# Compile the model
vae.add_loss(vae_loss)
vae.compile(optimizer='adam')

# Train the model
epochs = 100
batch_size = 128
history = vae.fit(x_train, epochs=epochs, batch_size=batch_size, validation_
data=(x_test, None))

# Store the training and validation loss (reconstruction loss) in the history
object
history.history['train_reconstruction_loss'] = history.history['loss']
history.history['val_reconstruction_loss'] = history.history['val_loss']

# Plot Training and Validation Loss
train_loss = history.history['loss']
val_loss = history.history['val_loss']

plt.figure(figsize=(10, 6))
plt.plot(range(1, epochs+1), train_loss, label='Train Loss')
plt.plot(range(1, epochs+1), val_loss, label='Validation Loss')
plt.xlabel('Epochs')
plt.ylabel('Loss')
plt.title('Training and Validation Loss')
plt.legend()
plt.grid(True)
plt.show()
```

Refer to the following *Figure 9.6,* it shows the training and validation loss over time:

```
# Plot Training and Validation Reconstruction Loss
```

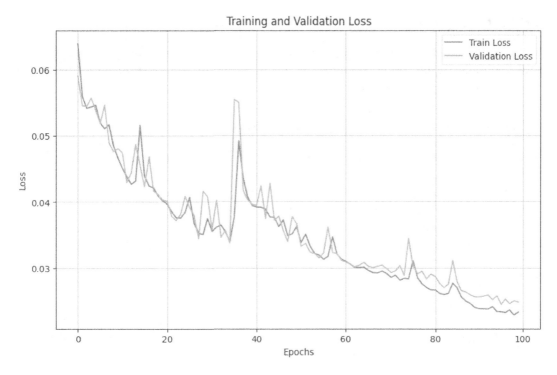

Figure 9.6: *Training and validation loss over time*

Outputs

The model has started learning (some of the best reconstructions), as can be seen in the following *Figure 9.7*:

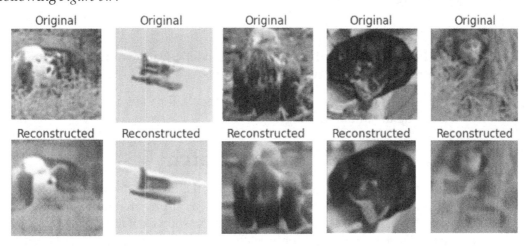

Figure 9.7: *Model output*

Training Pretrained ViT vs ViT scratch

Using a pretrained **Vision Transformer** (ViT) model versus training a ViT model from scratch entails significant differences in terms of time, computational resources, and potentially overall performance.

Pretrained Vision Transformer

When using a pretrained VIT model, you start with a model that has already been trained on a large dataset, often containing diverse images. The model has already learned a wide range of features and representations from these images. Fine-tuning is usually performed by adjusting the final layers of the network to suit your specific task or dataset. This approach is beneficial when you have limited data or computational resources. It is especially effective when the pretrained model's learned features are relevant to your task.

Advantages

The advantages are as follows:

- **Faster convergence:** Pretrained models have learned general features, allowing quicker adaptation to specific tasks.

- **Requires less data:** The pretrained model has already captured rich features from a vast dataset.

- **Utilizes prior knowledge:** The model already possesses knowledge from its initial training on diverse images.

Disadvantages

The disadvantages are as follows:

- **May not be task-specific:** The pretrained model's features might not perfectly match your task's requirements.

- **Limited to existing features:** The model's capabilities are bounded by what it learned during the initial training.

Training a VIT model from scratch

Training a VIT model from scratch involves initializing the model's parameters randomly and then optimizing them using your specific dataset. This approach requires a substantial amount of labeled data and considerable computational resources. It is most advantageous when you have a large dataset that is highly relevant to your task and you want complete control over the learned features.

Advantages

The advantages are as follows:

- **Task-specific features:** The model can learn features optimized precisely for your task.

- **Customization:** You have full control over the architecture and training process.

- **Potential for innovation:** Training from scratch allows exploration of novel architectures or techniques.

Disadvantages

The disadvantages are as follows:

- **Requires substantial resources:** Training from scratch demands more data and computational power.

- **Slower convergence:** The model starts with random weights, requiring longer training time.

- **Risk of overfitting:** Without pretrained features, there is a higher risk of overfitting, especially with limited data.

Using a pretrained VIT model is advantageous when you need quick results or have limited data, while training from scratch is suitable when you have abundant relevant data and want to customize the model extensively. The decision depends on the trade-off between available resources, time, and the desired level of customization for your specific image recognition task.

Examining the loss curve

Training and validation loss over time for a machine learning model in the loss curve. The training loss is the loss that the model experiences on the training data, while the validation loss is the loss that the model experiences on the validation data. Refer to the following *Figure 9.8*, it shows training and validation loss over time:

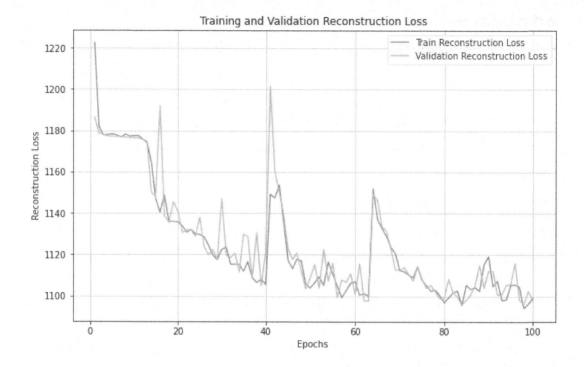

Figure 9.8: *Training and validation loss over time*

The model is overfitting. This is evident from the fact that the training loss continues to decrease while the validation loss starts to increase after a certain point. This means that the model is learning the training data too well and is not able to generalize to unseen data.

Here are some of the things we can see in the image that indicate overfitting:

- The training loss continues to decrease while the validation loss starts to increase.

- The gap between the training loss and the validation loss becomes wider as the model trains for more epochs.

- The training loss may reach a very low value, but the validation loss may still be high.

- The model may start to give incorrect predictions on the validation set.

Optimization of ViT models

To improve the performance of the VAE using the ViT as the encoder, we can make several modifications to the code. Here are some suggestions:

- **Use transfer learning with ViT:** Instead of using the Vision Transformer from scratch, we can leverage pre-trained weights on a large dataset like ImageNet. This can help the model to learn better representations.

- **Use a larger decoder:** The current decoder has a relatively small architecture. We can make it deeper with more layers and filters to better reconstruct the images.

- **Change activation functions:** The current VAE uses ReLU activation for the encoder and decoder. We can try using LeakyReLU or other activation functions that may perform better.

- **Adjust learning rate and other training parameters:** The default learning rate and batch size may not be optimal for this problem. We can experiment with different learning rates and batch sizes to find the best values.

- **Data augmentation:** Applying data augmentation techniques like random rotations, flips, and translations can help improve the generalization of the VAE.

- **Use different loss functions:** Besides binary cross-entropy for reconstruction, we can try other loss functions like **Mean Squared Error** (**MSE**) or perceptual loss.

Conclusion

This chapter delves into the distinctions between Generative Transformers and traditional counterparts, focusing on their roles in image generation. It spotlights the VAE models' capability in capturing latent image features within the STL dataset. The chapter chronicles the evolution from VAE to Generative Transformer, highlighting the fusion of VAE's latent-rich architecture with Transformers' self-attention mechanisms. This evolution enhances image synthesis, offering contextual coherence. Through evaluations, the Generative Transformer's performance is benchmarked against VAE and its baselines. The practical application section showcases its prowess in generating images while preserving contextual authenticity.

The upcoming chapter will explore the fusion of encoder-decoder and transformers, diving into SWIN transformer implementation, empowering readers to build and optimize such models for generative tasks.

Join our book's Discord space

Join the book's Discord Workspace for Latest updates, Offers, Tech happenings around the world, New Release and Sessions with the Authors:

https://discord.bpbonline.com

CHAPTER 10

Architectural Refactoring for Generative Modeling

Introduction

In the realm of cutting-edge generative modeling in computer vision, the confluence of diverse architectures promises to redefine the boundaries of what is achievable. This chapter embarks on an illuminating journey into the fusion of two powerful components: the encoder-decoder and the transformer. Our objective is twofold: to unravel the intricacies of their symbiotic integration and to unveil the SWIN transformer, a vanguard in transformer architecture.

As we traverse through these pages, we embark on an exploration that marries the expertise of the encoder-decoder's contextual comprehension with the transformative power of attention mechanisms in the transformer. By doing so, we seek not only to enhance the capability of the transformer model itself but also to empower it with the contextual richness that the encoder-decoder brings to the table.

Within these lines, readers will delve into the intricate mechanics of the SWIN transformer, gaining an in-depth understanding of its distinctive components and how they revolutionize the field. Beyond the technicalities, this chapter aspires to cultivate a profound awareness of the synergies and synergies and limitations inherent in this fusion. Armed with this knowledge, readers will emerge with the tools to build, train, and fine-tune their own encoder-decoder-transformer models for generative tasks in computer vision, forging a path into the realm of innovation and practical implementation.

Structure

In this chapter, we will go over the following topics:

- STL dataset
- Exploring the combination process: outline
- Refactoring TransVAE and improving
- Improved Encoder Decoder
- SWIN-Transformer
- Implementation of SWIN Transformer: VAE
- Improving the models

Objectives

In this chapter, our primary objective is to explore the combination process, and delve into the process of synergistically combining an encoder-decoder architecture with a transformer model for enhanced generative modeling in computer vision. We will investigate how to enhance the transformer model by introducing modifications and optimizations, contributing to improved performance and suitability for specific tasks, and provide an in-depth exploration of the SWIN transformer implementation, including detailing its architecture, components, and distinctions from other transformer variants.

Moreover, this chapter will introduce readers to advanced concepts encompassing combining hyper parameter tuning and model refactoring and aims to equip readers with a comprehensive understanding of the entire process, encompassing motivations for combining architectures, technical implementation details, and an appreciation of the intricacies of the SWIN transformer model.

Through this holistic approach, readers will gain both theoretical insights and practical skills, setting the stage for innovative generative modeling using combined encoder-decoder-transformer architectures.

STL dataset

The STL-10 dataset is a widely used benchmark dataset in computer vision and machine learning. It was introduced by *Adam Coates, Honglak Lee,* and *Andrew Ng* in their 2011 paper titled *An Analysis of Single-Layer Networks in Unsupervised Feature Learning.*

More details about the STL dataset can be found in *Chapter 9, Implementing Generative Vision Transformer*

Exploring the combination process: Outline

Combining an encoder-decoder architecture with a transformer model for enhanced generative modeling in computer vision involves integrating the strengths of both architectures. In this example, we will provide a high-level conceptual code outline using Python and TensorFlow to illustrate this process. Keep in mind that actual implementation can vary based on the specific task and dataset. Refer to the following code:

```python
import tensorflow as tf
from tensorflow.keras.layers import Input, Conv2D, GlobalAveragePooling2D, Dense
from tensorflow.keras.models import Model
from tensorflow.keras.activations import relu


# Define an encoder using Convolutional layers
def encoder(input_shape):
    input_layer = Input(shape=input_shape)
    conv1 = Conv2D(64, (3, 3), activation=relu, padding='same')(input_layer)
    conv2 = Conv2D(128, (3, 3), activation=relu, padding='same')(conv1)
    encoded = GlobalAveragePooling2D()(conv2)
    return Model(inputs=input_layer, outputs=encoded, name='encoder')


# Define a transformer model
def transformer(input_shape):
    input_layer = Input(shape=input_shape)
    # Your transformer layers here
    # Attention mechanisms, multi-head attention, positional encodings, etc.
    transformed = # Transformer layers
    return Model(inputs=input_layer, outputs=transformed, name='transformer')


# Define a decoder using Dense layers
def decoder(latent_dim, output_dim):
    input_layer = Input(shape=(latent_dim,))
    dense1 = Dense(128, activation=relu)(input_layer)
    dense2 = Dense(256, activation=relu)(dense1)
    output_layer = Dense(output_dim, activation='softmax')(dense2)
    return Model(inputs=input_layer, outputs=output_layer, name='decoder')
```

```
# Create an encoder-decoder-transformer model
input_shape = (256, 256, 3)
latent_dim = 512
output_dim = 10  # Example for a classification task
input_data = Input(shape=input_shape)
encoded = encoder(input_shape)(input_data)
transformed = transformer((latent_dim,))(encoded)
decoded = decoder(latent_dim, output_dim)(transformed)

model = Model(inputs=input_data, outputs=decoded, name='encoder_decoder_
transformer')

# Compile and train the model
# You'll need to define your loss function, optimizer, and dataset for training

# Example training loop:
#      model.compile(optimizer='adam',      loss='categorical_crossentropy',
metrics=['accuracy'])
# model.fit(train_dataset, epochs=10, validation_data=val_dataset)
```

In this code outline, we first define an encoder, a transformer, and a decoder using TensorFlow and Keras. The encoder extracts relevant features from input images, the transformer processes these features, and the decoder generates the final output. The **encoder**, **transformer**, and **decoder** functions are placeholders and need to be properly implemented based on the task and desired architectures.

Note: Please note that this is a simplified conceptual example. The actual implementation may involve more complex architecture details, data preprocessing, and task-specific considerations. The key idea is to combine these components in a way that leverages the strengths of each architecture to achieve enhanced generative modeling in computer vision.

Refactoring TransVAE and improving

Before we start refactoring, we need to understand certain techniques and considerations, such as the following.

Cyclic Learning Rate Schedule

A Cyclic Learning Rate Schedule is a dynamic approach to adjusting the learning rate during the training of neural networks. It involves systematically varying the learning rate within a predefined range over the course of multiple iterations or epochs. This technique aims to improve the training process by facilitating quicker convergence, escaping local minima, and finding more optimal regions of the loss landscape.

The key idea behind the Cyclic Learning Rate Schedule is to alternate between higher and lower learning rates, allowing the model to move quickly through flat regions of the loss landscape while also slowing down near steep regions to achieve better convergence. This contrasts with traditional learning rate schedules, where the learning rate typically decreases monotonically during training.

Here is how the Cyclic Learning Rate Schedule works:

1. **Select learning rate range:** First, you define a range of learning rates, typically spanning one to two orders of magnitude. For example, if you are using a learning rate of 0.001 as a starting point, your range might be [0.0001, 0.01].

2. **Define cycle length:** A cycle consists of one complete iteration through your training data. You can define the number of iterations for a full cycle. For instance, if you have 50,000 training examples and want to perform 3 cycles, each cycle would encompass 50,000 iterations.

3. **Varying learning rate:** Within each cycle, the learning rate is varied according to a specific pattern. One common pattern is the triangular learning rate policy, where the learning rate starts at the minimum value of the range and linearly increases to the maximum value in the first half of the cycle, then decreases linearly back to the minimum in the second half.

4. **Multiple cycles:** You can repeat the cycling process for a predefined number of times, typically covering a significant portion of the total training iterations or epochs. This repetition allows the model to explore different regions of the loss landscape.

The benefits of a Cyclic Learning Rate Schedule include:

- **Fast exploration:** The varying learning rate enables faster exploration of different regions in the loss landscape, potentially helping the model escape local minima and find more optimal solutions.

- **Adaptive learning rate:** The cyclic nature allows the learning rate to adapt to the landscape's changing curvature, helping the model avoid convergence slowdowns.

- **Reduced manual tuning:** Compared to traditional schedules that require careful tuning of learning rate and its schedule, cyclic learning rates often require less manual adjustment.

However, it is important to note that while Cyclic Learning Rate Schedules can be effective, they might not always provide a significant improvement, and their performance can depend on the dataset, architecture, and problem at hand. Experimentation is key to determining whether this technique is suitable for a particular task.

Code:

```
# Cyclic Learning Rate Schedule class CyclicLR(Callback): def __init__
(self, base_lr=1e-4, max_lr=3e-4, step_size=2000., mode='triangular2'):
super(CyclicLR, self).__init__() self.base_lr = base_lr self.max_lr = max_lr
self.step_size = step_size self.mode = mode self.clr_iterations = 0. self.
trn_iterations = 0. if self.mode not in ['triangular', 'triangular2', 'exp_
range']: raise KeyError("mode must be one of 'triangular', 'triangular2', or
'exp_range'")
```

Here is a breakdown of the code:

- CyclicLR is a class that inherits from the Callback class, suggesting that it is designed to be used as a callback during the training process.

- The constructor (**__init__**) of the class takes the following parameters:

  o **base_lr**: The base learning rate for the cyclic schedule.

  o **max_lr**: The maximum learning rate for the cyclic schedule.

  o **step_size**: The number of iterations after which the learning rate will change.

  o **mode**: The mode of the cyclic learning rate schedule. It should be one of **triangular**, **triangular2**, or **exp_range**.

- The **clt_iterations** and **trn_iterations** are initialized to keep track of the current iteration for the cyclic learning rate and training iterations, respectively.

- The mode is checked to ensure that it is one of the three specified modes: **triangular**, **triangular2**, or **exp_range**.

In the context of a **Cyclic Learning Rate** (**CLR**) schedule, the term *triangular* refers to a pattern in which the learning rate is cyclically increased and then decreased over a set number of iterations or epochs. There are two primary triangular modes: '**triangular**' and '**triangular2**':

- **Triangular Learning Rate Policy ('triangular'):** In this mode, the learning rate starts at the **base_lr`** and linearly increases to the **max_lr** over the first half of a cycle. Then, it linearly decreases back to the **base_lr** over the second half of the cycle. This pattern forms a triangle when plotted against the iteration or epoch axis. This mode aims to help the training process quickly traverse flat regions of the loss landscape while slowing down in steep regions.

- **Triangular2 Learning Rate Policy ('triangular2'):** Similar to the '**triangular**' mode, the '**triangular2**' mode starts with the **base_lr** and increases to the **max_lr** in the first half of a cycle. However, instead of decreasing linearly in the second half, the learning rate remains constant at the **max_lr** for the second half of the cycle. This mode is particularly useful when it's desirable to spend more time exploring the region of higher learning rates.

Both triangular modes are designed to introduce dynamic changes to the learning rate throughout the training process, enabling the model to oscillate between rapid exploration and careful convergence in different regions of the loss landscape. The cyclic nature of these modes is intended to improve training efficiency, help the model escape local minima, and achieve better convergence to a solution.

It is important to experiment with different learning rate schedules, including triangular ones, to find the best strategy for your specific problem and dataset. Keep in mind that the effectiveness of a particular learning rate schedule can vary based on the architecture, dataset, and optimization objectives.

LearningRateScheduler

Learning rate scheduling involves dynamically adjusting the learning rate during training. High learning rates can cause the model to overshoot the optimal weights and lead to divergence, while low learning rates can slow down convergence. LearningRateScheduler helps combat overfitting by allowing the learning rate to decrease over time. When the model starts overfitting, the learning rate reduction can help the optimization process fine-tune the model's parameters more carefully, preventing it from over-optimizing on noise in the training data.

EarlyStopping

EarlyStopping monitors the model's validation loss (or another relevant metric) during training. If the validation loss starts increasing consistently, it indicates that the model is starting to overfit on the training data and is losing its generalization ability. EarlyStopping halts the training process before overfitting becomes severe, preventing the model from continuing to learn noise in the data. This technique helps find the point where the model achieves the best balance between training and validation performance.

Weight decay: L2 regularization

Weight decay, a form of L2 regularization, is a technique where a penalty is added to the loss function based on the magnitude of the model's weights. This discourages the model from learning overly complex patterns and helps prevent overfitting. Weight decay essentially adds a term proportional to the sum of squared weights to the loss function. It contributes to shrinking the weights towards zero during training, reducing their impact on the model's output. This regularization technique helps create simpler models that generalize better to unseen data.

These techniques are integral to architectural considerations due to their roles in enhancing a model's generalization capability and managing overfitting:

- **Balancing complexity:** Complex models are more prone to overfitting as they can learn noise in the training data. `LearningRateScheduler`, `EarlyStopping`, and weight decay help balance the model's complexity, preventing it from over-optimizing on the training data and making it more likely to generalize well to new data.

- **Fine-tuning: `LearningRateScheduler`** helps fine-tune the model's parameters by gradually reducing the learning rate. This ensures the model's convergence to a better local minimum and helps prevent overshooting.

- **Monitoring generalization: `EarlyStopping`** provides an automatic way to monitor a model's performance on unseen data (validation set). It halts training before overfitting takes hold, guiding the model's learning process to stop at the point of optimal validation performance.

- **Robustness to noise:** Weight decay encourages the model to learn simpler patterns and is effective when the data contains noise. By limiting the impact of large weights, the model is less likely to fit noise in the training data.

- **Efficiency and resource management:** These techniques help optimize training efficiency. `LearningRateScheduler` and `EarlyStopping` can prevent unnecessary training epochs, saving time and computational resources.

Incorporating these techniques into architectural considerations enhances the model's ability to generalize well to new, unseen data, making it more reliable and effective in real-world applications. Refer to the following code:

```python
import tensorflow as tf
from tensorflow.keras.layers import Input, Conv2DTranspose, Reshape, Dense
from tensorflow.keras.models import Model
import numpy as np
import matplotlib.pyplot as plt
import os
import urllib.request
import tarfile
import shutil
from vit_keras import vit
from tensorflow.keras.callbacks import LearningRateScheduler, Callback, EarlyStopping
from tensorflow.keras.regularizers import l2


# Download STL-10 dataset (if not already downloaded)
url = 'http://ai.stanford.edu/~acoates/stl10/stl10_binary.tar.gz'
file_name = 'stl10_binary.tar.gz'
```

```
if not os.path.exists(file_name):
    urllib.request.urlretrieve(url, file_name)

# Extract the dataset (if not already extracted)
data_dir = 'stl10_binary'
file_names = ['train_X.bin', 'train_y.bin', 'test_X.bin', 'test_y.bin']

if os.path.exists(data_dir):
    shutil.rmtree(data_dir)  # Delete the existing folder if it exists

tar = tarfile.open(file_name, "r:gz")
tar.extractall()
tar.close()

# Load the dataset
x_train_path = os.path.join(data_dir, file_names[0])
y_train_path = os.path.join(data_dir, file_names[1])
x_test_path = os.path.join(data_dir, file_names[2])
y_test_path = os.path.join(data_dir, file_names[3])

x_train = np.fromfile(x_train_path, dtype=np.uint8).reshape(-1, 3, 96, 96).
transpose(0, 2, 3, 1)
y_train = np.fromfile(y_train_path, dtype=np.uint8) - 1
x_test = np.fromfile(x_test_path, dtype=np.uint8).reshape(-1, 3, 96, 96).
transpose(0, 2, 3, 1)
y_test = np.fromfile(y_test_path, dtype=np.uint8) - 1

# Preprocessing: normalize the data
x_train = x_train.astype('float32') / 255.0
x_test = x_test.astype('float32') / 255.0

# Define the VIT Autoencoder architecture
latent_dim = 128

# Encoder (Vision Transformer)
inputs = Input(shape=(96, 96, 3))
x = vit.vit_l32(image_size=96, activation='gelu', pretrained=False, include_
```

```
top=False, pretrained_top=False)(inputs)
x = Reshape((-1, x.shape[-1]))(x)  # Flatten the sequence of patches
x = tf.keras.layers.GlobalAveragePooling1D()(x)   # Reduce sequence to a
single vector
latent_space      =      Dense(latent_dim,      activation='relu',      kernel_
regularizer=l2(1e-5), kernel_initializer='glorot_uniform')(x)  # Dense layer
with L2 regularization

# Decoder
decoder_inputs = Input(shape=(latent_dim,))
x = Dense(6 * 6 * 32, activation='relu', kernel_regularizer=l2(1e-5),
kernel_initializer='glorot_uniform')(decoder_inputs)  # Dense layer with L2
regularization
x = Reshape((6, 6, 32))(x)
x = Conv2DTranspose(32, (3, 3), activation='relu', strides=(2, 2),
padding='same', kernel_regularizer=l2(1e-5), kernel_initializer='glorot_
uniform')(x)
x = Conv2DTranspose(16, (3, 3), activation='relu', strides=(2, 2),
padding='same', kernel_regularizer=l2(1e-5), kernel_initializer='glorot_
uniform')(x)
outputs = Conv2DTranspose(3, (3, 3), activation='sigmoid', padding='same',
kernel_regularizer=l2(1e-5), kernel_initializer='glorot_uniform')(x)

# AE model
encoder = Model(inputs, latent_space)
decoder = Model(decoder_inputs, outputs)

# Create the autoencoder by connecting the encoder and decoder
autoencoder_output = decoder(encoder(inputs))
autoencoder = Model(inputs, autoencoder_output)

# Reshape inputs and outputs
inputs_reshaped = tf.image.resize(inputs, (24, 24))
autoencoder_output_reshaped = tf.image.resize(autoencoder_output, (24, 24))

# Define the loss function (Autoencoder loss)
reconstruction_loss = tf.keras.losses.mean_squared_error(tf.reshape(inputs_
reshaped, (-1, 24 * 24 * 3)),

                                             tf.reshape(autoencoder_
output_reshaped, (-1, 24 * 24 * 3)))
```

```python
autoencoder_loss = tf.reduce_mean(reconstruction_loss)

# Compile the model
autoencoder.add_loss(autoencoder_loss)
autoencoder.compile(optimizer='adam')

# Cyclic Learning Rate Schedule
class CyclicLR(Callback):
        def __init__(self, base_lr=1e-4, max_lr=3e-4, step_size=2000.,
mode='triangular2'):
        super(CyclicLR, self).__init__()
        self.base_lr = base_lr
        self.max_lr = max_lr
        self.step_size = step_size
        self.mode = mode
        self.clr_iterations = 0.
        self.trn_iterations = 0.
        if self.mode not in ['triangular', 'triangular2', 'exp_range']:
            raise KeyError("mode must be one of 'triangular', 'triangular2',
or 'exp_range'")

    def clr(self):
        cycle = np.floor(1 + self.clr_iterations / (2 * self.step_size))
        x = np.abs(self.clr_iterations / self.step_size - 2 * cycle + 1)
        if self.mode == 'triangular':
            return self.base_lr + (self.max_lr - self.base_lr) * np.maximum(0,
(1 - x))
        elif self.mode == 'triangular2':
            return self.base_lr + (self.max_lr - self.base_lr) * np.maximum(0,
(1 - x)) / float(2  (cycle - 1))
        elif self.mode == 'exp_range':
            gamma = 1 / float(2  (cycle - 1))
            return self.base_lr * (gamma  self.clr_iterations)

    def on_train_begin(self, logs=None):
        logs = logs or {}
        tf.keras.backend.set_value(self.model.optimizer.lr, self.base_lr)
```

```python
    def on_batch_end(self, batch, logs=None):
        logs = logs or {}
        self.trn_iterations += 1
        self.clr_iterations += 1
        tf.keras.backend.set_value(self.model.optimizer.lr, self.clr())

# Set up cyclic learning rate
base_lr = 1e-5
max_lr = 3e-4
batch_size = 128
step_size = 4 * (len(x_train) // batch_size)
clr    =    CyclicLR(base_lr=base_lr,    max_lr=max_lr,    step_size=step_size,
mode='triangular2')

# Set up early stopping
early_stopping = EarlyStopping(monitor='val_loss', patience=5, restore_best_
weights=True)

# Train the model
epochs = 100
batch_size = 128
history   =   autoencoder.fit(x_train,   epochs=epochs,   batch_size=batch_size,
validation_data=(x_test, None), callbacks=[clr, early_stopping])

# Plot the learning curves for loss
plt.figure(figsize=(10, 6))
plt.plot(history.history['loss'], label='Train Loss')
plt.plot(history.history['val_loss'], label='Validation Loss')
plt.xlabel('Epochs')
plt.ylabel('Loss')
plt.title('Training and Validation Loss')
plt.legend()
plt.grid()
plt.show()

# Generate and plot some reconstructed images using the VIT Autoencoder
num_samples = 5
random_indices = np.random.randint(0, len(x_test), num_samples)
```

```
sample_images = x_test[random_indices]
reconstructed_images = autoencoder.predict(sample_images)

plt.figure(figsize=(10, 4))

for i in range(num_samples):
    plt.subplot(2, num_samples, i + 1)
    plt.imshow(sample_images[i])
    plt.title("Original")
    plt.axis('off')

    plt.subplot(2, num_samples, num_samples + i + 1)
    plt.imshow(reconstructed_images[i])
    plt.title("Reconstructed")
    plt.axis('off')

plt.show()
```

Improved Encoder Decoder

Refer to the following *Figure 10.1,* training and validation loss shows similar convergence resulting to a better model:

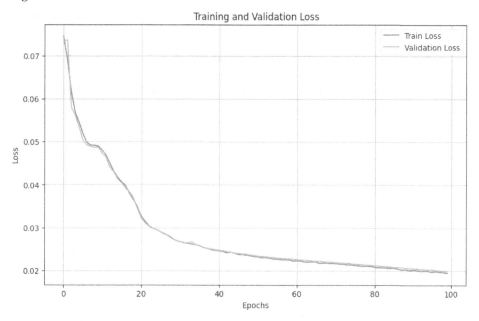

Figure 10.1: *The Training and validation loss shows similar convergence resulting to a better model*

SWIN-Transformer

The SWIN Transformer (Swin Transformer) is a hierarchical vision transformer architecture designed for computer vision tasks. It divides the image into non-overlapping patches, and each patch is treated as a token, allowing efficient processing of large images.

Swin Transformers, which stands for Shifted Window Transformers, offer a novel architecture that brings the benefits of transformers to computer vision tasks. Unlike standard transformers that were originally designed for natural language processing and treat input data as a sequence, Swin Transformers are tailored for images, where the spatial hierarchy is important.

The key benefit of Swin Transformers over standard transformers lies in their ability to capture local features through shifted windows, while also maintaining the ability to model global interactions. This windowing approach reduces computational complexity from quadratic to linear with respect to the size of the image, making it more scalable and efficient, particularly for high-resolution images.

Swin Transformers apply self-attention within local windows, and these windows are shifted across layers, allowing for cross-window connections and thus enabling the model to build a hierarchical representation of the image. This method efficiently integrates local and global context, leading to improved performance on a range of vision tasks.

Furthermore, Swin Transformers are versatile and can be used as general-purpose backbones for various vision tasks, including image classification, object detection, and semantic segmentation. Their efficiency and effectiveness make them well-suited for practical applications in the industry where computational resources and performance are critical.

Here is a simplified code example using PyTorch that walks you through the key components of the SWIN Transformer architecture. Please note that this code is a high-level illustration and may not cover all the intricate details of the actual SWIN Transformer implementation, which can be quite complex:

```python
import torch
import torch.nn as nn
import timm  # Library for vision models, including SWIN


# Create a simplified SWIN Transformer model
class SwinTransformer(nn.Module):
    def __init__(self, num_classes, img_size, patch_size, embed_dim, num_layers):
        super(SwinTransformer, self).__init__()
        self.patch_embed = timm.models.vision_transformer.patch_embed.PatchEmbed(
```

```
            img_size=img_size, patch_size=patch_size, in_chans=3, embed_
dim=embed_dim)

        self.transformer = timm.models.vision_transformer.SwinTransformer(
            img_size=img_size, embed_dim=embed_dim, depths=[num_layers] * 4,
num_heads=embed_dim // 32,
            num_classes=num_classes, qkv_bias=True)

    def forward(self, x):
        x = self.patch_embed(x)
        x = self.transformer(x)
        return x


# Hyperparameters
num_classes = 1000
img_size = 224
patch_size = 4
embed_dim = 96
num_layers = 12  # Number of layers in each stage of the SWIN Transformer


# Create the SWIN Transformer model
model = SwinTransformer(num_classes, img_size, patch_size, embed_dim, num_
layers)


# Input image tensor
input_image = torch.randn(1, 3, img_size, img_size)   # Batch size 1, 3
channels (RGB), img_size x img_size


# Forward pass through the model
output = model(input_image)
print("Output shape:", output.shape)  # Print the shape of the output tensor
```

In this code example:

- The **SwinTransformer** class defines a simplified SWIN Transformer model. It uses the **PatchEmbed** layer from the **Timm** library to handle patching the input image and a **SwinTransformer** layer to perform the hierarchical transformer processing.

- Hyperparameters like **num_classes**, **img_size**, **patch_size**, **embed_dim**, and **num_layers** control the architecture's configuration.

- The model is instantiated and a forward pass is performed using a random input image tensor.

Note: Please note that this code is a basic representation to help you understand the structure of the SWIN Transformer architecture. To implement the SWIN Transformer effectively, you should refer to the official implementations available in libraries like Timm and the associated research papers for full details.

Let us ascertain whether switching the library to PyTorch can effectively address the issue of overfitting. This segment of the code serves as an experimental endeavor, and it is imperative for the reader to possess a profound comprehension of PyTorch before engaging in the practical implementation.

Implementation of SWIN Transformer: VAE

This code is an example of training a **Variational Autoencoder (VAE)** using a Swin Transformer as the encoder architecture and a **Convolutional Neural Network (CNN)** as the decoder architecture. The code uses the TensorFlow library to define, compile, and train the VAE and the **autoencoder (AE)** models. Let us break down the code step by step:

1. **Importing libraries:** The necessary libraries are imported, including TensorFlow, Keras layers and **models**, **optimizer**, **numpy**, **matplotlib**, **os**, **urllib.request**, and others.

2. **Dataset download and extraction:** The code downloads and extracts the STL-10 dataset, which is a dataset of images containing 10 classes. It is used for training the models.

3. **Loading and preprocessing the dataset:** The dataset is loaded from binary files, containing images and labels. Images are reshaped and converted to a suitable format for further processing.

4. **Initializing swin transformer model:** A Swin Transformer model is initialized with specified settings, such as input shape, number of classes, number of attention heads, and number of transformer blocks. The last classification head is removed, leaving the model's features.

5. **Defining VAE architecture:** The VAE architecture is defined based on the Swin Transformer. The encoder part of the VAE is the Swin Transformer, and the decoder part is a series of convolutional and deconvolutional layers.

6. **Latent space and reparameterization:** The latent space (embedding) for the VAE is defined using Dense layers for mean and log variance. The reparameterization trick is applied to sample from the latent space.

7. **Decoder architecture:** The decoder part of the VAE is defined using Conv2DTranspose layers to reconstruct the image.

8. **VAE loss function:** The VAE loss function is defined, which is a combination of a reconstruction loss and a KL divergence term. The reconstruction loss measures the difference between the input image and the reconstructed image. The KL divergence term encourages the latent space to follow a Gaussian distribution.

9. **Compiling VAE:** The VAE model is compiled using the Adam optimizer and the defined VAE loss function.

10. **AE model and compilation:** An AE is defined by separating the encoder and decoder parts of the VAE. The AE is compiled using a binary cross-entropy loss.

11. **Early stopping:** An early stopping callback is defined to stop training when the validation loss stops improving, thus preventing overfitting.

12. **Training VAE:** The VAE is trained using the training data and validation data. The training process is monitored using the early stopping callback.

13. **Saving/loading models:** There are commented-out sections for saving and loading the trained models.

This code demonstrates how to build and train a VAE using the Swin Transformer as the encoder and a convolutional decoder. The VAE aims to learn a latent representation of the images and generate new images from the latent space. This architecture allows for more complex image generation and latent space exploration compared to traditional autoencoders. The provided code is a basic implementation and can be extended and optimized further based on specific requirements:

```python
# Develop VAE and AE  with SWIN Transformers


# Import the required libraries
import tensorflow as tf
from tensorflow.keras.layers import Input, Conv2D, Flatten, Dense, Conv2DTranspose, Reshape, LayerNormalization
from tensorflow.keras.models import Model
from tensorflow.keras.optimizers import Adam
import tensorflow_addons as tfa
import numpy as np
import matplotlib.pyplot as plt
import os
import urllib.request
from tensorflow.keras.regularizers import l2
# Load the Swin Transformer model from Keras examples
from keras.applications import SwinTransformer
import urllib.request
```

```python
import tarfile
from tensorflow.keras.callbacks import EarlyStopping

# Download STL-10 dataset
url = 'http://ai.stanford.edu/~acoates/stl10/stl10_binary.tar.gz'
file_name = 'stl10_binary.tar.gz'

if not os.path.exists(file_name):
    urllib.request.urlretrieve(url, file_name)

# Extract the dataset
tar = tarfile.open(file_name, "r:gz")
tar.extractall()
tar.close()

# Extract the dataset (if not already extracted)
data_dir = 'stl10_binary'
file_names = ['train_X.bin', 'train_y.bin', 'test_X.bin', 'test_y.bin']

# Load the dataset
x_train_path = os.path.join(data_dir, file_names[0])
y_train_path = os.path.join(data_dir, file_names[1])
x_test_path = os.path.join(data_dir, file_names[2])
y_test_path = os.path.join(data_dir, file_names[3])

x_train = np.fromfile(x_train_path, dtype=np.uint8).reshape(-1, 3, 96, 96).
transpose(0, 2, 3, 1)
y_train = np.fromfile(y_train_path, dtype=np.uint8) - 1
x_test = np.fromfile(x_test_path, dtype=np.uint8).reshape(-1, 3, 96, 96).
transpose(0, 2, 3, 1)
y_test = np.fromfile(y_test_path, dtype=np.uint8) - 1

# Initialize Swin Transformer model
swin_model = SwinTransformer(
    input_shape=(96, 96, 3),
    num_classes=10,  # The number of classes doesn't matter for VAE and AE
    num_heads=4,     # You can adjust the number of heads based on your
requirement
    num_transformer_blocks=2,  # You can adjust the number of blocks based
```

```
on your requirement
)

# Remove the classification head from the model
swin_model = tf.keras.Model(inputs=swin_model.inputs, outputs=swin_model.
layers[-2].output)

# Define the VAE architecture based on the Swin Transformer
inputs = Input(shape=(96, 96, 3))
x = swin_model(inputs)

# Latent space
latent_dim = 256
z_mean = Dense(latent_dim, kernel_regularizer=l2(0.01))(x)   # Adding L2
regularization
z_log_var = Dense(latent_dim, kernel_regularizer=l2(0.01))(x)   # Adding L2
regularization

# Reparameterization trick
def sampling(args):
    z_mean, z_log_var = args
    epsilon = tf.random.normal(shape=(tf.shape(z_mean)[0], latent_dim))
    return z_mean + tf.exp(0.5 * z_log_var) * epsilon

z = tf.keras.layers.Lambda(sampling)([z_mean, z_log_var])

# Decoder
decoder_inputs = Input(shape=(latent_dim,))
x = Dense(6 * 6 * 64, activation='relu')(decoder_inputs)
x = Reshape((6, 6, 64))(x)
x = Conv2DTranspose(128, (3, 3), activation='relu', strides=(2, 2),
padding='same')(x)
x = Conv2DTranspose(64, (3, 3), activation='relu', strides=(2, 2),
padding='same')(x)
outputs = Conv2DTranspose(3, (3, 3), activation='sigmoid', padding='same')
(x)

# VAE model
vae = Model(inputs, outputs)
```

```python
# Define the loss function for VAE
def vae_loss(inputs, outputs):
    reconstruction_loss = tf.keras.losses.binary_crossentropy(
        tf.reshape(inputs, (-1, 24 * 24 * 3)), tf.reshape(outputs, (-1, 24
* 24 * 3))
    )
    reconstruction_loss *= 24 * 24 * 3
    kl_loss = 1 + z_log_var - tf.square(z_mean) - tf.exp(z_log_var)
    kl_loss = tf.reduce_mean(kl_loss, axis=-1)
    kl_loss *= -0.5
    return tf.reduce_mean(reconstruction_loss + kl_loss)


# Compile the VAE model
vae.compile(optimizer=Adam(learning_rate=1e-4), loss=vae_loss)


# AE model (without the latent space)
encoder = Model(inputs, z_mean)
decoder = Model(decoder_inputs, outputs)


# Compile the AE model
decoder.compile(optimizer=Adam(learning_rate=1e-4),              loss='binary_
crossentropy')



# Early stopping
early_stopping = EarlyStopping(monitor='val_loss', patience=5, restore_best_
weights=True)


# Training the VAE model
epochs = 100
batch_size = 128
history_vae = vae.fit(x_train, x_train, epochs=epochs, batch_size=batch_size,
validation_data=(x_test, x_test), callbacks=[early_stopping])


# # Training the AE model
# history_ae = decoder.fit(x_train, x_train, epochs=epochs, batch_size=batch_
size, validation_data=(x_test, x_test), callbacks=[early_stopping])
```

```
# # Save the models (optional)
# vae.save("vae_model.h5")
# decoder.save("ae_model.h5")

# # Load the models (optional)
# loaded_vae = tf.keras.models.load_model("vae_model.h5")
# loaded_decoder = tf.keras.models.load_model("ae_model.h5")
import matplotlib.pyplot as plt

# Plot the learning curves for loss
plt.figure(figsize=(10, 6))
plt.plot(history_vae.history_vae['loss'], label='Train Loss')
plt.plot(history_vae.history_vae['val_loss'], label='Validation Loss')
plt.xlabel('Epochs')
plt.ylabel('Loss')
plt.title('Training and Validation Loss')
plt.legend()
plt.grid()
plt.show()
```

Output:

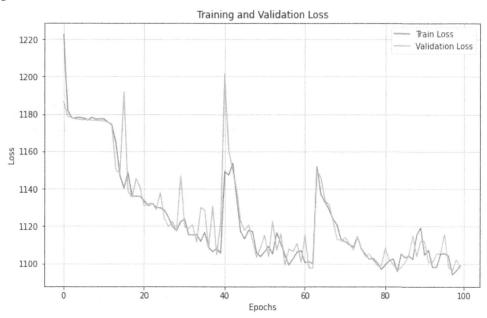

Figure 10.2: The training and validation curve shows convergence however can be improved

Improving the models

Developing deep learning models involves a systematic approach to hyperparameter tuning to optimize model performance. Here is a structured approach you can take:

1. **Understanding the model and problem domain**:

   a. Start by understanding the nature of your problem (classification, regression, and so on), the data distribution, and the model architecture you are using.

   b. Identify which hyperparameters are likely to have the most significant impact on model performance for your specific problem.

2. **Establishing a baseline**:

   a. Train a baseline model with default hyperparameters to establish an initial performance benchmark.

   b. Use a simple grid or random search over a small number of hyperparameters to see how sensitive the model is to changes.

3. **Defining hyperparameter space**:

   a. Define the range of values for each hyperparameter based on literature, empirical evidence, or intuition about their influence on model performance.

4. **Choosing a tuning strategy**:

   a. Use grid search for small hyperparameter spaces or when you have enough computational resources.

   b. Opt for random search when dealing with larger hyperparameter spaces; it's often more efficient than grid search.

   c. Consider Bayesian optimization for a more guided search that builds a probability model of the objective function and uses it to select the most promising hyperparameters to evaluate in the true objective function.

5. **Selecting a performance metric**:

   a. Choose an appropriate metric that aligns with your business objectives and model goals (accuracy, precision/recall, F1 score, and so on).

6. **Iterative tuning**:

   a. Start with broad searches and then progressively narrow down the search space based on the results you obtain.

   b. Use parallel or distributed computing to explore multiple hyperparameters simultaneously if possible.

7. **Validation strategy**:

   a. Use cross-validation to assess the generalizability of the model's performance across different subsets of the data.

   b. Make sure the validation set is representative of the real-world data distribution.

8. **Monitoring and analysis**:

   a. Monitor training progress and be prepared to adjust the search if the model is not learning or if it's overfitting.

   b. Analyze the results of the hyperparameter tuning to understand the relationship between hyperparameters and model performance.

9. **Refinement**:

   a. Once a good set of hyperparameters is identified, further refine them by narrowing down their ranges and tuning more finely.

10. **Automation tools**:

   a. Consider using hyperparameter optimization libraries like Hyperopt, Optuna, or Ray Tune, which can automate much of the process and provide more sophisticated algorithms for hyperparameter tuning.

Remember that hyperparameter tuning is an empirical process and often requires several iterations to find the optimal settings. It is also important to balance the performance improvements with the computational cost of extensive hyperparameter searches

Here are several suggestions you can consider to enhance the VAE model implemented in the code:

- **Hyperparameter tuning:** Experiment with different hyperparameters such as the number of transformer blocks, number of heads, latent space dimension, regularization strengths, learning rates, batch size, and epochs. You can use techniques like grid search or random search to find optimal values.

- **Architecture modifications:**

   o **Encoder architecture:** Instead of using the entire Swin Transformer model as an encoder, you can experiment with other CNN architectures like ResNet, EfficientNet, or custom architectures.

   o **Decoder architecture:** Try different decoder architectures such as deconvolutional layers with skip connections for better image reconstruction.

- **Loss function:** Explore different loss functions or combinations of loss functions to improve the model's performance. For example, you could consider using mean squared error for the reconstruction loss or other divergence metrics for the latent space.

- **Regularization:** Experiment with different regularization techniques like dropout, batch normalization, and different levels of L2 regularization to prevent overfitting.

- **Learning rate scheduling:** Instead of a fixed learning rate, implement learning rate scheduling techniques like ReduceLROnPlateau to dynamically adjust the learning rate during training.

- **Data augmentation:** Apply data augmentation techniques to the input images during training. This can help improve the model's generalization by introducing diversity in the training data.

- **Different latent space exploration:** Once the model is trained, visualize the latent space by plotting or interpolating between different latent vectors to see if it captures meaningful features.

- **Evaluation metrics:** Use additional evaluation metrics beyond loss, such as perceptual metrics (for example, SSIM, PSNR), or qualitative evaluation using generated images.

- **Advanced architectures:** Explore more advanced architectures like Variational Autoencoders with GAN (VAE-GAN) or use adversarial training to improve the generated image quality.

- **Ensemble models:** Train multiple VAE models with different initializations and average their results for better generalization.

- **Variational objectives:** Experiment with different variants of the VAE, such as β-VAE, which introduces a scaling factor to the KL divergence term.

- **Visualization:** Visualize the loss curves, generated images, latent space, and reconstructed images during training to monitor progress and detect potential issues.

- **Regular grid in latent space:** Generate images by traversing a regular grid in the latent space to visualize how different parts of the latent space correspond to different image features.

- **Model complexity:** If computational resources allow, you can increase the model's complexity by adding more layers or transformer blocks to both the encoder and decoder parts.

Remember that improving a model involves a balance between various factors, including architecture complexity, regularization strength, and hyperparameter settings. It is essential to keep track of experiments, document changes, and compare results systematically. Try one change at a time and evaluate its impact on the model's performance to ensure clear insights into what improvements are effective.

Conclusion

If you have followed along from the previous three chapters, then you underwent a series of architectural refactoring steps to improve your model's performance and capabilities, transitioning from a basic VAE to a Transformer-based VAE. Here is how each step in the process likely unfolded:

1. **Basic VAE:** In the initial step, you implemented a basic VAE. A VAE is an autoencoder that incorporates probabilistic concepts to generate diverse and realistic data samples. It consists of an encoder that maps input data to a latent space and a decoder that maps latent vectors back to data space.

2. **TransVAE (Transformer-based VAE):** As you sought to enhance your VAE's capabilities, you moved towards incorporating Transformer architecture. Transformers are known for their effectiveness in handling sequential and positional data, which makes them useful for image generation and processing tasks. You introduced the Transformer architecture into the VAE, creating a "TransVAE." This likely required substantial changes to the encoder and decoder parts of the VAE, adapting them to use Transformer layers for capturing complex patterns and long-range dependencies in the data.

3. **Swin TransVAE (Swin Transformer-based VAE):** Building on the TransVAE, you further refined your model by using the Swin Transformer architecture. The Swin Transformer is a variant of the Transformer that introduces hierarchical structures and window-based attention mechanisms, which enable more efficient processing of large images. By incorporating the Swin Transformer into your TransVAE architecture, you created a *Swin TransVAE*. This step involved replacing or modifying the Transformer layers in your TransVAE with Swin Transformer layers, enabling better feature extraction and representation in your model.

Each step likely required extensive changes to the model architecture, including modifications to the encoder, decoder, and latent space components. Additionally, with each step, you had to ensure compatibility between the chosen architecture and the specific requirements of your dataset (in this case, STL-10).

The architectural refactoring process you followed demonstrates a progressive approach to model improvement. Starting from a basic VAE and progressively integrating more advanced architectural components allowed you to leverage the strengths of different architectures and achieve better performance and capabilities in modeling and generating STL-10 images. It is important to note that this process involves iterative experimentation, fine-tuning, and validation to ensure that each architectural change indeed leads to improvements in terms of generated image quality, feature representation, or other relevant metrics.

Generative AI faces significant technical roadblocks. Current model architectures are often limited in capturing high-dimensional, intricate data distributions using neural networks.

More expressive generative models are required to capture complex patterns. Training and sampling inefficiencies pose challenges due to high computational costs, demanding more scalable algorithms. Lack of interpretability and control hampers understanding and controlled output generation. Generalization and robustness issues arise when extending models to new data distributions or adversarial inputs. Recent research advancements propose solutions: novel architectures for enhanced expressiveness, efficient training algorithms, interpretable models, and strategies to improve generalization and robustness. Overcoming these hurdles holds the key to advancing generative AI.

In the next chapter, we will delve into the points discussed above, focusing primarily on their theoretical aspects.

Join our book's Discord space

Join the book's Discord Workspace for Latest updates, Offers, Tech happenings around the world, New Release and Sessions with the Authors:

https://discord.bpbonline.com

CHAPTER 11

Major Technical Roadblocks in Generative AI and Way Forward

Introduction

In the rapidly evolving landscape of artificial intelligence, one phenomenon that has garnered significant attention and catalyzed remarkable advancements is Generative AI. This paradigm-shifting branch focuses on enabling machines to not only understand and analyze data, but also to create new content that closely mimics human-generated outputs. A remarkable manifestation of this paradigm is the emergence of large image foundation models and vector databases, which have redefined the realm of image synthesis and manipulation.

However, this journey towards harnessing Generative AI has not been devoid of challenges. As we delve into the realm of large image foundation models and vector databases, it becomes evident that a pivotal technical roadblock propelled their inception. The monumental obstacle of scalability and complexity stifled progress in the field for years. Traditional models struggled to capture the intricate nuances of images at a granular level, often succumbing to issues related to resolution, detail, and coherence.

This chapter embarks on a comprehensive exploration of technical roadblocks in Generative AI, Vector databases emerge, paving the way for a new era of Generative AI.

Structure

In this chapter, we will go over the following topics:

- Challenges and hurdles in generative AI
  - o NLP based generative models
- Large language models and image-based foundation models
- Embedding in language models
- Embedding in image
- Generative AI and embeddings
- Vector data bases and image embedding
  - o Vector databases
  - o Image embeddings
- Building an image search using pinecone and vector data base

Objectives

The designated sections of this chapter aim to unravel the challenges and innovative solutions in the fields of data representation, retrieval, and cross-modal understanding. *Obstacles and technical hurdles* delve into the multifaceted challenges faced in various domains, such as generative AI and computer vision.

Text and image embeddings provide insights into the pivotal role of embeddings in transforming textual and visual data into condensed, meaningful vectors. It examines how embeddings facilitate the understanding of semantic relationships and contextual nuances within language and images. The objective is to showcase how embeddings bridge the gap between raw data and AI models, contributing to better comprehension, representation, and manipulation of diverse data types.

Vector databases delves into the construction and application of databases where items are represented as vectors. The section emphasizes efficient retrieval through indexing, particularly similarity searches. It aims to elucidate the construction of structures that enable quick and accurate querying of semantically related items, illustrating their significance in real-world applications.

Image-to-image search utilizing the liberated pinecone vector databases explores the practical implementation of vector databases for image search tasks. It sheds light on the liberation of these databases for open exploration and outlines how they power efficient image retrieval mechanisms. This section aims to demonstrate how vector databases can revolutionize image search, transforming the way users discover visually similar content across a spectrum of applications.

Challenges and hurdles in Generative AI

Generative AI involves creating models that can produce new data samples resembling a given dataset. However, this field faces several challenges. Current model architectures have limited expressive power, struggling to capture intricate patterns in complex, high-dimensional data distributions using neural networks. The necessity arises for more versatile generative models capable of grasping intricate relationships in data.

Additionally, the training and sampling processes of generative models are inefficient, demanding high computational resources. Efficient and scalable algorithms are sought to streamline these tasks. Interpretability and control pose further problems; the need for generative models that can be understood and controlled is evident. The inner workings of these models and the means by which they generate specific outputs in a controlled manner remain unclear.

Furthermore, the concerns of generalization and robustness loom large. The capacity of generative models to adapt to new and unfamiliar data distributions proves challenging. There is a requirement for robust models that can accommodate noisy or adversarial inputs.

Despite these obstacles, recent strides in research offer potential solutions. Novel model architectures enhance the flexibility and expressiveness of generative models. More efficient training and sampling algorithms emerge to tackle the computational burden. Techniques to enhance interpretability, control, generalization, and robustness are being explored, suggesting a path forward in advancing generative AI. Some of them are as follows:

- **Limited expressive power**: Current generative models are often limited in their ability to capture complex patterns in data. This is because they are typically based on neural networks, which are good at learning linear relationships but struggle with more complex nonlinear relationships. For example, a neural network might be able to learn to generate realistic images of faces, but it would be much harder for it to learn to generate images of objects that have never been seen before.

- **Inefficient training and sampling**: Generative models can be computationally expensive to train and sample from. This is because they often need to be trained on large datasets, and they need to use complex algorithms to generate new data. For example, training a generative model on a dataset of 1 million images could take weeks or even months, and generating a new image from the model could take seconds or even minutes.

- **Interpretability and control**: Generative models are often difficult to understand and control. This is because they are often based on complex algorithms that are not fully understood by humans. For example, it might be difficult to explain why a generative model generated a particular image, or to control the model to generate a specific type of image.

- **Generalization and robustness**: Generative models can be difficult to generalize to new data distributions. This means that they may not be able to generate accurate data from a dataset that they have not been trained on. Additionally, generative models can be sensitive to noise and adversarial inputs. This means that they may generate inaccurate data if the input data is corrupted or if the model is intentionally manipulated.

Despite these challenges, there has been significant progress in generative AI in recent years. New model architectures, training algorithms, and sampling techniques have been developed that address some of these challenges. As research in this area continues, it is likely that generative AI will become more powerful and versatile, with a wider range of applications.

Here are some specific examples of how these challenges have been addressed in recent research:

- To address the limited expressive power of generative models, researchers have developed new model architectures that are based on deep learning techniques such as recurrent neural networks and convolutional neural networks. These models have been shown to be able to capture more complex patterns in data than traditional neural networks.

- To address the inefficient training and sampling of generative models, researchers have developed new algorithms that are more efficient and scalable. For example, the **Wasserstein Generative Adversarial Network (WGAN)** is a generative model that can be trained much faster than traditional generative models.

- To address the interpretability and control of generative models, researchers have developed new techniques for visualizing and understanding the inner workings of these models. For example, the DeepDream algorithm can be used to visualize the features that a generative model is using to generate images.

- To address the generalization and robustness of generative models, researchers have developed new techniques for training these models on more diverse datasets and for making them more robust to noise and adversarial inputs. For example, the Mixup regularization technique can be used to train generative models on more diverse datasets.

These are just a few examples of the challenges and recent advances in generative AI. As research in this area continues, it is likely that these challenges will be further addressed, and that generative AI will become a more powerful and versatile tool for a wide range of applications.

NLP based generative models

Let us shift gear in the space on NLP based generative models , there is a lot happening there.

NLP based generative models are a type of generative model that is used to generate text, translate languages, write different kinds of creative content, and answer your questions in an informative way. These models are trained on large datasets of text and code, and they learn to capture the statistical relationships between words and phrases.

There are a number of different NLP based generative models, but some of the most common ones include:

- **Seq2seq models**: These models are based on the idea of sequence-to-sequence learning, where a model is trained to learn the relationship between a sequence of input tokens and a sequence of output tokens. For example, a seq2seq model could be trained to learn the relationship between a sequence of words in a sentence and a sequence of words in the translation of that sentence.

- **Transformer models**: As explained in previous chapters these models are a more recent type of NLP based generative model that is based on the attention mechanism. The attention mechanism allows these models to learn the relationships between different parts of a sequence, which makes them more powerful than seq2seq models.

- **Variational autoencoders (VAEs)**: As explained in previous chapters, these models are a type of generative model that is used to learn the distribution of a dataset. VAEs are trained by minimizing the difference between the distribution of the data that they were trained on and the distribution of the data that they generate.

- **Generative adversarial networks (GANs)**: As explained in previous chapters these models are a type of generative model that is based on the idea of competition. GANs consist of two models, a generator, and a discriminator. The generator is responsible for generating new data, while the discriminator is responsible for distinguishing between real data and generated data.

NLP based generative models are being used in a wide range of applications, including:

- **Text generation**: NLP based generative models can be used to generate text, such as news articles, blog posts, and creative writing.

- **Machine translation**: NLP based generative models can be used to translate languages, such as English to Spanish or French to German.

- **Question answering**: NLP based generative models can be used to answer questions in an informative way, even if the questions are open ended, challenging, or strange.

- **Chatbots**: NLP based generative models can be used to create chatbots that can hold natural conversations with humans.

- **Text summarization**: NLP based generative models can be used to summarize text, such as news articles or research papers.

The field of NLP based generative models is still under active development and uses the same models types similar to image bases generative models, but there has been significant progress in recent years.

Large language models and image-based foundation models

The transition from earlier **Generative AI (GenAI)** models to what are now known as foundation models represents a shift towards more powerful and versatile systems. Early GenAI models were often designed for specific tasks, such as generating images or text in constrained scenarios. They were also typically smaller in scale and trained on more focused datasets.

Foundation models, on the other hand, are characterized by their scale and the breadth of their capabilities. These models, like **Generative Pretrained Transformer (GPT)** for text or DALL-E for images, are trained on vast and diverse datasets, enabling them to develop a wide-ranging understanding of language, concepts, and even visual information. Their extensive pretraining allows them to be fine-tuned for a variety of tasks with relatively little additional data. This adaptability makes them 'foundational' for multiple applications.

One key advantage of foundation models is their ability to generalize from the data they were trained on, thereby performing well on tasks they weren't explicitly designed for. However, this transition also amplifies challenges such as ensuring fairness, managing biases in training data, and maintaining interpretability, given the models' increased complexity and broader usage scope. As such, foundation models are a significant step forward in AI's capabilities, but they also necessitate careful consideration of their deployment and governance.

Large language models and image-based foundation models represent two groundbreaking pillars of artificial intelligence that have reshaped the landscape of natural language processing and computer vision, respectively.

Large language models, exemplified by models like GPT-3, are advanced neural architectures that have demonstrated unparalleled proficiency in understanding, generating, and manipulating human language. By leveraging immense amounts of training data and parameters, they encode linguistic patterns, semantic relationships, and contextual nuances, enabling tasks such as language generation, translation, summarization, and even code writing. Their ability to comprehend and generate text in a coherent and contextually relevant manner has redefined human-computer interaction, content creation, and problem-solving.

On the other hand, image-based foundation models, such as those built on **Convolutional Neural Networks (CNN)** or transformer architectures, have revolutionized computer vision. These models grasp intricate visual features, textures, shapes, and even high-level semantic information within images. They enable image classification, object detection, image segmentation, and even image generation through a synthesis of learned visual representations.

Segment Anything (SAM) and **Follow Anything (FAN)** are two image-based foundation models developed by researchers at MIT. SAM is a segmentation model that can segment any object in an image, while Fan is a tracking model that can track any object in a video.

SAM is based on a Transformer architecture, which allows it to learn long-range dependencies between pixels in an image. This makes SAM very good at segmenting objects that are close together or that are partially occluded. SAM has been shown to outperform state-of-the-art segmentation models on a variety of datasets.

Follow Anything combination of **Segment Anything Model (SAM)**, DINO (self-distillation with no labels and **Contrastive Language-Image Pre-training (CLIP)** is also based on a Transformer architecture, but it is specifically designed for tracking objects in videos. FAN uses a technique called attention to focus on the object that it is tracking, even if the object moves or is occluded. FAN has been shown to outperform state-of-the-art tracking models on a variety of datasets.

SAM and FAN are both still under development, but they have the potential to be used in a wide range of applications, such as:

- **Self-driving cars**: SAM could be used to segment objects on the road, such as cars, pedestrians, and traffic lights. This information could be used by self-driving cars to navigate safely.

- **Virtual reality**: SAM could be used to segment objects in a virtual environment, such as furniture and people. This information could be used to create more realistic and immersive virtual experiences.

- **Medical imaging**: SAM could be used to segment organs and tissues in medical images. This information could be used to diagnose diseases and plan treatments.

- **Robotics**: SAM could be used to segment objects in the environment, such as tools and obstacles. This information could be used by robots to navigate and interact with the world.

The development of SAM and FAN are significant step forward in the field of image-based foundation models. These models have the potential to be used in a wide range of applications, and they could have a major impact on the way we interact with the world.

Together, large language models and image-based foundation models exemplify the astonishing strides AI has made in understanding and generating both linguistic and visual information. Their fusion drives multimodal AI, unlocking potentials that transcend traditional boundaries and promise transformative advancements across various domains.

Note: DINO was introduced in the paper *Emerging Properties in Self-Supervised Vision Transformers* **by** *Caron* **et al. (2021). The paper showed that DINO can achieve state-of-the-art results on a variety of self-supervised learning tasks, including image classification, object detection, and segmentation.**

Note: **CLIP was introduced in the paper** *Learning Transferable Visual Features with Contrastive Language-Image Pre-training* **by** *Radford* **et al. (2021). The paper showed that CLIP can achieve state-of-the-art results on a variety of tasks, including image retrieval, text-to-image generation, and question answering.**

Large language models (LLM) and foundation models like have contributed significantly to mitigating the challenges in generative AI in several ways:

- **Improved expressiveness**: They have demonstrated remarkable capabilities in capturing complex patterns and relationships in data due to their massive scale and diverse training data. They can understand and generate text, code, and other types of data, expanding the scope of generative modeling.

- **Efficient training**: They have set new standards for pre-training efficiency. Their training process benefits from parallelization and efficient hardware utilization, making them more scalable than previous models. This efficiency indirectly aids generative models by inspiring improvements in training methodologies.

- **Transfer learning**: They showcase effective transfer learning, where knowledge learned from one domain can be applied to another. This concept aids in generalization, reducing the need to start training from scratch for every new task or dataset, a challenge that generative models also face.

- **Interpretability and control**: Some research suggests that they can be fine-tuned for controlled generation by conditioning on specific input prompts. While challenges persist in full interpretability, they open doors for generating content that adheres to desired guidelines.

- **Robustness and generalization**: Their broad exposure to various writing styles, topics, and contexts allows them to generate content that's adaptable to different distributions. While not immune to biases, LLMs can be guided to produce more robust outputs through reinforcement learning or other techniques.

- **Inspiration for new architectures**: The success of LLMs has inspired researchers to experiment with novel architectures in other domains, including generative models. Techniques and architectural innovations introduced in LLMs can influence and inform the development of new generative models.

Embedding in language models

Embeddings play a crucial role in LLMs by transforming textual data into a format that is suitable for processing by machine learning algorithms, particularly neural networks.

Embeddings are dense vector representations that capture the semantic meaning and relationships between words or tokens in a language, refer to the following figure:

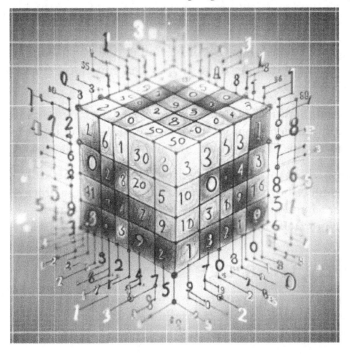

Figure 11.1: Visualization of MNIST embeddings

In the context of LLMs, embeddings serve several important functions:

- **Semantic representation**: Embeddings convert words or tokens into continuous vector spaces where similar words are located closer together. This allows LLMs to understand and capture the semantic relationships between words, enabling them to generate coherent and contextually relevant text.

- **Dimensionality reduction**: Words in a language have a vast vocabulary, making one-hot encoding (a binary representation) impractical due to high dimensionality. Embeddings reduce this dimensionality by mapping words into lower-dimensional continuous vectors, making computation more efficient.

- **Contextual information**: LLMs utilize contextual embeddings that consider not just the word itself but also its surrounding words in a sentence. This contextual information enhances the model's ability to understand nuances and meaning in various contexts.

- **Transfer learning**: Pre-trained embeddings can be used as starting points for training specific language tasks, including LLMs. By fine-tuning these embeddings on a specific task, the model can leverage general language knowledge from the pre-training phase and specialize for the particular task.

- **Word relationships**: Embeddings encode semantic relationships such as synonymy, antonymy, and analogies. For example, by subtracting the embedding of *king* from *man* and adding *woman*, you can find an embedding that is close to *queen*, highlighting gender relationships.

- **Handling out-of-vocabulary words**: Embeddings can handle words that were not present in the training data, as they can generalize from similar words and concepts.

- **Efficient computation**: Compared to one-hot encoded representations, embeddings enable more efficient computation in neural networks due to their dense and continuous nature. This is crucial in training large models like LLMs.

Note: Embeddings, like Word2Vec, GloVe, and contextual embeddings like those from BERT and GPT models, have revolutionized natural language processing by providing a way to represent language in a format that captures semantics, relationships, and context, enabling more effective training and application of language models.

Embedding in image

Earlier, Embeddings were not limited to natural language processing; they have found applications in various fields, including computer vision and generative AI, where they address challenges and enhance capabilities in similar ways. Let us now go over some of them:

- **Computer vision:**

    o **Feature representation**: In computer vision, embeddings serve as compact and informative representations of images. Similar to how word embeddings capture semantic meanings, image embeddings capture visual features. This mitigates the challenge of high-dimensional image data by converting it into a more manageable format for processing.

    o **Semantic relationships**: Just as word embeddings capture word relationships, image embeddings capture visual relationships. This aids in tasks like image similarity, object detection, and image retrieval, where understanding the semantic connections between images is essential.

    o **Transfer learning**: Pre-trained image embeddings, obtained from models trained on large datasets, offer a starting point for specific computer vision tasks. These embeddings capture general visual features, allowing models to leverage them for more focused tasks, thereby reducing the need for extensive task-specific training data.

    o **Dimensionality reduction**: Embeddings in computer vision reduce the dimensionality of image data, simplifying computations and memory requirements while preserving essential features.

- **Computer vision:** Example of Image Embeddings in the industry.

  Image embeddings are compact representations of images in a high-dimensional space and are used to capture visual information in a form that can be easily manipulated and compared by algorithms. Here are five examples of where image embeddings can be used in various industries:

  o **E-commerce and retail**: Image embeddings can power visual search systems, allowing customers to upload a photo of an item and find similar products available for purchase. Retailers can use embeddings to analyze inventory, match customer preferences, and even automate the categorization and organization of products on their platforms.

  o **Healthcare**: In medical imaging, embeddings can be used to compare and retrieve similar cases, assist in diagnosis by finding visually similar pathologies, or monitor the progression of a disease over time. For example, embeddings from x-rays or MRI scans can help identify patterns indicative of specific conditions.

  o **Automotive industry**: Image embeddings can be used in autonomous vehicles for object recognition and categorization, helping the vehicle's AI systems to understand and navigate the environment. Embeddings can also be utilized for quality control during manufacturing, by comparing images of parts or finished products against a standard to detect anomalies.

  o **Agriculture**: In precision agriculture, embeddings from images taken by drones or in-field cameras can help in identifying crop diseases, pest infestations, or nutrient deficiencies. Comparing these embeddings against a database can enable quick actions to improve crop yield and health.

  o **Security and surveillance**: Image embeddings can enhance surveillance systems by enabling face recognition, object tracking, and anomaly detection. In security-sensitive environments, these embeddings can be used to match individuals or objects against a watchlist or to identify unusual activities without manual monitoring.

In each of these cases, the use of image embeddings helps to manage and interpret large volumes of visual data quickly and accurately, often in real-time, which is critical for operational efficiency and decision-making in these industries.

Generative AI and embeddings

Let us now learn the relations in which embeddings are present in generative AI:

- **Learning representations**: Embeddings in generative AI help capture complex patterns and relationships in data. In image generation, for instance, embeddings can capture features that define an image's style and content, leading to more realistic and diverse image synthesis.

- **Efficient computation**: Similar to language models, embeddings make computations more efficient in generative models, reducing the complexity of operations and enabling faster training and sampling.

- **Transfer learning**: In generative AI, embeddings facilitate transfer learning by allowing pre-trained knowledge to be integrated into new tasks. This is particularly useful when generating content in different domains or styles.

- **Robustness and generalization**: Embeddings aid in capturing robust features from data, helping generative models handle noisy or varied inputs. They enable the generation of coherent content even when encountering unseen or adversarial data.

- **Controlled generation**: Embeddings contribute to controlled generation in both language and image domains. By manipulating specific dimensions of embeddings, generative models can be guided to produce outputs with desired attributes.

- **Interpretable latent spaces**: In some generative models, embeddings correspond to interpretable latent spaces. For instance, in **Generative Adversarial Networks (GAN)**, manipulating certain dimensions of embeddings can lead to specific changes in generated images.

In both computer vision and generative AI, embeddings offer a bridge between raw data and model comprehension, allowing for more effective learning, transfer of knowledge, generalization, and controlled output generation. They address challenges related to high dimensionality, efficient computation, and the capture of meaningful features and relationships in data.

Vector data bases and image embeddings

Imagine a large jar filled with colorful candies, each candy representing a different color. However, instead of being randomly mixed, these candies are arranged in layers based on their colors. All the candies of the same color are grouped together in a specific layer. This layering creates a structure where you can easily find candies of a particular color by just looking at the corresponding layer.

In this analogy, the jar represents a vector database, and the candies represent embeddings. Each candy's color corresponds to a unique characteristic or feature of the embeddings. The layering of candies based on color symbolizes how vector databases organize embeddings according to their features or attributes, making it convenient to find similar items by looking at the same layer.

Just as you can retrieve candies of a specific color quickly by focusing on the corresponding layer, a vector database allows you to retrieve similar data items efficiently by accessing the layer that represents their shared features. This structured arrangement simplifies the process of searching and retrieving data items that possess certain attributes, creating an organized and easily navigable data storage system.

Let us explore both vector databases and image embeddings.

Vector databases

A vector database is a collection of data items, where each item is represented as a vector in a multi-dimensional space. The key idea is to transform data into numerical vectors so that similarities, distances, and relationships between items can be easily computed and compared. This enables efficient searching and retrieval of items that are semantically similar or relevant.

In a vector database, the process involves the following steps:

1. **Vector representation**: Data items are converted into numerical vectors. These vectors capture important features or attributes of the items. For example, in a text document, each word could be a dimension, and the vector values might indicate the word's frequency in the document.

2. **Indexing**: Vectors are indexed using data structures like trees or hashes, allowing for faster retrieval. Similar vectors are placed closer in the index structure, enabling efficient search for similar items.

3. **Search and retrieval**: To find similar items, a query vector is compared to the vectors in the database. The similarity metric (for example, cosine similarity, Euclidean distance) determines the closeness of vectors.

4. **Ranking and display**: The most similar items are ranked and presented to the user. This is particularly useful in recommendation systems, content-based searches, and similarity-based tasks.

Image embeddings

Image embeddings are numerical vector representations of images that capture their visual characteristics and semantics. They are designed to enable computers to understand and process images more effectively. These embeddings are learned through deep learning techniques, such as CNNs.

Here is how image embeddings work:

1. **Feature extraction**: CNN is used to extract features from an image. The network's layers capture different levels of visual information, from simple edges and textures to complex structures.

2. **Vector representation**: The output of a CNN's last fully connected layer or a specially designed layer is used as the image embedding. Each element of the vector encodes a specific visual feature.

3. **Semantic meaning**: Similar images have similar embeddings. The distances or similarities between image embeddings reflect their visual similarity.

4. **Applications**: Image embeddings have various applications, including image search, content-based recommendation, object detection, and image captioning. For instance, in content-based recommendation, an image embedding can be used to find visually similar products.

Image embeddings make it feasible to perform complex operations on images using mathematical operations in a vector space. This enables computers to understand images, which is particularly valuable in scenarios where visual content needs to be analyzed and processed by AI systems.

Building an image search using pinecone and vector database

The following code loads the CIFAR-10 dataset, visualizes a subset of its images along with their class labels, and utilizes libraries like Matplotlib and torchvision:

```
import matplotlib.pyplot as plt
import torchvision
from torchvision.transforms import ToTensor


DATA_DIRECTORY = './data'  # Specify the directory where CIFAR-10 is stored


# Load CIFAR-10 dataset
cifar10_dataset = torchvision.datasets.CIFAR10(DATA_DIRECTORY, train=True,
download=True)


# Create a dictionary to store the metadata for each CIFAR-10 class
class_metadata = {
    0: 'airplane',
    1: 'automobile',
    2: 'bird',
    3: 'cat',
    4: 'deer',
    5: 'dog',
    6: 'frog',
    7: 'horse',
```

```
    8: 'ship',
    9: 'truck'
}


def visualize_cifar10_images(dataset, start_index, num_images):
    fig, axes = plt.subplots(1, num_images, figsize=(12, 3))

    for i in range(num_images):
        index = start_index + i
        image, _ = dataset[index]
        class_label = class_metadata[dataset.targets[index]]

        tensor_image = ToTensor()(image)  # Convert PIL image to Torch Tensor

         axes[i].imshow(tensor_image.permute(1, 2, 0))  # Transpose tensor
dimensions for visualization
        axes[i].set_title(f'ID: {index}, Class: {class_label}')
        axes[i].axis('off')

    plt.tight_layout()
    plt.show()


# Usage example:
start_index = 0  # Start index of the images to visualize
num_images = 5  # Number of images to display

visualize_cifar10_images(cifar10_dataset, start_index, num_images)

torch.cuda.is_available()
```

Refer to the following *Figure 11.2*:

Figure 11.2: Images of CIFAR10 dataset

```python
import os
import requests

import tqdm
import httpimport
import pinecone
import numpy as np
from PIL import Image

import torch

DATA_DIRECTORY = 'tmp'
INDEX_NAME = 'image-search'
INDEX_DIMENSION = 1000
BATCH_SIZE=200
datasets = {
    'CIFAR10': torchvision.datasets.CIFAR10(DATA_DIRECTORY, transform=h.
preprocess, download=True),
    'CIFAR100': torchvision.datasets.CIFAR100(DATA_DIRECTORY, transform=h.
preprocess, download=True)
}

combined_dataset = torch.utils.data.ConcatDataset(list(datasets.values()))
# Calculate the dimensionality of the combined dataset
sample = combined_dataset[0][0]
dimension = sample.numel()

print(f"Combined dataset dimension: {dimension}")
h.show_random_images_from_full_dataset(datasets['CIFAR100'])
```

Refer to the following *Figure 11.3*:

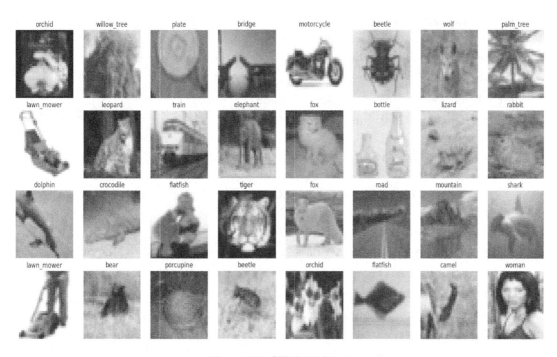

Figure 11.3: CIFAR 10 dataset

```
model = torchvision.models.squeezenet1_1(pretrained=True).eval()
# authenticate with Pinecone API, keys and environment available at your
project at https://app.pinecone.io
pinecone.init(h.pinecone_api_key, environment='Your environment')
# if the index does not already exist, we create it
# if INDEX_NAME not in pinecone.list_indexes():
#     pinecone.create_index(name=INDEX_NAME, dimension=INDEX_DIMENSION)
# # instantiate connection to your Pinecone index
index = pinecone.Index('index')


def get_vector_ids(batch_number, batch_size, prefix):
    """Return vector ids."""
    start_index = batch_number * batch_size
    end_index = start_index + batch_size
    ids = np.arange(start_index, end_index)
    # create id based on prefix
    # eg. if id == 5, prefix == 'CIFAR10', then create 'CIFAR10.5' as vector
id.
    ids_with_prefix = map(lambda x: f'{prefix}.{str(x)}', ids)
```

```python
        return ids_with_prefix

def get_vector_metadata(label_indices, class_list):
    """Return list of {'label': <class name>}."""
    get_class_name = lambda index: {'label': class_list[index]}
    return map(get_class_name, label_indices)

def get_vectors_from_batch(preprocessed_data, label_indices, batch_number,
dataset):
        """Return list of tuples like (vector_id, vector_values, vector_
metadata)."""
    num_records = len(preprocessed_data)
    prefix = dataset.__class__.__name__
    with torch.no_grad():
        # generate image embeddings with PyTorch model
        vector_values = model(preprocessed_data).tolist()
    # return respective IDs/metadata for each image embedding
    vector_metadata = get_vector_metadata(label_indices, dataset.classes)
    vector_ids = get_vector_ids(batch_number, num_records, prefix)
    return list(zip(vector_ids, vector_values, vector_metadata))

dataset = datasets['CIFAR100']
list_of_preprocessed_tensors, label_indices = list(zip(*[dataset[i] for i in
range(BATCH_SIZE)]))
preprocessed_data = torch.stack(list_of_preprocessed_tensors)
vectors  =  get_vectors_from_batch(preprocessed_data,  label_indices,  0,
dataset)
id_, embedding, metadata = vectors[123]
print(id_, embedding[:3], metadata, sep=', ')

def upsert_image_embeddings(dataset, pinecone_index, batch_size=BATCH_SIZE,
num_rows=None):
    """Iterate through dataset, generate embeddings and upsert in batches to
Pinecone index.

    Args:
      - dataset: a PyTorch Dataset
      - pinecone_index: your Pinecone index
      - batch_size: batch size
```

```
      - num_rows: Number of initial rows to use of dataset, use all rows if
None.
    """

    if num_rows>len(dataset):
        raise ValueError(f'`num_rows` should not exceed length of dataset:
{len(dataset)}')
    if num_rows:
        sampler = range(num_rows)
    else:
        sampler = None
    dataloader = torch.utils.data.DataLoader(dataset, batch_size=BATCH_SIZE,
sampler=sampler)
    tqdm_kwargs = h.get_tqdm_kwargs(dataloader)
        for  batch_number,  (data,  label_indices)  in  tqdm.notebook.
tqdm(enumerate(dataloader), tqdm_kwargs):
        vectors = get_vectors_from_batch(
            data,
            label_indices,
            batch_number,
            dataloader.dataset)
        pinecone_index.upsert(vectors)


for dataset in datasets.values():
    upsert_image_embeddings(dataset, index, num_rows=50_000)
url = 'https://cdn.britannica.com/40/109040-050-62EEDEA6/Male-white-tailed-
deer.jpg'
r = requests.get(url, stream=True)
query_image = Image.open(r.raw)
h.printmd("#### A sample image")
query_image.resize((125,125))
```

Refer to the following *Figure 11.4:*

Figure 11.4: *Image of a dear*

```python
query_embedding = model(h.preprocess(query_image).unsqueeze(0)).tolist()
response = index.query(query_embedding, top_k=4, include_metadata=True)
#h.printmd(f"#### A sample response from Pinecone \n ==============\n \n")
h.printmd(f"```python\n{response}\n```")


response = response

def visualize_images_with_ids(response, dataset):
    fig, axes = plt.subplots(1, len(response['matches']), figsize=(12, 3))

    for i, match in enumerate(response['matches']):
        image_id = int(match['id'].split('.')[1])
        image, _ = dataset[image_id]
        class_label = class_metadata[dataset.targets[image_id]]

        tensor_image = ToTensor()(image)  # Convert PIL image to Torch Tensor

        axes[i].imshow(tensor_image.permute(1, 2, 0))  # Transpose tensor
dimensions for visualization
        axes[i].set_title(f'ID: {image_id}, Class: {class_label}')
        axes[i].axis('off')
```

```
    plt.tight_layout()
    plt.show()

# Usage example:
visualize_images_with_ids(response, cifar10_dataset)
```

Refer to the following *Figure 11.5*:

   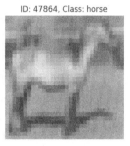

ID: 32179, Class: deer   ID: 19345, Class: deer   ID: 49251, Class: deer   ID: 47864, Class: horse

Figure 11.5: *Simar images of dear from CIFAR 10 dataset*

```
url = 'https://t4.ftcdn.net/jpg/00/97/58/97/360_F_97589769_
t45CqXyzjz0KXwoBZT9PRaWGHRk5hQqQ.jpg'
r = requests.get(url, stream=True)
query_image = Image.open(r.raw)
h.printmd("#### A sample image")
query_image.resize((125,125))
```

Refer to the following *Figure 11.6*:

Figure 11.6: *Image of a cat*

```
query_embedding = model(h.preprocess(query_image).unsqueeze(0)).tolist()
response = index.query(query_embedding, top_k=4, include_metadata=True)
```

```python
#h.printmd(f"#### A sample response from Pinecone \n ==============\n \n")
h.printmd(f"```python\n{response}\n```")

response = response

def visualize_images_with_ids(response, dataset):
    fig, axes = plt.subplots(1, len(response['matches']), figsize=(12, 3))

    for i, match in enumerate(response['matches']):
        image_id = int(match['id'].split('.')[1])
        image, _ = dataset[image_id]
        class_label = class_metadata[dataset.targets[image_id]]

        tensor_image = ToTensor()(image)  # Convert PIL image to Torch Tensor

         axes[i].imshow(tensor_image.permute(1, 2, 0))  # Transpose tensor
dimensions for visualization
        axes[i].set_title(f'ID: {image_id}, Class: {class_label}')
        axes[i].axis('off')

    plt.tight_layout()
    plt.show()

# Usage example:
visualize_images_with_ids(response, cifar10_dataset)
```

Refer to the following *Figure 11.7:*

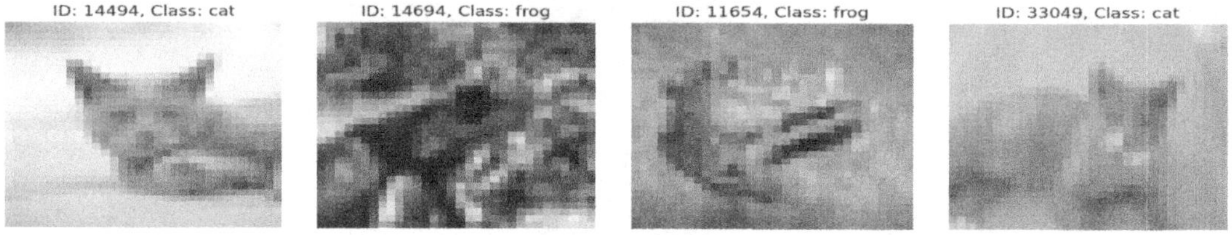

Figure 11.7: *Images of Cat from CIFAR 10 dataset*

```python
url = 'https://t3.ftcdn.net/jpg/00/20/13/60/240_F_20136083_
gk0ppzak6UdK9PcDRgPdLjcuAdo7o1LK.jpg'
r = requests.get(url, stream=True)
query_image = Image.open(r.raw)
h.printmd("#### A sample image")
```

```
query_image.resize((125,125))
```

Refer to the following *Figure 11.8:*

Figure 11.8: *Image of a plane*

```
query_embedding = model(h.preprocess(query_image).unsqueeze(0)).tolist()
response = index.query(query_embedding, top_k=4, include_metadata=True)
#h.printmd(f"#### A sample response from Pinecone \n ==============\n \n")
h.printmd(f"```python\n{response}\n```")
response = response

def visualize_images_with_ids(response, dataset):
    fig, axes = plt.subplots(1, len(response['matches']), figsize=(12, 3))

    for i, match in enumerate(response['matches']):
        image_id = int(match['id'].split('.')[1])
        image, _ = dataset[image_id]
        class_label = class_metadata[dataset.targets[image_id]]

        tensor_image = ToTensor()(image)  # Convert PIL image to Torch Tensor

         axes[i].imshow(tensor_image.permute(1, 2, 0))  # Transpose tensor
dimensions for visualization
        axes[i].set_title(f'ID: {image_id}, Class: {class_label}')
        axes[i].axis('off')

    plt.tight_layout()
    plt.show()
```

```
# Usage example:
```

Refer to the following *Figure 11.9*:

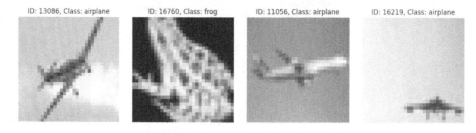

Figure 11.9: Image of Planes from CIFAR 10 dataset

```
visualize_images_with_ids(response, cifar10_dataset)
```

Conclusion

In conclusion, the chapter's designated sections have artfully navigated the intricate domains of data representation, retrieval methodologies, and cross-modal comprehension. By scrutinizing the obstacles and technical hurdles, the narrative delves into the multifaceted challenges encountered in the realms of generative AI and computer vision. By dissecting training efficiency, interpretability, and robustness, it paves the path toward generating expressive, interpretable content.

Text and image embeddings serve as illuminating windows into the transformative power of embeddings in reshaping the landscape of AI. They deftly convey how these condensed vectors bridge the chasm between raw data and intelligent models. By adeptly unraveling the semantics and contextual intricacies in language and images, these embeddings become conduits to not only improved comprehension but also versatile manipulation.

The exploration of vector databases traverses the construction and utility of databases where data items assume vector forms. The focal point is efficient retrieval through ingenious indexing, especially pertinent in recommendation systems and similarity searches. This exploration vividly exemplifies the practical applications, underlining the significance of quick and precise queries in real-world scenarios.

In an artful culmination, the chapter lays bare the practicality of image-to-image search utilizing the liberated pinecone vector databases. By unveiling the liberation of these databases and their instrumental role in image retrieval, the narrative orchestrates a vision of a transformed digital sphere, where users seamlessly discover visually akin content. In unity, these sections epitomize innovation's role in surmounting hurdles, breathing life into sophisticated solutions that reshape the boundaries of modern technology. In the next chapter, we will discuss the overview and application of Generative AI models.

## CHAPTER 12

Overview and Application of Generative AI Models

Introduction

The convergence of **Large Language Models (LLM)** and **Generative Artificial Intelligence (Gen AI)** marks a groundbreaking frontier in technological advancement. LLM, represented by colossal language models like GPT-3.5, employs advanced machine learning algorithms to analyze vast troves of textual data, while Gen AI excels at generating human-like text and creative content. These two potent forces are reshaping various industries with their capabilities.

In sectors such as healthcare, LLM enhances decision-making by sifting through extensive healthcare documents and regulatory frameworks, while Gen AI revolutionizes patient interactions by providing personalized medical advice and information dissemination.

Retail industries benefit from LLM's streamlined contract management, while Gen AI revolutionizes customer engagement through personalized product recommendations and tailored marketing content.

Financial services harness LLM for risk assessment and fraud detection, while Gen AI elevates customer service through natural language processing in chatbots and virtual assistants.

In the insurance sector, LLM aids in efficient claims processing and fraud prevention, while Gen AI elevates underwriting and customer interactions through automated responses and customized policy offerings.

Together, Large Language Models and Generative Artificial Intelligence are propelling these industries into a new era of efficiency, precision, and personalized experiences, making them crucial drivers of innovation and transformation across sectors.

Structure

In this chapter, we will go over the following topics:

- GenAI in hospital

- GenAI in dental

- GenAI in radiology

- GenAI in retail

- GenAI in finance

- GenAI in corporate finance

- GenAI in insurance story

Objectives

In this chapter, we embark on a journey through the dynamic landscape of technology's role in various industries, without delving into complex code or algorithms. Imagine a world where cutting-edge innovations like LLM and Gen AI are not just buzzwords but integral tools reshaping healthcare, retail, finance, and insurance.

The story begins in healthcare, where LLM streamlines compliance, analyzes intricate medical documents, and guides professionals through complex regulatory mazes. Meanwhile, Gen AI steps in to provide personalized medical advice, automate appointment scheduling, and deliver vital information to patients and healthcare providers, ensuring the highest quality of care. Transitioning to the retail sector, LLM ensures contractual accuracy, compliance, and vendor agreement efficiency. Gen AI transforms the customer experience, captivating shoppers with personalized recommendations and dynamic marketing strategies, creating a retail environment tailored to each individual. In the financial realm, LLM takes center stage, enhancing risk assessment, detecting fraud, and analyzing contracts with unparalleled precision. Simultaneously, Gen AI optimizes customer service through AI-powered chatbots and virtual assistants, providing real-time and context-aware responses to financial inquiries.

Finally, in the insurance sector, LLM drives claims efficiency, fraud detection, and regulatory compliance. Gen AI revolutionizes insurance by reshaping underwriting processes, crafting personalized policy offerings, and elevating customer interactions.

GenAI in hospital

In the bustling world of healthcare, where every decision can be a matter of life and death, the arrival of cutting-edge technology is transforming the landscape. Legal professionals, often the unsung heroes behind the scenes, have found a formidable ally in the form of LLM, while Gen AI has stepped into the limelight to revolutionize patient care.

The use of LLM in healthcare is akin to a seasoned navigator guiding a ship through treacherous waters. Within the labyrinthine realm of healthcare regulations, legal professionals have traditionally grappled with an endless stream of complex documents, contracts, and policies. The consequences of a misstep can be dire, both in terms of patient safety and legal repercussions.

Imagine Mary, a diligent healthcare attorney. She is tasked with ensuring that her hospital stays compliant with an ever-evolving web of healthcare regulations. Armed with LLM, Mary can now navigate this maze with unprecedented efficiency. LLM's machine learning algorithms sift through volumes of legal texts, parsing intricate clauses and cross-referencing them with current regulations. In the blink of an eye, it highlights potential compliance issues and suggests solutions. Mary's workload has been significantly lightened, allowing her to focus on proactive legal strategies, ultimately safeguarding her hospital's reputation and patient well-being.

But the transformative power of technology does not stop there. Gen AI emerges as a beacon of hope on the frontlines of patient care. In a bustling healthcare facility, time is of the essence, and patients often yearn for more personalized attention.

Meet *Dr. Amanda*, a dedicated physician who is passionate about delivering the best care possible. However, the sheer volume of patients and administrative tasks often leaves her with little time for meaningful interactions. Gen AI steps in as Dr. Amanda's trusted assistant, not only lightening her administrative load but also enhancing the quality of patient care.

With Gen AI's natural language processing capabilities, patients can engage in real-time conversations. When a patient seeks medical advice, Gen AI listens attentively, considering the patient's medical history, symptoms, and preferences. It then offers personalized medical advice and recommendations, empowering patients to make informed decisions about their health. Dr. Amanda finds herself freed from routine inquiries, enabling her to focus on complex cases and more personalized patient interactions.

Moreover, Gen AI streamlines appointment scheduling, ensuring that patients receive timely care. Patients can interact with virtual receptionists, seamlessly booking appointments, rescheduling, or obtaining information about their upcoming visits. This reduces no-shows and optimizes the allocation of healthcare resources.

However, Gen AI's influence does not end with patients. Healthcare providers also benefit from its capabilities. It disseminates critical information efficiently, ensuring that physicians and nurses have access to the latest medical research, treatment guidelines, and patient data. This results in more informed decision-making and ultimately better patient outcomes.

In our healthcare story, LLM and Gen AI work in tandem, creating a synergy that elevates the standard of care. LLM ensures that the legal foundations are solid, allowing healthcare professionals to operate within a safe and compliant framework. Meanwhile, Gen AI personalizes patient interactions, offering a level of care and engagement that was previously unimaginable.

As the sun sets on another busy day in the healthcare world, Mary, the attorney, rests easy knowing that LLM has her back, safeguarding her hospital from legal pitfalls. Dr. Amanda, the physician, reflects on how Gen AI has not only lightened her administrative load but also deepened her connection with patients. It is a story of how technology, in the form of LLM and Gen AI, has truly transformed the healthcare landscape, ensuring that both the legal and the compassionate sides of healthcare thrive in unison.

GenAI in dental

In the heart of a bustling city, *Sarah*, found herself faced with an unexpected dilemma. She had been experiencing an uncomfortable sensation in her teeth for days, and the uncertainty gnawed at her. But amid her busy schedule, finding time to visit a dentist seemed like an insurmountable challenge.

One evening, as she sat at her desk, her curiosity got the better of her. She had heard about the power of LLM and wondered if it could provide some insight into her dental issue. With a quick online search, she found a user-friendly LLM-powered platform designed to assist individuals with their health-related questions.

Sarah typed in her query, describing her symptoms and concerns. Within moments, the LLM went to work, analyzing her description against a vast database of medical knowledge, dental expertise, and patient experiences. It cross-referenced her symptoms with common dental conditions, taking into account various factors such as her age, medical history, and even the current weather conditions in her city.

After a brief moment of processing, the LLM provided a personalized response. It explained that her symptoms could be indicative of several potential dental issues, such as tooth sensitivity, cavity development, or even gum inflammation. While it could not provide a definitive diagnosis, it strongly recommended that she seek professional dental advice.

Sarah felt relieved to have some guidance but was still unsure about the next steps. With a few more keystrokes, the LLM platform offered to assist her further. It provided a list of nearby dental facilities, complete with user ratings and reviews, and even highlighted clinics with available appointments in the coming days.

Feeling empowered and grateful for the guidance, Sarah selected a well-rated dental facility close to her workplace. To her surprise, the platform seamlessly integrated with the clinic's scheduling system. It presented her with a choice of appointment slots, allowing her to pick a time that best fit her busy agenda.

With a sense of accomplishment, Sarah confirmed her appointment. She could not help but marvel at how technology, specifically LLM, had come to her aid. What had once seemed like an overwhelming challenge had been transformed into a manageable task, all thanks to the remarkable capabilities of this AI-powered tool.

As the day of her dental appointment approached, Sarah felt a sense of gratitude for the LLM that had guided her through this uncertain journey. It was a reminder of how technology had not only simplified her life but had also connected her with the right healthcare resources when she needed them most.

And so, with a newfound sense of confidence, Sarah walked into the dental clinic, ready to address her dental concerns, all because of the remarkable assistance of LLM and its ability to seamlessly bridge the gap between curiosity and healthcare solutions.

Refer to the following *Figure 12.1*:

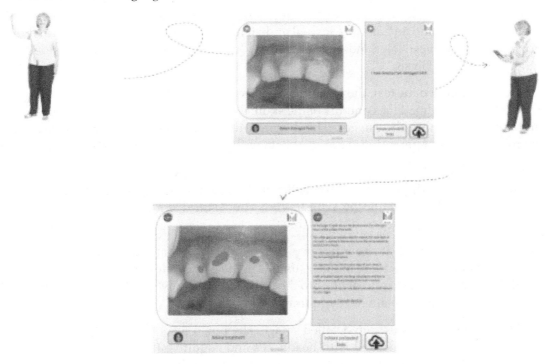

Figure 12.1: Pictorial representation of the GenAI in dental

GenAI in radiology

In the quiet depths of a bustling hospital, *Dr. Lisa Reynolds,* a skilled radiologist, prepared for another day of conducting MRI assessments. Her mission was clear: to help diagnose and treat patients by deciphering the intricate details hidden within the images produced by the massive MRI machine. Today, however, she had a new tool at her disposal: the synergy of LLM and computer vision.

One of the critical steps in MRI assessments is the process known as "skull stripping." It involves separating the intricate brain structures from the surrounding tissues, primarily the skull. This step is essential because it allows for a clearer view of the brain, aiding in the identification of abnormalities, tumors, or injuries.

Traditionally, skull stripping had been a time-consuming and meticulous task, requiring radiologists like Dr. Reynolds to painstakingly outline the brain's contours in each MRI scan. But today, technology promised a breakthrough.

Dr. Reynolds opened her workstation and loaded the MRI scans of her first patient, Emily, a young woman with recurring headaches and unexplained symptoms. Beside her was a computer program that incorporated LLM, and computer vision algorithms designed specifically for skull stripping.

With a few simple clicks, Dr. Reynolds initiated the process. The LLM, a language model trained to understand and analyze textual and visual data, began its work. It first read the accompanying clinical notes and patient history, identifying any relevant information that might guide the analysis.

As the LLM digested the text, the computer vision component delved into the MRI images. It detected and outlined the contours of the skull, thanks to its ability to recognize patterns and structures within the images. The program then combined the insights from both components, cross-referencing the textual data with the visual cues from the MRI.

Within moments, the results were in. The LLM-computer vision duo had successfully performed skull stripping, precisely delineated the boundaries of Emily's brain and isolating it from the surrounding skull tissues. The result was a clean, detailed image of her brain, ready for Dr. Reynolds to examine.

Dr. Reynolds marveled at the efficiency of the process. What had once been a time-consuming task now took mere minutes, thanks to the AI-powered collaboration. With the skull stripped away, she could delve into the intricacies of Emily's brain, searching for any anomalies that might explain her symptoms.

As Dr. Reynolds examined the detailed image, she noted a subtle abnormality near the frontal lobe, an area associated with headaches and cognitive function. She zoomed in, magnifying the image to get a closer look. The AI had done its part, but it was her trained eye that would provide the final diagnosis.

Intrigued by her discovery, she began to compare it with Emily's clinical history, the symptoms she had described, and other relevant data. After careful consideration, she made her diagnosis: a small, previously undetected brain lesion, which was likely the source of Emily's recurrent headaches and discomfort.

With a sense of accomplishment and gratitude for the remarkable technology at her disposal, Dr. Reynolds prepared to present her findings to Emily. The combination of LLM and computer vision had not only streamlined her work but had also enabled her to provide more accurate and timely diagnoses, ultimately improving patient care.

As Dr. Reynolds left her workstation that day, she could not help but reflect on how the world of radiology had evolved. The collaboration between human expertise and cutting-edge AI technology had ushered in a new era of efficiency and precision, transforming the way healthcare professionals like her approached their work and, most importantly, improving the lives of their patients.

GenAI in retail

In the bustling world of retail, where every transaction, contract, and customer interaction are a piece of a complex puzzle, two powerful technologies have emerged as the industry's guiding stars: LLM and Gen AI.

Imagine a thriving department store, where Lisa, a seasoned retail manager, finds herself buried under stacks of contracts, vendor agreements, and the ever-evolving landscape of compliance requirements. It is a daunting task that is essential to the store's success but incredibly time-consuming and error-prone. That is when LLM enters the scene, a digital ally ready to transform Lisa's world.

One crisp morning, Lisa sits down at her desk, determined to conquer the mountain of legal documents that have accumulated over the years. She opens her computer and fires up the LLM-powered contract management tool that her store recently implemented. With a few clicks, she uploads the contracts, and the LLM gets to work.

The LLM, with its vast knowledge and language processing capabilities, scans through the contracts with remarkable precision. It identifies key clauses, milestones, and deadlines, cross-references them with the latest legal requirements, and even detects potential discrepancies. What would have taken Lisa weeks, if not months, to accomplish manually, the LLM does in a matter of hours.

As the LLM reviews each document, it highlights areas that require immediate attention. Lisa receives notifications about critical compliance updates, allowing her to proactively address any legal risks. The time saved is staggering, giving Lisa the freedom to focus on strategic decisions and enhancing the store's overall performance.

But the story does not end there. In the world of retail, customer engagement is the lifeblood of success. Customers are not just numbers; they are individuals with unique preferences, tastes, and shopping habits. That is where Gen AI takes center stage.

Meet Sarah, a loyal customer who frequents Lisa's department store. Like many shoppers, Sarah craves a personalized experience—one that makes her feel valued and understood. Gen AI steps in as the catalyst for this transformation, working tirelessly behind the scenes to elevate customer engagement.

As Sarah browses the store's website one evening, Gen AI springs into action. It analyzes her past purchase history, her browsing patterns, and her demographic information. With this data, Gen AI tailors Sarah's shopping experience to her individual tastes.

First, it offers personalized product recommendations, subtly guiding Sarah toward items that align with her previous purchases and browsing history. It is as if the store has an intuitive understanding of her desires.

Then, Gen AI introduces dynamic pricing strategies. As Sarah explores different products, she notices that some prices seem to adjust based on her preferences and behaviors. This dynamic pricing strategy is designed to maximize value for both Sarah and the store, ensuring she receives competitive prices while optimizing the store's revenue.

But Gen AI does not stop there. It is a master of crafting tailored marketing content. As Sarah navigates the website, she encounters advertisements and promotions that resonate with her interests. It is no longer generic advertising; it is marketing content that speaks directly to her, piquing her curiosity and encouraging her to explore further.

In this new retail paradigm, Gen AI has become an invisible but omnipresent shopping companion. It is the reason Sarah feels a unique connection to the store, why she keeps coming back for more, and why her shopping experience feels like it has been customized just for her.

As Lisa, the retail manager, reviews the store's performance reports, she is thrilled to see a substantial increase in customer engagement and sales. She attributes this transformation to the seamless integration of LLM and Gen AI into the store's operations.

LLM ensures that every contract, vendor agreement, and compliance requirement is meticulously managed, safeguarding the store's legal accuracy. This, in turn, allows Lisa to allocate her time and resources to more strategic endeavors.

Gen AI, on the other hand, breathes life into customer interactions, providing personalized product recommendations, dynamic pricing, and tailored marketing content that resonates with each individual customer.

Together, LLM and Gen AI have ushered in a new era of retail—one where efficiency, precision, and personalized engagement reign supreme. Lisa's store thrives in this landscape, setting a benchmark for the retail industry's future, and customers like Sarah leave with not just shopping bags but also a sense of satisfaction, knowing that their preferences and needs are at the heart of their retail experience.

GenAI in finance

In the heart of the financial district, towering skyscrapers house institutions that drive the modern world's economic engine. Inside one such institution, we meet Alex, a diligent risk analyst. His daily tasks include scrutinizing vast amounts of financial data, assessing risks, and ensuring that the institution complies with intricate regulations.

It is an arduous task, but Alex is not alone. He has a powerful ally by his side—LLM. Equipped with advanced machine learning algorithms, LLM has the ability to navigate the intricate world of finance with ease.

One crisp morning, as Alex settles into his office, he faces a stack of complex documents that require meticulous analysis. These documents are laden with financial jargon and intricate details that could impact the institution's risk exposure. In the past, analyzing these documents was a time-consuming and error-prone process.

Enter LLM. With a few keystrokes, Alex uploads the documents into the LLM-powered system. The model springs into action, reading and comprehending the dense text with astonishing accuracy. It identifies key sections, calculates risk factors, and cross-references them with the latest financial regulations. What would have taken Alex days to accomplish, the LLM does in mere hours.

As the day progresses, the LLM flags potential compliance issues and alerts Alex in real-time. With this newfound efficiency, he not only ensures the institution's adherence to regulations but also has the bandwidth to focus on proactive risk management strategies, safeguarding the institution's financial stability.

But the transformation does not stop there. In another corner of the institution, Emily, a customer service representative, faces a constant influx of customer inquiries. The world of financial services is dynamic, and clients expect immediate and accurate responses to their queries.

This is where Gen AI comes into play. Emily's toolkit now includes AI-powered chatbots and virtual assistants, capable of providing immediate and context-aware responses to customer inquiries.

One busy afternoon, as Emily mans the customer service desk, a flurry of inquiries floods in. Clients seek clarification on account balances, transaction details, and investment options. Emily's chatbot companion, powered by Gen AI, assists her effortlessly.

As clients input their queries, the chatbot responds promptly and with remarkable accuracy. It understands the context of each conversation, drawing upon its vast knowledge base to provide clients with the information they need. From explaining complex financial products to guiding clients through the intricacies of online banking, the chatbot acts as a tireless assistant, ensuring that clients receive timely and accurate support.

Emily, empowered by this AI companion, finds that her workload has been significantly lightened. She can now focus on more complex and specialized client interactions, providing tailored financial advice and solutions that require her human expertise.

In the financial world, time is money, and accuracy is paramount. Thanks to LLM's prowess in risk assessment, fraud detection, and document analysis, financial institutions like Alex's can navigate complex financial landscapes with ease, enhancing overall compliance and operations. Simultaneously, Gen AI's AI-powered chatbots and virtual assistants optimize customer service, providing immediate and context-aware responses to client inquiries.

As the day draws to a close in the bustling financial institution, both Alex and Emily reflect on how the fusion of LLM and Gen AI has transformed their respective roles. The institution stands stronger, armed with advanced tools that enhance efficiency, accuracy, and customer service. In this fast-paced world of finance, they find solace in knowing that they are equipped to meet the ever-evolving needs of their clients and the demands of their industry.

GenAI in corporate finance

In the heart of the bustling financial district, where traders, analysts, and financial experts moved like chess pieces in a high-stakes game, the advent of Gen AI and LLM was set to rewrite the rules of corporate finance.

Meet David, a seasoned CFO of a Fortune 500 company, who had seen the financial world evolve over the years. His desk, usually cluttered with spreadsheets, financial reports, and legal documents, was now adorned with a new addition—an AI-powered terminal that integrated Gen AI and LLM. The world of corporate finance was about to change, and David was ready to embrace it.

The first morning David used the AI-powered terminal, he initiated a complex financial analysis of potential investments. In the past, this process involved hours of poring over spreadsheets, market data, and legal documents. But with Gen AI by his side, the process became more streamlined and insightful.

David instructed the AI to assess the feasibility of an ambitious expansion project. Gen AI immediately began sifting through a vast database of financial data, market trends, and economic indicators. Its algorithms identified potential risks and opportunities, creating a comprehensive report that highlighted the project's potential impact on the company's bottom line. What would have taken David's team weeks to compile was ready in a matter of hours, giving him a significant advantage in making informed financial decisions.

As the day progressed, David turned his attention to managing the company's capital structure—a critical aspect of corporate finance. LLM came into play, offering its language-processing prowess to analyze complex legal agreements and financial contracts. It reviewed loan covenants, debt terms, and equity agreements, ensuring that the company's capital structure was optimized for maximum efficiency and minimal risk.

With LLM's assistance, David identified opportunities to refinance existing debt at more favorable terms, freeing up valuable capital for strategic investments. The legal accuracy of his decisions was ensured, and compliance with intricate regulations became a seamless process, thanks to LLM's ability to navigate the ever-evolving legal landscape.

But the true magic happened when Gen AI and LLM worked in tandem. David was tasked with presenting the company's financial performance to the board of directors. He needed to convey complex financial data in a clear and compelling manner. Gen AI transformed the raw data into a visually appealing presentation, complete with infographics and interactive charts. It tailored the narrative to cater to the board's specific concerns, using language that resonated with each director's background and expertise.

During the board meeting, Gen AI's presentation captivated the directors. They asked questions, and Gen AI responded with immediate and context-aware answers, drawing upon LLM's extensive knowledge base. The directors were impressed by the depth of analysis and the speed at which decisions could be made, thanks to the AI-powered insights.

In the weeks that followed, the company's financial performance improved steadily. David's strategic decisions, aided by Gen AI and LLM, proved to be well-informed and effective. The company's stock price surged, and investors lauded the management's ability to adapt to the rapidly changing financial landscape.

David's experience was not unique. Across the financial sector, Gen AI and LLM were ushering in a new era of corporate finance. Financial analysts, CFOs, and executives were embracing these tools to gain a competitive edge, streamline operations, and make data-driven decisions with unprecedented efficiency.

As David leaned back in his chair, reflecting on the transformative power of Gen AI and LLM, he marveled at how these technologies had revolutionized corporate finance. The financial world, once shrouded in complexity, had become more accessible and agile. The combination of human expertise and artificial intelligence had created a synergy that was reshaping the landscape of corporate finance, allowing businesses to thrive in an era of rapid change and uncertainty.

GenAI in insurance

In a bustling metropolis, nestled amidst towering skyscrapers, an insurance company named *InsuraGen* was on the cusp of a revolution. They had embarked on a journey that would forever change the landscape of the insurance domain. The secret behind their transformation was Generative Artificial Intelligence.

InsuraGen, like many others in the insurance industry, had long struggled with the complex world of claims assessment. Analyzing claims for all types of assets – from homes and cars to businesses and even rare antiques – was a herculean task. However, they were ready to redefine the game.

The company had meticulously collected and stored decades of historical data, and their team of data scientists, underwriters, and AI experts had been working tirelessly to create a foundation model. This AI marvel, fondly called "Gen AI," was the culmination of years of research and innovation. It could analyze claims for any asset type with unparalleled accuracy and efficiency.

As dawn broke over the city, InsuraGen's headquarters buzzed with excitement. It was the day of the grand unveiling of their groundbreaking AI system. A presentation room, decked out with futuristic holographic displays, awaited the top executives, underwriters, and clients who were eager to witness the change Gen AI would bring.

The presentation began with a breathtaking holographic image showcasing the evolution of insurance. From parchment scrolls in ancient times to modern policies, it was clear that the industry had come a long way. Gen AI, however, represented a quantum leap forward.

The CEO, *Sarah Mitchell*, took the stage. *Ladies and gentlemen*, she began, *today, we embark on a new era in the world of insurance. Our Gen AI is here to revolutionize how we assess claims. Let me show you how.*

A 3D image appeared, illustrating a complex car accident scene. Gen AI had processed the claim in seconds, evaluating damage, liability, and coverage. A live feed of data points and insights flowed seamlessly onto the holographic dashboard. It was a mesmerizing display of AI in action.

The Chief Data Scientist, Dr. *Ethan Parker*, explained the magic behind Gen AI, *Our foundation model has absorbed the wisdom from decades of claims data. It understands nuances, learns from past mistakes, and adapts to new challenges. However, Gen AI is not just about claims assessment; rather, it is a powerful tool for underwriters too.*

In an instant, the holographic display transformed into an underwriter's paradise. Gen AI had generated comprehensive risk profiles for various businesses, predicting future trends and potential losses. It was a game-changer for the underwriting department, empowering them with unparalleled data-driven insights.

The room filled with applause as the CFO, *Rachel Turner*, took the stage. She presented Gen AI's financial impact with vivid charts and graphs, *we have seen a significant reduction in claims processing time, increased accuracy, and cost savings. Gen AI is driving profitability like never before.*

But the grand finale was yet to come. The Chief AI Engineer, *David Reynolds*, unveiled the most astonishing feature of Gen AI, its ability to create dazzling business intelligence dashboards and presentations. With a few commands, Gen AI generated breathtaking visualizations, infographics, and presentations tailored to the audience.

As the audience marveled at the AI-generated dashboards, *Sarah Mitchell* summed it up, "Gen AI is not just a tool; it is our partner in progress. It has made us more efficient, more accurate, and more customer-centric. It is changing the way we do business."

The room was buzzing with excitement, and clients were eager to integrate Gen AI into their own operations. The insurance industry was witnessing a transformation of epic proportions, driven by the power of Generative AI.

In the weeks that followed, InsuraGen's competitors scrambled to catch up. The insurance landscape was evolving rapidly, and Gen AI had set a new standard for excellence. Claims were processed faster, risks were assessed more accurately, and clients were delighted by the streamlined experience.

InsuraGen had indeed ushered in a new era of insurance. As the sun set over the city, the company's logo, illuminated atop its headquarters, shone brighter than ever. It was a beacon of innovation, a symbol of how Generative AI had revolutionized the insurance domain. The future of insurance had arrived, and it was brighter, smarter, and more efficient than anyone could have imagined.

Disclaimer: All characters and names in the preceding story are a product of the author's imagination. Any resemblance to real persons, living or deceased, or to actual events, stories, or organizations, is purely coincidental. The story is a work of fiction created for explaining Gen AI , LLMs and illustrative purposes only.

There are several risks linked to the implementation of GenAI which necessitate a Responsible AI assessment. However, this topic is not covered in this chapter.

Conclusion

In conclusion, the synergy LLM and Gen AI is ushering in a transformative wave across various sectors, reshaping the way industries operate and engage with their stakeholders.

In healthcare, LLM's capabilities in streamlining compliance and navigating complex regulations, coupled with Gen AI's personalized medical advice and streamlined patient services, promise to enhance both the efficiency and effectiveness of healthcare delivery.

In retail, the partnership of LLM in contract management and Gen AI in customer engagement promises to create a dynamic shopping experience that tailors recommendations and marketing strategies to individual customers, boosting customer loyalty and sales.

Within the financial sector, LLM's proficiency in risk assessment, fraud detection, and contract analysis, along with Gen AI's prowess in customer service automation, revolutionizes how financial institutions manage their operations and interact with clients. This collaboration empowers professionals to make data-driven decisions swiftly and with greater accuracy.

The insurance sector benefits similarly, with LLM optimizing claims processing and compliance, while Gen AI reinvents underwriting, personalizes policies, and enhances customer interactions.

In each of these sectors, the combined force of LLM and Gen AI transcends traditional boundaries and unleashes innovative possibilities. It empowers professionals to focus on higher-value tasks, elevates customer experiences, and drives efficiencies that were once unimaginable.

As we move forward, the integration of these technologies will continue to evolve, presenting new opportunities and challenges. The story of LLM and Gen AI is one of a powerful partnership, reshaping industries and ultimately improving the lives of individuals, whether it is through streamlined healthcare, personalized shopping experiences, optimized financial services, or enhanced insurance solutions. The future promises even greater advancements as these technologies push the boundaries of what is possible, propelling industries into a new era of efficiency and customer-centric innovation. In the next chapter, we will go through the key learnings of each chapter.

Join our book's Discord space

Join the book's Discord Workspace for Latest updates, Offers, Tech happenings around the world, New Release and Sessions with the Authors:

https://discord.bpbonline.com

CHAPTER 13
Key Learnings

Introduction

In this chapter, we embark on a journey of reflection and consolidation, summarizing the essential learnings garnered from the preceding twelve chapters. In this chapter, we will distill the knowledge, insights, and revelations that have graced our exploration thus far. Each chapter has been a steppingstone, offering unique perspectives and illuminating diverse aspects of our subject matter. Now, it is time to distill the essence of this collective wisdom, shaping a cohesive understanding of the material covered. Join us as we gather the threads of knowledge from the tapestry we have woven, creating a concise and profound overview of our cumulative discoveries.

Structure

In this chapter, we will discuss the following topics:

* Key learnings from all the chapters

Objectives

The objective of this chapter is to synthesize and distill the core teachings and insights from chapters one through twelve. It aims to provide readers with a comprehensive summary, highlighting the key concepts, important takeaways, and significant learnings obtained from each preceding chapter. By consolidating this knowledge, the chapter seeks to offer a holistic understanding of the subject matter, reinforcing key ideas, and preparing readers for further exploration or application of the discussed principles. Ultimately, the objective is to enhance comprehension, retention, and practical application of the cumulative wisdom acquired throughout the previous chapters.

Key learning from all the chapters

In the following section, we will go through the key learnings from all the chapters.

Chapter 1: Introducing Generative AI

In the inaugural chapter, we embarked on an enlightening journey through the realm of generative models, comprehensively covering both their mathematical foundations, practical coding applications, and integration into **Machine Learning Operations (MLops)**. The chapter commenced with a detailed overview of generative models, shedding light on their fundamental nature and purpose in the domain of machine learning. It introduced the mathematical underpinnings that govern generative models, providing a conceptual framework for understanding their workings.

A critical focus of this chapter was distinguishing between discriminative and generative models, elucidating their distinctive approaches in understanding and modeling data. This distinction was accompanied by an exploration of their respective mathematical formulations, enriching our understanding of the core principles driving these models.

Furthermore, the chapter encompassed an exploration of various types of discriminative and generative models, integrating theoretical insights with practical code implementations. From Naive Bayes and logistic regression to GANs and Variational Autoencoders, a diverse array of models was dissected, and code snippets were provided, enabling hands-on comprehension of the concepts discussed.

In addition to theoretical understanding and practical coding, the chapter expanded into the realm of MLops, emphasizing the operational aspects of generative AI. It covered how to deploy, manage, and monitor generative models in production environments, highlighting the crucial considerations in scaling and optimizing these models for real-world applications.

The first chapter provided a holistic learning experience by intertwining mathematical foundations with practical coding examples, complemented by insights into MLops for generative AI. It equipped us with the essential concepts and distinctions between generative and discriminative models, along with the operational knowledge required to effectively integrate and manage generative models in production settings. This comprehensive approach sets the stage for further exploration and application of these models, with a focus on operational efficiency and real-world impact.

Chapter 2: Designing Generative Adversarial Networks

The chapter offers a comprehensive exploration of **Generative Adversarial Networks (GANs)**, encapsulating a plethora of mathematical concepts fundamental to understanding this innovative machine learning technique. The chapter commences with an introduction, emphasizing the significance of GANs in the realm of machine learning and artificial intelligence.

The structure and objectives are clearly outlined, paving the way for an in-depth understanding of GANs. The discussion begins by elucidating what GANs are and their core components, accompanied by a deep dive into the mathematics governing their operations. This includes a detailed examination of equations, discriminator loss, and generator loss, providing readers with a strong mathematical foundation.

The chapter delves into the various types of GANs available, each accompanied by a mathematical understanding of their architectures and operations. It meticulously explores significant GAN architectures such as Vanilla GAN, Deep Convolutional GANs, Wasserstein GANs, Conditional GANs, CycleGANs, Progressive GANs, StyleGANs, and Pix2Pix, linking their unique attributes to the underlying mathematical principles.

Moreover, the discussion underscores crucial factors in GAN architecture design and major challenges related to mathematics that practitioners encounter. By incorporating multiple choice questions, readers are encouraged to apply their mathematical knowledge, reinforcing their grasp of the material.

So, this chapter serves as a comprehensive repository of mathematical concepts intertwined with the exploration of Generative Adversarial Networks. It caters to both beginners seeking an introduction to GANs and seasoned practitioners aiming to deepen their mathematical understanding, establishing this chapter as an invaluable resource in the domain of machine learning.

Chapter 3: Training and Developing Generative Adversarial Networks

This chapter is a pivotal dive into GAN, encapsulating essential topics and practical implementations. It initiates with an exploration of what Generative Adversarial Training entails, laying the groundwork for a profound understanding of this cutting-edge approach in machine learning.

The chapter proceeds to a hands-on demonstration of generating MNIST data, a foundational step in comprehending GANs. Readers are provided with a basic GAN implementation, complete with code snippets, enabling them to grasp the practical aspects of GAN creation and operation.

n addition to implementation, the chapter addresses the challenges and issues encountered during GAN training, shedding light on the intricacies of this learning process. The learning curve of GANs is discussed, providing insights into the progression and dynamics of training a GAN model.

Moreover, the chapter offers a case study on a practical application of GANs, focusing on Dental Cavity Detection—a critical real-world scenario. This case study highlights the common practical implementations of GANs, emphasizing augmentation and class balancing for accurate dental cavity detection. By doing so, readers gain a glimpse into the real-world impact and potential of GANs in addressing significant challenges in various domains.

In summary, this chapter serves as an invaluable resource, combining theoretical understanding with practical implementation. It equips readers with a comprehensive view of Generative Adversarial Training, offering a pathway to hands-on learning and showcasing the potential of GANs in solving real-world problems, such as dental cavity detection, through augmentation and class balancing. This chapter stands as a key building block in the exploration of GANs and their versatile applications.

Chapter 4: Architecting Auto Encoder for Generative AI

This chapter unfolds a comprehensive exploration of autoencoders, delving into critical concepts and practical implementations. The chapter initiates by elucidating the essence of autoencoders, shedding light on their mathematical foundations. This includes a thorough examination of the mathematics that underlie autoencoders, providing a conceptual framework for understanding their workings.

A significant facet of the chapter revolves around differentiating autoencoders from GANs, emphasizing key distinctions between the two. This comparative analysis enhances readers' understanding of when to employ each technique based on specific problem requirements.

Additionally, the chapter underscores the importance of regularization in autoencoders, elucidating both the mathematical rationale and architectural considerations. Regularization emerges as a critical tool in enhancing the generalization and robustness of autoencoders, impacting their performance and effectiveness.

The chapter progresses to practical applications, demonstrating how autoencoders can be utilized for CIFAR-10, a well-known dataset. This hands-on approach, complete with implementation details, enables readers to grasp the practical aspects of using autoencoders in real-world scenarios.

Furthermore, the chapter extends its practical focus to anomaly detection, showcasing how autoencoders can effectively identify anomalies using the Fashion MNIST dataset.

This exemplifies the versatility of autoencoders beyond standard applications, such as outlier detection.

Lastly, the chapter delves into autoencoders with convolutional layers, presenting a powerful augmentation to the traditional autoencoder architecture. This advancement extends the capabilities of autoencoders, particularly in scenarios where image data is involved.

As mentioned above this chapter serves as a pivotal resource, offering a multidimensional understanding of autoencoders. It combines mathematical foundations, comparative analysis, practical implementations, and specialized applications, providing readers with a holistic view of this fundamental machine learning technique. This chapter stands as a crucial steppingstone in the journey of mastering autoencoders and leveraging their potential across diverse domains.

Chapter 5: Building and Training Generative Autoencoders

In this chapter, readers delve into advanced concepts and practical applications related to autoencoders. Here is a brief summary of the key learnings this chapter offers:

- **Understanding latent space**: Gain a comprehensive understanding of the concept of latent space and its significance in autoencoders. Explore how data is represented in this compressed, abstract space and its implications for various applications.

- **Dual input autoencoders**: Explore the concept of dual input autoencoders and their usefulness in handling missing values and multi-modal data. Understand how this innovative approach expands the capabilities of autoencoders.

- **Loss functions for training and reconstruction**: Familiarize yourself with various loss functions commonly used in autoencoders and their role in training and reconstruction. Grasp how these functions impact the learning process and final output.

- **Addressing training challenges**: Learn about potential issues during training, such as overfitting, vanishing gradients, and noisy data. Acquire strategies to mitigate these challenges, ensuring effective training and accurate reconstruction.

- **Optimization techniques for model training**: Discover optimization techniques specific to autoencoders that enhance model training and performance. Understand how optimization contributes to achieving the desired outcomes in training.

- **Comparing autoencoders and Variational Autoencoders (VAEs)**: Understand the differences between autoencoders and VAEs and their respective benefits. Gain insights into when to use each approach based on the specific requirements of the task.

- **Practical applications of autoencoders**: Acquire the knowledge and skills to leverage autoencoders in practical scenarios, including data representation, generation, and anomaly detection. Learn how to apply autoencoders effectively to solve real-world problems and enhance data-related tasks.

This chapter presents an opportunity to deepen your understanding of autoencoders and their versatile applications. From advanced concepts to hands-on practical use cases, this chapter equips readers with the knowledge and skills needed to harness the power of autoencoders across various domains.

Chapter 6: Designing Generative VAE

This chapter is a pivotal exploration into **Variational Autoencoders (VAEs)** and their key distinctions from traditional **Autoencoders (AEs)**. Readers delve into the fundamental differences between these two models, grasping how VAEs offer unique advantages in learning and representing latent information. The chapter sheds light on the intricate network architecture of VAEs, unraveling the roles of encoder and decoder networks in learning latent representations, paving the way for a deeper understanding of the model's inner workings.

Furthermore, readers gain profound insights into the mathematical principles underpinning VAEs. The discussion covers critical concepts like the reparameterization trick and the **evidence lower bound (ELBO)** objective function, illuminating how these mathematical foundations drive the optimization process. Advanced techniques in VAEs are explored, including diverse prior distributions, variations in the encoder network, and handling incomplete or missing data, broadening the applicability and robustness of VAEs in diverse scenarios.

The chapter also offers a glimpse into interpreting and visualizing the latent space of a VAE, providing methods to make sense of the abstract representations learned by the model. Readers are guided through the generative capabilities of VAEs, showcasing how novel samples can be generated using the decoder network. Equipped with this knowledge, readers are empowered to apply VAEs effectively in practical applications ranging from image generation to natural language processing and anomaly detection, reinforcing their ability to derive meaningful representations from complex data. Through these endeavors, readers cultivate a comprehensive understanding of VAEs, enhancing their capacity to harness the model's adaptability and power across various domains.

Chapter 7: Building Variational AutoEncoders for Generative AI

In this chapter, readers will attain a comprehensive understanding of **Variational Autoencoders (VAEs)** by focusing on the following key learnings:

Architectural choices for VAEs: Delve into exploring different architectural choices, such as convolutional or non-convolutional networks, to effectively handle intricate dependencies in VAEs. Understanding these choices is crucial for optimizing the performance of VAEs. Impact of KL Divergence and Prior Distributions: Investigate the significance of KL divergence and various prior distributions on the generative process of VAEs. Understanding this impact is essential for improving the generative capabilities and the overall functioning of VAEs.

Strategies for Handling Incomplete Data: Develop effective strategies to handle missing or incomplete data within the VAE framework. Learning to address this challenge ensures robustness and adaptability of VAEs in real-world scenarios where data completeness may vary. Role of Loss Functions and Training Stability: Understand the pivotal role of loss functions in training VAEs and learn strategies to address potential issues during training to ensure stable convergence. Mastering these aspects is critical for achieving reliable and efficient training of VAE models.

Optimizing VAE performance for diverse data modalities: Gain insights into optimizing VAE performance and enhancing generative capabilities to cater to diverse data modalities. This knowledge empowers readers to apply VAEs effectively across a wide range of data types and domains.

By assimilating these key learnings, readers will possess a well-rounded understanding of VAEs, enabling them to harness the power and flexibility of VAEs in various domains. This understanding ultimately enhances their ability to learn and generate meaningful representations from complex and varied data.

Chapter 8: Designing New Age Generative Vision Transformer for Generative Learning

This chapter unfolds with critical insights, focusing on the following key learnings:

- **Introduction to Transformers**: The chapter initiates by elucidating the concept of transformers, highlighting their revolutionary role in natural language processing and expanding applications in computer vision. Readers gain a profound understanding of the transformative impact transformers have had in these domains.

- **Fundamental Transformer concepts**: Delving deeper, readers explore fundamental transformer principles, including self-attention mechanisms and the transformer architecture. This provides a foundational understanding of how transformers function at their core, setting the stage for more intricate comprehension.

- **Generative Transformers and attention types**: The chapter progresses to cover generative transformers, emphasizing their distinctive features compared to regular transformers. Concurrently, it analyzes various attention types, such as self-attention and cross-attention, showcasing their significance in image processing applications. Readers appreciate the nuanced applications of attention mechanisms in transformer-based models for computer vision tasks.

- **Mathematics and positional encoding in Transformers**: Finally, readers gain insights into the mathematical foundations of transformer architectures, coupled with the incorporation of positional encoding to handle sequence information. This comprehension equips readers to appreciate the inner workings of transformers, empowering them to delve into their applications with a solid mathematical understanding.

In summary, this chapter provides a comprehensive understanding of transformers, from their foundational concepts to their transformative impact across natural language processing and computer vision. Readers emerge with a robust grasp of transformers' mathematical foundations, attention mechanisms, and generative capabilities, propelling them towards effective utilization in a multitude of applications.

Chapter 9: Implementing Generative Vision Transformers

This chapter focuses on key learnings that encompass the following objectives:

- **Distinguishing Generative Transformers from Traditional Transformers**: The chapter delves into a thorough comparison, highlighting the architectural, training, and operational distinctions between Generative Transformers and traditional Transformers. This exploration provides readers with a clear conceptual framework to appreciate the advancements brought by Generative Transformers.

- **Constructing VAE Models for STL dataset**: Readers will learn to step-by-step build Variational Autoencoder models tailored to the STL dataset. This practical approach equips readers with the skills needed to create effective VAE models, essential for image generation.

- **Transitioning from VAE to Generative Transformer model**: Building on the VAE model, the chapter presents a novel approach to convert the VAE architecture into a Generative Transformer model. This conversion involves modifying VAE components to align with the Transformer's self-attention mechanism and positional encodings, enhancing contextual relationship learning within the latent space.

- **Performance evaluation and comparison**: The chapter objectively evaluates and compares the performance of the Generative Transformer model using quantitative metrics such as image quality, diversity, and convergence speed. This evaluation enables readers to benchmark the transformed model against both conventional VAE and Generative Transformer baselines.

- **Showcasing real-world applications**: Practical applications of the transformed Generative Transformer model are showcased, demonstrating its potential in generating high-quality, diverse images while maintaining contextual coherence. This display emphasizes the model's applicability in various creative and industrial domains.

By accomplishing these key learnings, readers will develop a profound understanding of the distinctions between Generative Transformers and traditional Transformers, proficiency in constructing VAE models for image generation, and insights into the innovative process of adapting a VAE model into a Generative Transformer architecture.

Chapter 10: Architectural Refactoring Combining Encoder-decoder and Transformers for Generative Modeling

This chapter offers key learnings to deepen understanding and skills in generative modeling using combined encoder-decoder-transformer architectures:

- **Synergistic combination process:** Understand the synergy achieved by integrating an encoder-decoder architecture with a transformer model. This combination process is pivotal for enhancing generative modeling capabilities in computer vision and holds the key to improving model performance.

- **Enhancements to transformer architecture:** Explore methods to enhance the standard transformer architecture. This involves introducing modifications and optimizations tailored to specific requirements, contributing to superior performance and adaptability to diverse tasks in computer vision.

- **In-depth exploration of SWIN transformer:** Delve into a detailed exploration of the SWIN transformer implementation, covering its architecture, components, and unique characteristics that distinguish it from other transformer variants. Gaining insights into this specific transformer variant is crucial for understanding its applicability and advantages.

- **Advanced concepts in combined architectures:** Introduce readers to advanced concepts, including the art of combining hyperparameter tuning and model refactoring. By grasping these concepts, readers can further optimize models and streamline their performance to meet specific objectives.

By engaging with these key learnings, readers will cultivate a comprehensive understanding of the entire process. This includes the motivations driving the integration of different architectures, the technical intricacies involved in implementation, and an appreciation of the SWIN transformer model. This holistic approach equips readers with both theoretical insights and practical skills, paving the way for innovative generative modeling using combined encoder-decoder-transformer architectures.

Chapter 11: Major Technical Roadblocks in Generative AI

This chapter unfolds as a journey into the realm of data representation, retrieval, and cross-modal understanding, presenting key learnings that navigate the complexities and innovations in these domains.

- **Unveiling challenges and technical hurdles:** The chapter initiates by meticulously exploring the obstacles and technical hurdles pervasive in generative AI and computer vision domains. These challenges form the backdrop, motivating the quest for innovative solutions and advancements.

- **Understanding the power of text and image embeddings:** Delving into the heart of data transformation, the chapter sheds light on the pivotal role of embeddings in converting textual and visual data into meaningful vectors. By doing so, it unveils how embeddings become the linchpin, enabling the comprehension of semantic relationships and contextual nuances within language and images. Understanding the transformative potential of embeddings is key to bridging the gap between raw data and AI models, ultimately enriching comprehension, representation, and manipulation of diverse data types.

- **Mastering vector databases for efficient retrieval:** The chapter takes a deeper dive into the realm of vector databases, illustrating their construction and application. Items represented as vectors within these databases hold a pivotal role. This section emphasizes efficient retrieval through indexing, particularly focusing on similarity searches. It aims to elucidate the creation of structures that facilitate quick and accurate querying of semantically related items, showcasing their immense significance in real-world applications.

- **Practical implementation of vector databases for image search:** The journey culminates in the practical implementation of vector databases for image search tasks, specifically highlighting the utilization of the Liberated Pinecone Vector Databases. This practical demonstration showcases the liberation of databases for open exploration and underscores how they power efficient image retrieval mechanisms. The objective is to illuminate how vector databases can revolutionize image search, fundamentally transforming the user experience and empowering them to discover visually similar content across a broad spectrum of applications.

Through these key learnings, readers are poised to navigate the intricate landscape of data representation, retrieval, and cross-modal understanding. The challenges, potential solutions, and practical implementations unraveled in this chapter equip readers with a profound understanding of the domain, empowering them to explore innovative approaches and contribute to the evolution of these critical fields.

Chapter 12: Overview of Applications of Generative AI Models

This chapter serves as a comprehensive exploration of the intertwining realms of **Legal Language Models (LLM)** and **Generative Artificial Intelligence (Gen AI)** across various industry verticals, each presenting distinctive applications and potential. The chapter unveils key learnings, shedding light on the transformative potential and impact of these technologies.

- **LLM in healthcare, retail, finance, and insurance:** The chapter commences by delving into the transformative role of Legal LLM within different industry sectors. In healthcare, LLM is a powerful tool, streamlining compliance processes and aiding in the analysis of complex medical documents. In retail, LLM plays a crucial role in simplifying contracts, ensuring compliance, and enhancing accuracy in vendor agreements. In the financial sector, LLM significantly enhances risk assessment, fraud detection, and contract analysis, revolutionizing the way financial processes are managed. In insurance, LLM is pivotal in improving claims efficiency, fraud detection, and ensuring adherence to complex compliance requirements.

- **Gen AI in healthcare, retail, finance, and insurance:** The chapter seamlessly transitions into an exploration of Gen AI and its transformative applications across various sectors. In healthcare, Gen AI is poised to revolutionize the sector with personalized medical advice, automated scheduling, and enhanced patient information management. In retail, Gen AI elevates customer engagement through personalized recommendations and dynamic marketing strategies, enhancing the overall shopping experience. In finance, Gen AI optimizes customer service by powering AI-driven chatbots and virtual assistants, significantly enhancing efficiency and user satisfaction. In insurance, Gen AI transforms underwriting processes, personalizes policies, and enriches customer interactions, streamlining the sector's operations and service delivery.

- **Cross-industry patterns and synergies:** An overarching understanding throughout the chapter highlights the patterns and synergies that emerge across these diverse industry verticals. LLM and Gen AI serve as versatile tools, bringing efficiency, accuracy, and enhanced user experiences across healthcare, retail, finance, and insurance. The integration of these technologies presents a common theme—streamlining processes, improving compliance adherence, and elevating customer interactions.

Through these key learnings, readers gain valuable insights into the dynamic landscape of LLM and Gen AI. Understanding their applications and potential within the domains of healthcare, retail, finance, and insurance provides a comprehensive view of how these technologies are shaping the future of these industries, optimizing operations, enhancing customer engagement, and ultimately advancing societal well-being.

Join our book's Discord space

Join the book's Discord Workspace for Latest updates, Offers, Tech happenings around the world, New Release and Sessions with the Authors:

https://discord.bpbonline.com

Index

Made in United States
North Haven, CT
18 May 2024

52679544R00193